THE SCIENTIFIC BASIS OF PSYCHIATRY

General Editor
Professor Michael Shepherd
Editorial Board
Professor H. Häfner
Professor P. McHugh
Professor N. Sartorius

The achievements of modern medicine have been largely derived from the understanding of biological structure and function which has accrued from advances in a number of basic sciences. On the foundations of such well-established fields as anatomy, physiology, pathology, bacteriology, pharmacology, genetics and immunology it has been possible to construct a clinical science directed towards the causation and rational treatment of many physical diseases. The slower development of psychological medicine can be attributed partly to historical factors bearing on its development and status. In addition, however, progress has been retarded by the innate complexity of a subject which one of its most distinguished representatives has defined as 'the study of abnormal behaviour from the medical standpoint'. The study of human behaviour goes beyond structure and function to incorporate the psychological and social sciences, and so calls for a wider range of scientific inquiry than is required for most other branches of medicine. The purpose of this series of monographs is to provide individual accounts of those disciplines which constitute the scientific basis of psychiatry.

Each volume is written by a practising scientist whose work is related to psychiatric practice and theory so that his/her review of a particular subject reflects a personal contribution and outlook. Together they are intended to provide a conspectus on the problems and challenges posed by a major and growing branch of medicine.

Hormones and human behaviour

BERNARD T. DONOVAN

Department of Physiology, Institute of Psychiatry
University of London

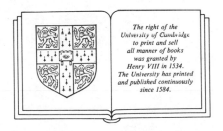

The right of the
University of Cambridge
to print and sell
all manner of books
was granted by
Henry VIII in 1534.
The University has printed
and published continuously
since 1584.

CAMBRIDGE UNIVERSITY PRESS

Cambridge

London   New York   New Rochelle

Melbourne   Sydney

Published by the Press Syndicate of the University of Cambridge
The Pitt Building, Trumpington Street, Cambridge CB2 1RP
32 East 57th Street, New York, NY 10022, USA
10 Stamford Road, Oakleigh, Melbourne 3166, Australia

First published 1985

Printed in Great Britain at the University Press, Cambridge

Library of Congress catalogue card number: 85–4230

British Library cataloguing in publication data

Donovan, Bernard T.
  Hormones and human behaviour. — (The Scientific
  basis of psychiatry; 2)
  1. Human behaviour   2. Hormones
  I. Title   II. Series
  612'.405   BF121

ISBN 0 521 25881 2

CONTENTS

PREFACE

Some years ago I summarized current thinking on the neural control of the endocrine system and brain–hormone interactions in a small book on *Mammalian Neuroendocrinology* (Donovan, 1970). As it happened, that work just preceded the widespread application of new and highly sensitive radioimmunoassay techniques to neuroendocrine problems, and little space was devoted to considerations of behaviour. In the ensuing years progress has been rapid, particularly in the application of minimally invasive research techniques to the human subject, so that we now know more about brain–endocrine reactions in man than in the laboratory rat. Correlations are now possible that were once considered to be totally impracticable, but the information available is scattered among a wide variety of journals and difficult of access. Thus, this book represents an attempt to review present knowledge concerning hormones and human behaviour in a concise and intelligible manner. It has no pretensions toward definitiveness, and cannot be comprehensive, but aims to provide an up-to-date account with sufficient references to the literature to justify the statements made and to guide further independent exploration. There is much that is fascinating in this field and it would be splendid if a little of the excitement rubbed off on to the reader. In any case, the book will be of considerable help to those working in the behavioural sciences and psychiatry, as well as to those studying for specialist qualifications in psychological medicine and for the Membership of the Royal College of Psychiatrists.

From the early 1950s the interdisciplinary subject of neuroendocrinology has promised much for the understanding of human behaviour, but only now has it begun to deliver the goods. As will be apparent from the pages to come, the doors are being opened to a sympathetic understanding of seemingly abnormal behaviour and to the rational treatment of psychiatric disorders. This is not to say that few problems remain, but simply that we can now gauge the dimensions of the problems and know where to look for the answers. Perhaps these considerations are underlined by a coincidence, in that after the first draft of this book was completed I came across the response of Manfred Bleuler, an eminent Swiss psychiatrist, to the question: How do you reconcile the claims made by biological scientists with your opinion of psychiatry's basic facts? He replied:

> I am aware, of course, of the rich variety of research findings in modern biology and brain physiology, anatomy and chemistry. I admire the complicated and difficult techniques used by modern biologists. I think, however, that the significance of all this knowledge for psychology and psychiatry can be summarised and expressed in a few clear and impressive theses; we should neglect sophisticated, uncertain speculations and keep to the main facts and to well-elaborated theories. Such a summary should point out principally the probable relationships between the neurotransmitters at the neural synapses and activation, sedation and mood changes; the interaction between nervous, endocrinological and emotional functions; the functions of cerebral systems which regulate primitive drives such as hunger, thirst, breeding instincts and sexuality; and the significance of the oxygen supply to the brain. It should bring together a few of the theories on memory; and it should mention what we know and do not know with regard to the localisation of elementary psychological functions.
>
> (Bleuler, 1982.)

Remarkably, and inadvertently, the present work comes close to matching these requirements.

Finally, a word about the illustrations, or rather the lack of them. This book could have been rendered more visually attractive, and costly, by the use of diagrams and photographs to delineate some of the salient points of anatomy and certain behavioural events. However, a detailed knowledge of the location and layout of structures within the brain is not essential to the understanding of the material presented, although it may well serve to comfort the reader.

Acknowledgements

I am most grateful for the constructive comments of a number of colleagues. This book emerged as the result of encouragement from Professor Michael Shepherd, and has benefited greatly from his advice. Helpful criticisms were also provided by Professor I. Marks, and Drs F. Besag, I. C. Campbell, S. Checkley, and J. C. Crammer, who were able to exercise influence without responsibility. I am indebted to them all.

1

Introduction and overview

Studies of the influence of hormones upon human behaviour have a long, and occasionally disreputable, history. Nevertheless, to those seeking biological explanations of aspects of human behaviour, or of the genesis of psychiatric disease, observations of the striking effects of hormone inadequacy or hormone excess point the way to progress. Clinicians have long associated emotional apathy and intellectual deterioration with thyroid insufficiency. In fact, Fodéré, a celebrated French authority on forensic medicine who suffered from thyroid enlargement in the form of a goitre, wrote in 1800 concerning cretinism:

> Here, one does not recognize a human being. Struck in his distinctive characteristics, the thought and spoken word, this is no longer the lord of the earth, who calculates the immensity of the skies and describes their very movements; it is the weakest of all existing human beings, since he is even incapable to provide himself for his own subsistence. This is no more the animated countenance, the proud eye, which reflects the will; it is a dumb face, similar to those old pieces of coin, where [continuous] use has erased the imprint of the coin-face.
> (Medvei, 1982.)

Fodéré believed that goitre was inherited, usually from the father's side.

Analysis of hormonal influences on sexual conduct looms large in the development of modern research on hormones and behaviour (Beach, 1981). In view of the importance of a knowledge of breeding patterns and of the effects of castration this is to be expected, but the stereotyped and repetitive nature of patterns of sexual behaviour has facilitated experimental study. Scientific research may be said to have begun in 1849, when the hormonal activities of the testes were delineated by Berthold, who castrated six cockerels and returned one testis to the abdomen in three, whereupon the birds with transplanted testes showed full cockerel behaviour, in contrast to the three caponized birds. It was in the same year that Thomas Addison outlined the consequences of disease of the adrenal glands and drew attention to the behavioural changes (Major, 1945).

Another nineteenth century physician interested in adrenal function was Charles Brown-Sequard, but he is best remembered for his interest in rejuvenation, which led to a series of self-injections of a mixture of testicular blood, fluid and semen derived from a dog and a guinea-pig. Although he was aware of the dangers of auto-suggestion (but not of antibody reactions), he reported an increase in muscular strength, improved bladder tonus, a greater regularity of bowel function and a heightened resistance to mental fatigue. These benefits could be conferred upon other aging scientists, but his offers of treatment were scorned. Later, Eugen Steinach adopted the simpler expedient of ligating the vas deferens of old rats, dogs and horses and described renewed hair growth, an increase in general activity and an enhanced responsiveness to external stimuli, as well as to females. This procedure was rapidly applied to elderly men, including Sigmund Freud, and enjoyed considerable popularity for a while (Money, 1983). Of course, the studies of such experimentalists were performed in the absence of any information concerning the nature and activities of hormones. Thus, use was made of aqueous extracts of testicular tissue, although we now know that the active androgens are not water-soluble and would have been lost in the discarded tissue residue.

Despite a lack of understanding of fundamental endocrine physiology, perceptive clinicians over the years have long been interested in the potential significance of a link between psychiatric disorders and disturbances of endocrine function. The Committee on Myxoedema, set up by the Clinical Society of London in 1883 to investigate the disease, reported in 1888 that 'delusions–hallucinations occur in nearly half the cases, mainly where the disease is advanced. Insanity as a complication is noted in about the same proportion as delusions and hallucinations. It takes the form of acute or chronic manias, dementia, or melancholia, with a marked predominance of suspicion and self-accusation' (Medvei, 1982). Soon after, the first patient, a woman of 46, was treated with a glycerol extract of sheep thyroid tissue and that lady survived until the age of 74 (Murray, 1920). Over the 28 years of treatment she was provided with extract derived from the glands of more than 870 sheep, with no apparent ill-effect.

Freud believed that many of the disturbances that he tried to understand from the psychological point of view might become amenable to treatment with hormones (van Ophuisen, 1951), and the first papers on 'Psychiatrie Endocrinienne' were published by Laignel-Lavastine in 1908 (Scharrer & Scharrer, 1963). At the opening of the Phipps Psychiatric Clinic in

Baltimore, Harvey Cushing, a leading neurosurgeon of the time, was prompted to reflect upon the association of psychic disturbances with disorders of the endocrine glands, and reminded his audience that the ranks of giants supplied more drum majors than prime ministers (Cushing, 1913). He was concerned with the consequences of over-activity of the pituitary gland as seen in acromegaly, and the recurring periods of hopelessness, lethargy and depression manifest in such cases were graphically set out. Cushing describes attempts to treat the converse situation, hypopituitarism, by the use of pituitary glands collected from still-born children and implanted into the brain. In a case reported in detail 'there was an unexpected and astonishing improvement in his mental capacity', which sadly did not last. Others were concerned with more commonplace situations, and in 1915 Walter B. Cannon, the eminent Harvard physiologist, published the first edition of his *Bodily Changes in Pain, Hunger, Fear and Rage: An Account of Researches into the Function of Emotional Excitement*, in which emphasis was laid on the interaction of nervous and hormonal responses in emotional disturbance. He was particularly concerned with the role of adrenal hormones in the reactions to excitement and pain; yet at this time only the activities of the adrenal medulla were beginning to be appreciated and the functions of the adrenal cortex remained unknown territory (Cannon, 1929). Much of his work was carried out with dogs and cats, where the 'natural enmity' of the two species proved useful, but he cites numerous instances of glycosuria associated with emotional stress in man.

Involvement of the adrenal cortex in the physiological response to stressful stimuli was highlighted by Hans Selye in the 1930s. Selye was an experimental endocrinologist and from 1936 he championed the concept of a 'general adaptation syndrome' which could be divided into an 'alarm' stage, corresponding to activation of the adrenal gland; 'resistance', during which adrenal function was reset at a higher, coping, level; and an 'exhaustion phase', which ensued if adaptation was insufficient to contend with the stress or trauma encountered (Selye, 1957). These ideas generated a great deal of interest in the relationship between the brain and adrenocortical function and the many publications that resulted merited review in a series of annual volumes devoted entirely to 'Stress'.

Another student of the relationship between hormones and mental states was Max Reiss, who enthusiastically promoted psychoendocrinology some thirty years ago, despite dissatisfaction with the cumbersome term. Psychiatrists of the prominence of Freud and Kraepelin had expected much of endocrinology in providing explanations of psychopathological disturbances, and treatment of schizophrenic patients with thyroid hormone was once a popular form of therapy, although the clinical failures far outnumbered the successes. Nowadays, diagnosis of hypo- or hyperthyroidism has been greatly simplified by laboratory procedures, yet cases of hypo-thyroidism still find their way into psychiatric rather than medical wards. Reiss wrote in 1958 that a feeling of utter frustration must come over anyone, be he psychiatrist or endocrinologist, who attempts to survey the thousands of biochemical and endocrinological investigations into schizo-phrenia, and that when Bleuler undertook such a survey (published as *Endokrinologische Psychiatrie* in 1954) he found the facts so contradictory that he could not permit himself to draw any definite conclusions.

Reiss was somewhat over-pessimistic, for alongside the somewhat tenta-tive explorations of the clinical investigators, scientists were busy delineat-ing the basic configuration of the neuroendocrine system, for if the brain was influential in the control of endocrine function, how might the control be exercised? Some believed that the anterior pituitary gland was innervated for this purpose by nerve fibres from the nearest part of the brain, the hypothalamus, as was the case for the posterior lobe, but such fibres proved difficult to detect. Others drew attention to a plexus of blood vessels running along the pituitary stalk between the hypothalamus and hypophysis, but interpretation of their functional significance was complicated by the belief that blood was conveyed in them in the opposite direction, from the pituitary gland to the brain. Once this misconception was corrected by the presentation of strong arguments to the contrary (Green & Harris, 1947), progress was rapid. This is not the place to relate the fascinating story, for the controversies concerning the function of the hypophysial portal vessels have been described in detail elsewhere (Donovan, 1978a; Wade, 1981), and first-hand accounts of the work of some of the scientists involved are available (Meites, Donovan & McCann, 1975). Suffice it to add that with the realization that the hypophysial portal vessels carried chemical messengers (neurohumors) from the hypothalamus to the pituitary gland to govern hormone output the way was clear for the analysis of brain–endocrine system interactions.

Neuroendocrine relationships

The nervous and endocrine systems provide the two major modes of intercellular and inter-organ communication within the body, and underpin all homeostatic processes. Until relatively recently, that is until the 1950s, they were regarded as functionally distinct, but it is now clear that there is considerable overlap between them. The change in outlook can be traced to the discovery by Ernst Scharrer in 1928 that certain hypothalamic neurons specialize in secretory activity to a degree comparable to that of endocrine gland cells, and to the suggestion that the secretory activity was related to hypophysial function (Scharrer, 1974), particularly in connection with the secretion of the antidiuretic hormone (vasopressin) and oxytocin (Chapter 2). It was also proposed that there was a class of neuron that could function as glands of internal secretion and merited the term 'neurosecretory cells'. These suggestions were not readily accepted and generated much controversy, particularly as the first observations were made in fish, and decades passed before the wide applicability of the concept was appreciated.

Originally, only those nerve cells in which the secretory products could be visualized by histological techniques were regarded as neurosecretory, and the neurohypophysial system, producing the hormones vasopressin and oxytocin in this way for discharge from the posterior lobe of the hypophysis, emerged as the classical neurosecretory system. Neurosecretory cells retain all of the attributes of nerve cells, including the ability to generate and transmit nerve impulses, while nerve cells synthesize and release other materials, in particular the neurotransmitters acetylcholine, noradrenaline, dopamine and serotonin. Thus it becomes difficult to limit the application of the term 'neurosecretion' to the elaboration and release of particular products. In fact, current developments in the identification and localization of a variety of neural products have shown that peptides are widely used by the nervous system in conveying signals from one area to another, and since peptides possess hormonal activity in addition to their signalling capacity within the nervous system, it becomes increasingly difficult to distinguish between neurotransmitters, neuromodulators (a term introduced to cope with this dilemma), and hormones.

There are other complications, in that many peptide hormones have been identified recently in the brain cells and peripheral nerves of vertebrates and multicellular invertebrates, where they were not previously expected. It is now realised that cancers of non-endocrine tissues, such as the lung, may produce and release large amounts of hormonal peptides, with disastrous consequences. Further, neuropeptides, so-called because they were thought to be produced by and limited to the central nervous system, have been found in non-neural tissue, while familiar gastrointestinal or pancreatic hormones, like insulin, have been found in the brain, as well as in the nervous system of insects. Thus, as will be described in more detail later on, the boundaries between neural and endocrine function become increasingly blurred. This is not as surprising as it might seem, for it has long been known that plants produce compounds like the adrenal and gonadal steroids of the human, that they also produce alkaloids (muscarine, nicotine, morphine, ephedrine, yohimbine) with actions on the nervous system that are so familiar as to be taken for granted, and that they even produce peptides with effects that mimic hypothalamic gonadotrophin-releasing factor, thyrotrophin-releasing factor, interferon, and the endogenous opiates (Roth, Le Roith, Shiloach & Rubinovitz, 1983)–peptides that will be shown to be important in human physiology and behaviour.

Conventionally, the neuroendocrine system embraces the hypothalamus and pituitary gland, with the rest of the brain superimposed upon, and influencing, the hypothalamus, and most peripheral glands lying under the control of the pituitary gland. In addition, some endocrine glands, like the adrenal medulla, are directly innervated and governed by the hypothalamus. Because of its hierarchical character, the functions of the neuroendocrine system can be investigated at various levels. Assays of hormones in samples of peripheral blood provide information on the secretory activity of target endocrine glands, like the adrenals, thyroid gland, ovaries and testes, as well as on the concentration of the various pituitary hormones in circulation. But changes in the hypothalamus can only be assessed indirectly through alterations in the output of pituitary hormones, or in a particular pattern of behaviour. Stimulation of the brain by electrical or chemical means can be carried out, but several physiological processes are interposed between the stimulus and response. Further, the brain is susceptible to the influence of hormones, and this feedback action, completing a functional circuit, can be exercised in a variety of ways. In the end, so many factors (hormonal, nutritional, environmental) contribute to the operation of the neuroendocrine system that it is surprising that consistent patterns of behaviour and hormonal activity ever result.

Take, for example, the variety of ways in which hormones can be used for signalling purposes (Yates, 1981). Cells, whether neurons or not, may respond directly to the concentration of hormone in the blood, as for thyroxine or the sex hormones. Or the rate of change in hormone concentration may serve as a vital signal, as in the case of the hypothalamo-pituitary–adrenal response to fluctuations in plasma adrenal steroid concentration. In other circumstances an unstable equilibrium operates, where there is an inability to achieve a stable balance between stimulus and response, so that fluctuations on either side of a mean level ensue. The response of the islets of Langerhans in the pancreas to the blood level of glucose provides a good example, in that if a glucose solution is infused into a dog at a constant rate over a long period, and the plasma level of insulin measured at intervals, then the concentration of insulin is seen to fluctuate on either side of an 'ideal' value, rather as might be expected if 'hunting', in engineering parlance, were taking place. A fourth type of response is seen in cases where the reaction of a tissue depends upon the frequency with which it is driven to activity by a trophic factor. The tissue itself, through the hormone receptors it fabricates, determines the level of response, as in cases of 'down-regulation' or 'up-regulation' (Chapter 5).

The effects of hormones on behaviour

With regard to the brain, the effects of hormones can be grouped into a number of categories (McEwen, 1980). There is the inductive or organizational effect of hormones on the brain in determining future patterns of behaviour. Sexual behaviour could be determined in this way, as will be discussed at length in Chapter 7. Once induced, the latent patterns of behaviour can be elicited or activated by hormones, as with the restoration of sexual activity by sex hormones after gonadectomy. The feedback action of hormones upon the brain has already been mentioned and can be negative or positive in effect, with negative feedback serving to inhibit the secretion of the appropriate trophic hormone, and positive feedback acting on occasion to enhance the output, as when oestrogen causes luteinizing hormone release and ovulation at mid-cycle in women. Hormones can influence adaptive behaviour, learning and memory, and also can act indirectly by maintaining the optimal biochemical parameters for brain function by controlling the blood sugar level, or that of calcium or phosphorus. This latter category should not be taken for granted, and a little elaboration is merited.

Hormones, metabolism, and behaviour

Diabetes mellitus might be regarded as a classic endocrine or metabolic disease. It centres around an absolute or relative lack of the pancreatic hormone, insulin, or an insensitivity to the actions of that hormone. As a consequence, the metabolism of glucose is disturbed and the blood level of glucose is high, spilling over into the urine. Three hundred years ago, Thomas Willis wrote that sadness, or long sorrow, as likewise convulsions, and other depressions and disorders of the animal spirits, are used to generate or foment this morbid disposition, and more recently the pioneer British psychiatrist Henry Maudsley noted in 1899 that diabetes is sometimes caused by mental anxiety (Wilkinson, 1981). Maudsley went on to add that diabetes is a disease that often shows itself in families in which insanity prevails, but this has not been substantiated. There have also been suggestions that stressful situations can precipitate the onset of diabetes, but it is difficult to decide in retrospect whether any emotional problems preceded the onset of the illness, or arose as an early sign of disturbed carbohydrate metabolism. Wilkinson (1981) concludes that there is a lack of evidence to support the belief that psychiatric factors, acting directly, cause diabetes mellitus.

Less is known about the effects of persistent hyperglycaemia upon brain function, while the episodes of hypoglycaemia that may be suffered by the diabetic patient as the result of a temporary excess of insulin may cause brain damage. In acute cases, hypoglycaemia is characterized by malaise, anxiety, a loss of connection with reality, palpitations and restlessness. Conscious-ness is clouded and coma may ensue, but glucose administration is immediately corrective. With a smaller fall in blood sugar level the anxiety and restlessness may be lacking, but spontaneous activity is reduced, performance is impaired and the patient may appear drunk. However, most neuropathological reports concern patients dying of hypoglycaemic coma and not patients who had minor hypoglycaemic attacks (Wilkinson, 1981; Gibbons, 1983).

Hypocalcaemia follows from parathyroid hormone deficiency, but can arise in other circumstances, including renal failure, lack of vitamin D, and nutritional deficiencies. Tetany is the most prominent feature of this syndrome and generalized seizures are common.

Secondary hypoparathyroidism can arise acutely through interference with the parathyroid glands as a complication of thyroidectomy. Then, features of an organic brain syndrome with disorientation, memory impair-ment, auditory or visual hallucinations and agitation ensue (Jefferson & Marshall, 1981). Earlier, the literature on the mental changes associated with hypoparathyroidism had been sifted by Denko & Kaelbling (1962) and Smith *et al.* (1972), who concluded that a major degree of cognitive impairment was present in half of the patients. In general, hypocalcaemic states may simulate functional excitement, irritability, paranoia and cyclic, bipolar, mood disturbances, while in animals reductions in the concen-tration of calcium in the cerebrospinal fluid of less than 10 per cent produce excitement, hyperactivity and irritability. Conversely, increasing the con-centration of calcium in the brain produces sedation and catatonic behaviour in cats and goats (Carman *et al.*, 1984). Normally, substantial increases in serum calcium alter the concentration of the metal in the CSF to a minor degree, but Carman *et al.* (1984) point out that in 'rapid-cycling' manic–depressive patients entering their manic phase, serum calcium increases by as much as CSF calcium decreases. It appears that overcompensation of one of the homeostatic mechanisms regulating CSF calcium may occur, so that periodic serum calcium spikes trigger longer-lasting reductions in CSF calcium, which may in turn generate periodic episodes of psychotic agi-tation.

Since the majority of the changes caused by hyperparathyroidism follow from the resultant hypercalcaemia, other conditions raising the blood calcium level, such as renal failure, excessive ingestion of vitamin D, bone disease, adrenal insufficiency and prolonged immobilization, can mimic hyperparathyroidism. Further, pseudohyperparathyroidism can arise from tumours outside the parathyroid glands which produce peptides acting like parathyroid hormone.

Although there is a high incidence of mental disturbance in cases of raised blood calcium levels (Petersen, 1968; Smith *et al.*, 1972), the psychiatric changes are insidious in onset and non-specific. Patients suffer from depressed mood, become listless and apathetic, lose their sense of spontaneity and their initiative, and experience a loss of drive. Often these changes are recognized only retrospectively, when therapy has restored mineral metabolism to normal (Jefferson & Marshall, 1981).

There is a good correlation between the blood calcium concentration and mental state. The normal serum calcium level is about 9–11 mg/100 ml, and personality changes with affective disorders and disturbances of drive set in at the 12–16 mg/100 ml range (Petersen, 1968). Acute organic psychosis appears at high serum calcium levels and values of 16–19 mg/100 ml are associated with alterations in consciousness, with hallucinations and paranoia, before somnolence or coma is observed with calcium concentrations above 19 mg/100 ml. In patients with acute renal failure, the concentration of calcium in the brain is increased and linked with abnormalities in the EEG (Cooper, Lazarowitz & Arieff, 1978).

Hormones and sensory function

A less obvious way in which hormones can affect behaviour is by altering the impact of peripheral stimuli upon the brain. Abnormalities of taste and smell have been reported in a variety of endocrine disorders, including adrenocortical insufficiency, an excess of adrenal hormones as in Cushing's syndrome or congenital adrenal hyperplasia, hypogonadotrophic hypogonadism, pseudohypoparathyroidism and hypothyroidism, and may contribute to any accompanying anorexia or decreased food intake (McConnell *et al.*, 1975). In the majority of cases sensory function returns to normal with treatment. The changes in dietary preferences can be life-saving, as in the case of a $3\frac{1}{2}$-year-old boy suffering from Addison's disease in the days before the basis of this condition was understood. Because of damage to the adrenal cortex in Addison's disease there is a lack of the salt-retaining steroid, aldosterone, and consequently a devastating loss of sodium from the body. In this case, the child was able to keep himself alive at home by spontaneously eating salt in seemingly excessive amount, but when he was admitted to hospital, fed the usual hospital diet, and inadvertently deprived of his salt supplement, death came quickly (Wilkins & Richter, 1940). Similarly, rats preferentially drink saline solution after adrenalectomy, although before the operation plain water is selected.

Later work showed that the increased ability of patients suffering from adrenal insufficiency to detect salt extended to sweet, sour and bitter tastes and could be corrected by treatment with glucocorticoids. Unfortunately, the more delicate palate of the patient is counterbalanced by an impairment of the ability to recognize tastes, so that in a case where the detection acuity for sodium chloride was 1000 times more sensitive than normal, the ability to integrate sensory information about taste was about one-fifth to one-tenth of the customary level. Patients with untreated adrenal cortical insufficiency are also more sensitive to sound, so that the familiar noises of a hospital ward can appear so loud as to cause distress. Again, the ability of such patients to discriminate between sounds or to recognize words is impaired, but happily, as with taste, is restored to normal upon hormone therapy. Conversely, an excessive concentration of adrenal steroid hormones in the blood, as with Cushing's syndrome, lessens the ability of patients to detect and discriminate between tastes, odours and sounds. Hypothyroid patients also show a reduced ability to detect and recognize tastes, odours and sounds. Treatment with thyroid hormone is beneficial, but may not restore normality (Henkin, 1980).

Studies of normal women have shown that several sensory modalities may be affected by the hormonal changes occurring during the menstrual cycle. In one survey (Parlee, 1983) it was concluded that, although substantial variations in stimulus conditions and procedures made generalization difficult, sensitivity to visual and olfactory stimuli appeared to be greatest around the time of ovulation. Sensitivity to painful stimuli was generally found to be lower in the premenstrual phase of the cycle, and auditory performance showed one peak around the time of ovulation and another at the onset of menstruation. No generalizations emerged from the scattered research on menstrual changes in taste, temperature sensitivity or two-touch thresholds. Gandelman (1983) pertinently comments that many of the data concerning the relationship between gonadal hormones and sensory function are quite indirect and consist in many cases of stated preferences and aversions, or choice behaviour for certain stimuli. There is also the need to verify that any change in sensory function is directly mediated by the independent variable. Thus an effect attributed to oestrogen could arise from the action of an adrenal hormone, for oestrogen can alter the activity of the pituitary–adrenal axis. And then there is the possibility that the material available represents a biased sampling of data. Because of the reluctance of most journal editors to publish research reporting a lack of effect in a particular situation (otherwise referred to as the null hypothesis), information refuting any endocrine involvement in sensory function may not be available in the literature.

The limbic system

Most of the phylogenetically old cerebral cortex (including the cingulate gyrus, hippocampal gyrus and uncus) surrounding the brain stem forms part of the limbic system, which is important in the genesis of emotional behaviour. This part of the brain, which can be viewed as a ring of cerebral cortex around the corpus callosum and associated deep structures, was once termed the rhinencephalon, but it is now clear that smell is but one of the sensations represented. From the evolutionary point of view, some components of the limbic system (septum and hippocampus) are more developed in higher primates and man than in lower mammalian species, whereas the olfactory bulb and olfactory cortices are smaller (Stephan, 1983). These trends clearly imply a shift in functional emphasis. Neural discharges in or near to the limbic lobe, which tend to be confined to the limbic system, may trigger a broad spectrum of vivid affective feelings which include those of hunger, thirst, nausea, somatic sensations such as pain and tingling, and general feelings of fear, terror, sadness, a desire for solitude, familiarity and, rarely, anger. It seems that the limbic system can give rise to free-floating, strong affective feelings of conviction attached to revelations and beliefs, whether they be true or false (MacLean, 1976). The limbic system is a prime target of corticosteroid and gonadal steroid action (Stumpf, 1980; Chapter 5).

The amygdaloid nuclei in the temporal lobes of the brain provide links between the olfactory system, hippocampus and basal ganglia, and between the cerebral cortex, septal complex and hypothalamus. They receive an input from all sensory modalities and connect with most parts of the brain. From the behavioural point of view, the amygdala can be regarded as concerned with emotionality and the response to noxious stimuli (Goddard, 1964), as well as with the genesis of fear (Chapter 12).

Olfactory stimuli

There is a tendency to regard the influence of the olfactory system in human behaviour as of little significance, but this view may well be ill-advised. The olfactory system remains a major component of the brain and provides the foundation upon which many emotional responses are built. Much anecdotal information is available concerning the significance of smell in sexual life in man, but little hard evidence. Havelock Ellis, at the turn of the century, was concerned with the relationship between olfaction and sexuality, as well as the generation of odours of sexual significance. The role of odours in the development of bonds between mother and child has also attracted attention, while the association of olfactory hallucinations with sexual manifestations has not escaped notice (Kalogerakis, 1963). In reviewing the literature, Mary Rogel (1978) felt that there was a curious bias in the reported research toward searching for a sex attractant produced by females, and thought that this probably stemmed from the personal biases of the predominantly male investigators. Such a sexual slant seemed to be particularly odd in the light of olfactory studies reporting a greater sensitivity of females to male odours and suggesting the operation of a male sex attractant.

Among vertebrates, olfactory stimuli serve as potent triggers of sexual behaviour. Dogs are attracted by the scent of oestrous bitches, the behaviour of an oestrous cat changes upon encountering the scent of urine from the male, and the odour produced by a female in heat serves as a potent sexual stimulant in a number of farm animals. Olfactory stimuli were shown to be significant in sexual communication between monkeys by Michael, Zumpe, Keverne & Bonsall (1972), with short chain fatty acids in the vaginal secretions of the females seeming to exercise an important role as a sex attractant and rising in phase with the concentration of oestrogen in the plasma. However, it was later established that the peak concentrations of the fatty acids occurred in the luteal phase, several days after ovulation has occurred, and at a time when the animals were least likely to copulate. In turn, Michael, Bonsall & Zumpe (1976) argued that because of the changes in the viscosity of vaginal fluids, with the vaginal contents being least viscous at mid-cycle, more of the fatty acids could reach the exterior during this phase, and be effective.

The idea that fatty acids in the vaginal fluid, termed 'copulins' by Michael *et al.* (1972), might act in this way gained support from the observation that male monkeys lost their libido when rendered anosmic. On the other hand Goldfoot, Kravetz, Goy & Freeman (1976) were not persuaded that vaginal lavages obtained from oestrogen-treated donor female monkeys possessed any special sexual stimulating properties, and preferred the view that sexual interaction was governed to a large extent by the female: that soliciting by the female was important. They also pointed out that anosmic males studied outside the laboratory mated readily, and were fertile. Sexual experience was essential in order for olfactory cues to be effective, but other odours could replace those of the 'copulins'. One such was produced by a mixture of grisalva and galbazine, that smelled somewhat like green peppers.

Several reasons may be advanced in favour of the persistence of olfactory factors in human interaction. One is the presence of a complete system of apocrine glands associated with conspicuous hair tufts; another is that oral–genital contact is common in a number of cultures; and a third is that olfaction remains significant in parental recognition and imprinting in higher primates and in man. Fatty acids like those produced by the rhesus monkey have been identified in vaginal secretions collected from women. The ability of women to smell a macrocyclic ketone, exaltolide, is maximal at ovulation and declines during the luteal phase of the menstrual cycle. Children, men and post-menopausal or ovariectomized women are hardly able to detect this musk-like odour unless oestrogens are administered.

Seemingly, the sex of an individual can be identified solely on the basis of the smell of the breath (Doty, Green, Ram & Yankell, 1982). Both male and female judges correctly guessed the sex of individuals exhaling into a tube passing through a concealing screen on up to 95% of tests. Female judges were better at identifying males, and male judges slightly better at identifying females. Likewise, many more women than men can detect the smell of 5α-androstenone, the steroid responsible for the boar taint smell of roasting pig meat. Exposure to this odour altered the judgements of women asked to evaluate written, and hypothetical, interview descriptions of possible candidates for a responsible job. Only the assessments of men made by women were affected (Cowley, Johnson & Brooksbank, 1977). Twenty-five years ago it was suggested that certain schizophrenic patients produced an intense, characteristic odour that was heavy, unpleasant and slightly pungent—and remained after the patients were scrubbed with surgical soap (Smith & Sines, 1960).

The operation of olfactory signals in human neuroendocrine function may be demonstrable in other ways. Several studies have shown that the menstrual cycles of women living together tend to become synchronous. In one investigation, the women housed on one floor of a prison showed a synchrony that was out of phase with that of similarly synchronous women on another floor. The onset of all cycles on the top floor fell within a 7-day period, a full week before those on the bottom floor. In an analysis of women undergraduates living in Scotland in single sex flats with six single bedrooms, a significant coincidence over 4 months in the cycles of close friends, but not in those of neighbours, was evident (Graham & McGrew, 1980). Menstrual synchrony was also evident in room-mates and close friends in an American context (Quadagno, Shubeita, Deck & Francoeur, 1981).

By themselves, observations of menstrual synchrony reveal little about the possible mechanisms involved, but there is information pointing to the driving force. Russell, Switz & Thompson (1980) collected sweat from the axillae of a female donor who had been shown to influence the menstrual cycle of a friend. When the two lived together the cycle of the friend became synchronous with the sweat donor, and asynchrony developed when the two separated. For the experiment, the donor wore axillary pads for 24 hours. They were then collected, cut into quarters, a few drops of 70 per cent alcohol added, and frozen in individual vials on dry ice for storage. For testing purposes, a pad was thawed for 2 minutes before being rubbed upon the upper lip of the subject, who was then asked not to wash for 6 hours. Initially, the mean difference between the onset of the menstrual cycle of the donor and the test subjects was 9.3 days, but after treatment with axillary product the difference was reduced to 3.4 days. The comparable figures for controls were 8.0 days pre-treatment and 9.2 days post-treatment. Four of the five test subjects became synchronous to within 1 day of the onset of menstruation of the driver. The influence of men should not be ignored, in that women who spent two or more nights with men during a 40-day study period exhibited a significantly higher rate of ovulation ($P < 0.05$) than those spending no or one night. Menstrual cycle length was not affected (Veith *et al.*, 1983). Much more information is needed before these phenomena can be regarded as proven, and much needs to be done in the investigation of the mechanisms involved. But, at the very least, these observations point to a largely unexplored field.

Hormonal influences in motivation

Motivated behaviours such as seeking water or food, building a shelter from the cold, or escaping from a predator, are, as Mogensen (1977) points out, typically goal-directed, with Curt Richter (1943) being credited with the demonstration that a number of such behaviours contribute to homeostasis. Thus, rats given a choice between relatively pure sources of amino acids, carbohydrates and fats will select them in proportions that provide a balanced diet. Children offered a range of foods will do likewise, while children suffering from hypoparathyroidism and a deficiency of calcium display a craving for chalk. Motivated behaviours can occur periodically, and, naturally, with interruptions: feeding, drinking and mating are examples of this kind, and in human society the interruptions can be prolonged.

Hormones can exert direct effects upon motivated behaviour, as with the initiation of drinking by angiotensin (Chapter 2), or operate indirectly through changes in metabolic activity. However, caution needs to be exercised in the interpretation of direct effects because it can be argued that the drinking induced by angiotensin is not truly a behavioural response, but simply activation of the motor component of the response mechanism. For this, and other, reasons discussion of the psychological concept of motivation in connection with activities such as eating, drinking, thermo-regulation, and sexual behaviour has been avoided. The term is ill-defined and conveys different ideas, in tune with the interests of the writer or reader. Long and complex texts have concerned themselves with motivation (e.g. Bolles, 1975), but controversy remains and some psychologists will have nothing to do with the notion. Grossman (1979) expressed his puzzlement in a rather technical way by commenting that we have, as yet, not the slightest idea of what the biological substrate of the directing function might be that is the essential aspect of the definition of specific motivational states; how arousal mechanisms might organize complex behaviour so as to control the level of brain activation; or how arousal mechanisms might interact with specific motivational mechanisms so as to gate relevant sensory input. This may represent an extreme attitude, but the point is well worth making. Much more needs to be learned about the physiological basis of the behavioural activities mentioned above before meaningful psychological constructs can be erected. The various approaches to the analysis of motivation have been discussed by Pfaff (1982), who calls attention to the fact that authors with great experience in the analysis of animal behaviour can describe comprehensively the biology of a wide range of behavioural patterns with no references to the term 'motivation'. Instead, the exact nature of the external stimuli, receptors, threshold, and response sequences is set out. There would seem to be a resultant gain in precision.

Another way of organizing a discussion of behaviour in a logical fashion is to utilize the efforts of the systems analysts (Scott, 1980). Nine general classes of behaviour can be distinguished, with four types being universal. The four include *ingestive* behaviour, related to the intake of nourishing materials, *shelter-seeking* behaviour, which needs little description, *investigatory* behaviour, which is concerned with the exploration of the environment with the aid of different senses, and *sexual* behaviour. The five other senses are less catholic in their incidence and tend to be limited to higher forms. These are the epimeletic, et-epimeletic, agonistic, allelomimetic, and eliminative behaviours. *Epimeletic* behaviour has the function of providing care and attention to the young of the species, while *et-epimeletic* behaviour signals a need for care and attention. *Agonistic* behaviour is intended to protect against injury, but may be extended to inflict injury, and to regulate the use of space and territory. *Allelomimetic* behaviour is defined as doing what another individual does and serves to co-ordinate the behaviour of individuals within a group, and *eliminative* behaviour covers the disposal of excretory products and the associated signalling activities seen in some species. Almost all of these behavioural phenomena are influenced by hormones, as we shall see. One exception is provided by et-epimeletic behaviour, where there is no obvious humoral control of the expression of a demand for help. On the other hand, the responses to such appeals can have a considerable impact upon the endocrine system of the young.

The complexities involved in the analysis of behavioural patterns are well-illustrated by a consideration of drinking behaviour, which can be divided into initiation, procurement and consummatory phases. The initiation phase may involve the detection of peripheral and central signals of an impending water deficit, the evaluation of sensory information from the external environment, and cognitive factors. Then the procurement phase is characterized by a general state of behavioural arousal, and by foraging behaviour, utilizing locomotor activity, sensory information and previous experience. If these efforts are successful, the final consummatory phase involves preprogrammed motor responses, such as licking and swallowing, while taste and smell can also be influential (Swanson & Mogensen, 1981). Clearly, drinking behaviour is not simple.

The hypothalamus

The hypothalamus is that part of the brain most deeply involved in homeostatic processes. Weighing but 4 g, and dwarfed by the thalamus and cerebral cortex lying above, it integrates almost all higher functions. In 1929, Cushing regarded the hypothalamus as the mainspring of primitive existence in governing vegetative, emotional, and reproductive function, and the succeeding years have served merely to underline his emphasis.

The hypothalamus is the most rostral part of the brain in which lesions can abolish the performance of integrated adaptive responses. Separate eating, drinking, sexual and thermoregulatory centres have been discerned within the hypothalamus although none has been defined in terms of the anatomical circuitry and neurophysiology of specific cell groups. Rather do there appear to be collections of neurons functionally linked for the generation of a particular response on a particular occasion. Located anteriorly, the medial preoptic area is concerned with drinking behaviour, male sexual behaviour and thermogenesis and contains neurons responding to osmotic stimuli, to androgens and to changes in local temperature. It is not clear how selective the response may be, or whether separate populations of neurons are involved (Swanson & Mogensen, 1981), but it should be recalled that the ventromedial nuclei in the middle part of the hypothalamus stand out as being uniquely sensitive to the effects of sex hormones in influencing behaviour (Everitt & Hansen, 1983). Further, a number of investigators have demonstrated changes in neural activity in the hypothalamus as well as in other areas of the brain when an animal is exposed to food or water, engages in ingestive or food- or water-rewarded instrumental behaviour, or merely awaits the delivery of food or water in response to a conditioned signal. What has not been convincingly demonstrated in most of these experiments is that the observed electro-physiological changes are, in fact, specifically related to hunger or thirst rather than to increments in general arousal, the processing of sensory information, the organization of motor reactions, or perhaps the generally rewarding effects of food and water (Grossman, 1979).

The way knowledge is progressing is well illustrated by recent studies of the paraventricular and supraoptic nuclei, the magnocellular nuclei close to the optic chiasma that produce oxytocin and vasopressin. In the rat, the paraventricular nuclei, with some 10000 neurons, occupy less than one-third of a cubic millimetre of tissue on either side of the third ventricle and yet can be subdivided into at least eight clearly distinguishable subdivisions, within which some thirty different putative neurotransmitters have been identified either in cell bodies or in presumed terminals. It may be that, together with involvement in kidney and uterine function through their production of vasopressin and oxytocin, the paraventricular nuclei are concerned with cardiovascular regulation and with the visceral and behavioural responses associated with eating and drinking (Swanson & Sawchenko, 1983). Neural projections from the supraoptic and paraven-tricular nuclei have been traced to distant structures, such as the substantia nigra in the basal ganglia, nuclei in the medulla, the substantia gelatinosa of the spinal cord, and elsewhere (Doris, 1984; Chapter 2).

Quite apart from its role in the control of the pituitary gland, and, in turn, hormonal secretion, the hypothalamus influences at least six major and fairly distinct non-endocrine functions: consciousness and sleep, cognition, emotional behaviour and affect, autonomic balance, caloric balance and water–osmolar balance (Plum & van Uitert, 1978). Several of these activities will be discussed in detail later on, with the control of hormone secretion being accorded more extensive discussion in the next chapter, but others merit brief review here.

Consciousness and sleep–wake behaviour
Lesions in the posterior hypothalamus cause drowsiness, stupor, or an unresponsive coma, depending upon size. Conversely, stimulation of this area produces arousal. These responses stem from involvement of the most rostral parts of the reticular activating system, which extends through much of the brain stem up to the thalamus and reaches caudally through the pons and medulla. Because stimulation of the anterior hypothalamus was de-pressive in character, and lesions of the anterior hypothalamus induced wakefulness, the anterior hypothalamus has been regarded as a 'sleep centre' and the posterior hypothalamus as a 'wake centre' (Plum & van Uitert, 1978). However, these effects are mediated through the reticular activating system and are not special properties of the hypothalamus. Clinically, there are numerous examples of disturbances of sleep associated with damage to the hypothalamus, although large, slowly progressing lesions occasionally invade all regions of the hypothalamus without disturb-ing consciousness or sleep–wake patterns. It is assumed in such patients that either the mesencephalic portion of the reticular activating system and part of the hypothalamus remains functionally intact, or that other regions possess the capacity to establish a diurnal rhythm of consciousness.

Cyclic functions

Alongside participation in the sleep–wake cycle, the hypothalamus is directly concerned with the generation of behavioural and hormonal rhythms. These are discussed in more detail elsewhere, particularly in connection with events that recur with a frequency approximating to twenty-four hours, and are called circadian rhythms (Chapter 6).

The key to many circadian rhythms may be found in the suprachiasmatic nuclei, which are located close to the third ventricle in the midline over the optic chiasma. The nuclei are provided with a direct neural projection from the retina, and destruction of the nuclei, or of the retino-hypothalamic tracts to them, prevents the entrainment of rodent activity rhythms, or of rhythms of adrenal corticosterone secretion, to light–dark cycles. Destruction of the suprachiasmatic nuclei does not simply disconnect endogenous rhythms from the influence of the environment, but causes loss of the rhythm itself, with the production of irregular, arrhythmic, patterns.

Despite the mass of evidence implicating the suprachiasmatic nuclei in the generation of circadian rhythms, little is known about the way in which the rhythm comes to be generated. Electrophysiological studies of islands of hypothalamic tissue containing the suprachiasmatic nuclei show that periodicity continues within the island, but is lost outside. The nuclei also continue to show rhythmic electrical discharges when studied under *in vitro* conditions. The suprachiasmatic nuclei may serve to couple or integrate a population of individual neuronal oscillators, although it is less certain that single neurons can support a circadian rhythm (Block & Page, 1978).

Control of autonomic function

The hypothalamus has long been known to control autonomic function. Stimulation of small loci within the hypothalamus of experimental animals increases or depresses blood pressure, speeds or slows the heart rate and induces vasoconstriction or vasodilation in the peripheral circulation (Mancia & Zanchetti, 1981). Overall, pressor effects can be evoked from a large zone beginning at the supraoptic area and extending caudally through much of the hypothalamus, whereas depressor effects come from a more rostral zone which begins in the preoptic area and extends upwards into the septum and nearby structures.

The cardiovascular responses accompanying emotional behaviour have been utilized in work on the hypothalamic control of autonomic reactions, and the hypothalamic area controlling emotional responses has been delineated. This encompasses the perifornical region and most medial portion of the lateral hypothalamus. There is also good evidence for the existence of direct neural connections between the hypothalamus and the intermediolateral cell column in the spinal cord which gives rise to autonomic nerve fibres. Small groups of neurons may project to one level of the spinal cord and be interspersed with others projecting to a different level, so providing the basis for a differentiation or localization of autonomic output. In turn, hypothalamic function is modulated or regulated by the amygdala and anatomical studies have led to suggestions that all sensory systems send projections to the amygdaloid complex and that, except for the olfactory system, the projections relayed from the amygdala to the hypothalamus arise only from the later stages of the cortical processing of sensory information. The various areas of the amgydala may each be primarily influenced by one major sensory system, with the cortical efferents supplying the amygdala also sending collaterals to influence the input to the hippocampus. These connections thus transmit all kinds of sensory information to the amygdala and so facilitate the modulation of hypothalamic function by the amygdala. However, the point of transfer from psychological processes to central autonomic control still seems to lie at the lower level of the hypothalamus (Smith & DeVito, 1984).

The secretion of adrenaline and noradrenaline from the medullary part of the adrenal glands can be enhanced by hypothalamic stimulation, as can that of renin from the kidneys. Animal studies, particularly with cats, have shown that increases in blood pressure, heart rate, and kidney, intestinal and skin vasoconstriction are produced by stimulation of those areas of the hypothalamus that also produced behavioural changes in conscious animals indicative of anger and rage. This integrated response has been termed the defence reaction, and underscores the point that the hypothalamus is concerned with the generation of a complete behavioural reaction, and establishing the pattern of cardiovascular and metabolic adjustments necessary for a particular response, whether it be fight or flight.

Clinical observations accord with the results of experimental studies in that tachycardia, tachypnoea, hypertension and pupillary dilation are evoked by stimulation of the posteromedial part of the hypothalamus. More lateral stimulation elicited hypotension, bradycardia and pupillary constriction (Sano *et al.*, 1970). However, these effects in man do not necessarily reflect a marked increase in the activity of the adrenal medulla, for in the course of a major review of the literature, Ungar & Phillips (1983) could find no evidence for a significant output of noradrenaline from the adrenal glands of humans, although under most circumstances there is 5–10 times as much of this catecholamine in peripheral blood than there is of other amines. In their eyes, the wide variations in the ratio of adrenaline to noradrenaline in peripheral blood, and in the ratios of the urinary metabolites of these compounds, reflect changes in the balance between adrenal secretory drive and noradrenaline overflow from peripheral nerve endings and should not be taken as evidence of selective release. This point is relevant in any discussion of the effects of emotional stress upon catecholamine secretion (Chapter 12).

Sometimes, as in cases of phaeochromocytoma, an excessive production of catecholamines can be generated within the adrenal medulla itself. A phaeochromocytoma is usually a tumour of the adrenal medulla, but in 10 per cent of cases the growth may occur somewhere along the sympathetic chain. The tumour cells periodically discharge adrenaline and noradrenaline and thus mimic phases of sympathetic overactivity. Discharges may be precipitated by exercise, change of posture or emotion, and generate an indescribable alarming sensation followed by palpitations, epigastric fullness, profuse sweating and headache. There may be severe anxiety, with the condition being mistaken for psychogenic anxiety attacks (Gibbons, 1983). Once again, these behavioural changes argue for the participation of the sympathetic system in the generation of emotional feelings.

Metabolic functions

The control of carbohydrate metabolism is another major concern of the hypothalamus. In part this function is exercised through the endocrine system, both indirectly through the pituitary gland and its target endocrine glands, and, more directly, through the adrenal medulla. In addition, the hypothalamus can influence the endocrine pancreas, and the secretion of insulin and glucagon, through nervous pathways (Benzo, 1983), so providing a means whereby emotional stress can affect the blood sugar level. Studies of rats in which the pancreas was vascularly isolated from the rest of the body, but in which the innervation was preserved, indicate that the brain tonically inhibits glucose-stimulated insulin secretion by about 40 per cent, probably through the sympathetic system (Curry, 1983). Electrical stimulation of the ventrolateral area of the hypothalamus can increase the secretion of insulin and glucagon, with the reaction being blocked by division of the vagus nerves. Interruption of the vagal nerve supply to the pancreas also inhibits conditioned insulin secretion, and, in man, vagotomy can impair the secretion of insulin and glucagon. Stimulation of the ventromedial area of the hypothalamus can elicit an increase in glucagon secretion, and a concomitant decrease in insulin output, as can stimulation of the splanchnic nerve. Receptors in the liver may monitor the blood level of glucose, and signal the brain through the vagus and splanchnic nerves. These processes may also be influential in the control of food intake (Chapter 11).

Thermoregulatory behaviour

The machinery influencing thermoregulatory behaviour shows two major components: the physiological mechanisms concerned with the maintenance of a near-constant body temperature and that involve heat loss or gain; and those concerned with purely behavioural adjustments, such as seeking shade in hot weather, or shelter in cold. They are centred upon the hypothalamus, where the processes governing heat loss are located in the preoptic area, and those concerned with the conservation of heat are situated posteriorly. Damage to the anterior hypothalamus results in chronic hyperthermia, while stimulation of this region suppresses shivering and causes cutaneous vasodilation. Conversely, lesions in the posterior hypothalamus damage the mechanisms conserving heat, and stimulation produces shivering.

For the human, behavioural responses to changes in temperature are of considerable importance. Bligh (1973) made it clear that it is the use of shelter and clothing, rather than shivering and sweating, that enables man to inhabit a wide range of climatic areas, with behavioural rather than autonomic thermoregulation determining the environmental limits within which man can exist. Behavioural responses to heat and cold are also important in the fine balance of body temperature, for we prefer to open and shut windows and adjust our dress rather than sweat and shiver. In the same way, rats given access to a supply of paper build insulating nests when exposed to cold (Richter, 1943), and monkeys readily learn to operate a fan to provide warm or cold air as appropriate.

Behavioural patterns

The distinctions just made are necessarily artificial in that various hypothalamic activities are discussed in isolation although they are often executed in concert. One might consider, like Jürgens (1974), that the behavioural patterns generated through the hypothalamus can be grouped into agonistic (dominance gestures, attack, defence, flight, submission), sexual, eating and drinking, grooming and preening, exploratory behaviour, and sleep. Even so, there is a considerable overlap in the regions concerned with these activities, considerable individual variation in the representation of the patterns, and a very high degree of integration. The attack behaviour evoked by hypothalamic stimulation in cats is highly stimulus responsive and directed: it is as if the behaviour is aimed toward a specific end so that the muscles activated and the movements generated differ according to circumstance. There is no simple activation of a particular set of nerves and muscles.

Immune function

A less well-developed area of hypothalamic function concerns its role in immune reactions. With the explosive resurgence of interest in immunology in recent years, the influence of the brain in the reactions to antigens is attracting increasing attention, for hormones influence the production of antibodies, and antibody production is depressed by removal of the pituitary gland. Lesions in the hypothalamus seem to be protective in the case of anaphylactic reactions, and could operate, at least in part, through changes in the release of hormones from the pituitary gland. Treatment with thyroid hormone reduces the protective effect of hypothalamic lesions, apparently by enhancing immune responses, whereas the reaction to adrenal cortical steroids depends upon the plasma concentration of the hormone. Other factors that may affect immune processes include growth hormone and the sex hormones. The hypothalamus may also influence immune activity through its connections with the autonomic system, for β-adrenergic stimulation inhibits the immune system, whereas β-adrenergic blockade enhances immune function. The way is evidently very clear for immune reactions to be affected by environmental or behavioural perturbations acting through the hypothalamus (Stein, Keller & Schleifer, 1981).

That psychosocial factors can influence the response to infection is beyond dispute. This has been established in a variety of ways, as by examining the personalities of students recently recovered from infectious mononucleosis, by studying the incidence of streptococcal disease in families in relation to 'stress', and by tracing the incidence of upper respiratory tract disease in students or of other conditions in officer cadets. The life span of mice inoculated with malarial parasites or *Salmonella* is inversely related to the number of mice in a cage, and there are many other concordant observations (Plaut & Friedman, 1981). Such effects may be attributed to 'stress', if the term is equated with any adverse circumstance, and might in turn be regarded as being derived from an activation of the adrenal glands and the consequent rise in plasma adrenal steroids. But that would be an oversimplification, for the adrenal steroids have many and diverse effects, one of which may be interference with the production or activity of the prostaglandins (fatty acid derivatives having a bewildering array of local actions on tissues) or similar agents (Chapter 3).

2

The pituitary gland and behaviour: the neurohypophysis

The hypothalamus influences the activity of the endocrine system in a variety of ways. There is the production of the hormones within that part of the brain, followed by the transport of the materials through the blood–brain barrier for discharge into the circulation: this procedure is adopted for the synthesis and release of the neurohypophysial hormones vasopressin and oxytocin. Then there is the direct neural control by the hypothalamus of the release of hormones synthesized elsewhere, as for adrenaline and nor-adrenaline in the adrenal medulla; and, finally, there is the production of chemical messengers by the hypothalamus, the releasing factors, that are carried by a short vascular link to an endocrine gland to control hormone secretion directly. This is the method adopted to govern the activity of the anterior pituitary gland. All of these modes are used to regulate the secretion of hormones influencing behaviour. There can also be a combination of methods, in that it seems that the hypothalamus can directly influence adrenal and ovarian function by neural means, as well as through control of the secretion of the appropriate pituitary hormones. This has been shown by studies involving the removal of one endocrine gland and examining the effects of ipsilateral or contralateral interruption of the pathways from that pair of glands to the hypothalamus, or by the production of unilateral hypothalamic hemi-islands, so cutting nerve fibres supplying that part of the brain (Nance, White & Moger, 1983). More attention will need to be paid to the nerve supply to, and from, endocrine glands in the future.

The pituitary gland

There are three parts to the pituitary gland: the anterior lobe, the posterior lobe, and lying between them, the intermediate lobe. Embryologi-cally, the pituitary gland arises from two different sources. The neural lobe, or pars nervosa, develops as an outpocketing of the hypothalamus, and the anterior and intermediate lobes differentiate from Rathke's pouch, an outgrowth from the roof of the mouth. The pouch meets and envelops the neural lobe and then loses its connection with the buccal epithelium, although residual clusters of cells along the route may persist in a very few individuals as a pharyngeal hypophysis. The intermediate lobe, or pars intermedia, differentiates from the part of the wall of Rathke's pouch in contact with the neural lobe, while that part of Rathke's pouch anterior to the residual lumen enlarges and becomes the anterior lobe.

Among vertebrates, the components of the pituitary gland remain remarkably constant. The most conspicuous phylogenetic changes have been the development of a consolidated neural lobe, the development of a system of portal vessels passing from the median eminence to the anterior lobe, and the disappearance of the pars intermedia in birds and a few mammals, such as the whale, Indian elephant and armadillo. In man, the intermediate lobe is well developed in infancy but loses its integrity, and in adults is merged with the neural lobe (Turner & Bagnara, 1976).

The neurohypophysis or posterior pituitary gland

This system is considered as a whole because the hormones produced are fabricated in the supraoptic and paraventricular nuclei and transported down a nerve tract to the posterior lobe of the pituitary gland for storage and release. Vasopressin and oxytocin, the hormones concerned, are nonapeptides (peptides comprised of nine amino acid residues) produced in the cell bodies in the hypothalamus along with larger molecules, the neurophysins. The neurophysins are found in the same secretory granules as vasopressin and oxytocin, and may serve to retain the hormones within the granules as they pass along the axons from the cell bodies in the brain for release at the nerve terminals in the posterior lobe. The concentration of neuropeptides is greatest in the synaptic region of the neuron, like that of the more familiar neurotransmitters. Neuropeptide release occurs with depolarization of the neuron and is dependent upon the uptake of calcium. Once in the general circulation, vasopressin serves as an antidiuretic hormone through its action on the kidney to enhance the permeability of tubule cells to water and to promote water reabsorption. Oxytocin is released at the time of nursing to cause ejection of milk from the lactating mammary gland, as well as at other times to cause contraction of the smooth muscle of the uterus.

The supraoptic and paraventricular nuclei are very prominent and well-defined nuclei within the hypothalamus, and for many years it was believed that they were concerned solely with the control of kidney, mammary gland and uterine function; however, it had long been known that the antidiuretic hormone possessed vasomotor activity–as indicated by the name vasopressin, which was applied before the much more important action on the kidneys had been discovered. With the aid of immunological techniques selectively staining vasopressin in neural tissue, the existence of a widespread network of nerve fibres in the brain that contains this peptide has come to light. Projections extend from cell bodies in the paraventricular nuclei into the dorsal and ventral hippocampus, amygdaloid nuclei, substantia nigra, the medulla, and much further caudally to reach the substantia gelatinosa of the spinal cord (De Wied & de Kloet, 1980). Thus, the presence of vasopressin is far from limited to the hypothalamus.

Vasopressin- and oxytocin-containing terminals are also present in high density in monoaminergic nuclei, especially the locus ceruleus (Iversen, 1983), and vasopressin can alter the turnover of catecholamines in various brain regions, including the locus ceruleus, the centre of catecholamine production in the pons. In line with its effects on the kidneys, vasopressin can increase the permeability to water of neurons in the locus ceruleus (Meisenberg & Simmons, 1983a, b). Oxytocin networks are similarly distributed, but are particularly prominent in the brain stem where the ratio of oxytocin to vasopressin fibres at the level of the caudal medulla oblongata is about 4 : 1. Caution is still advisable in regarding the cells of the supraoptic and paraventricular nuclei as the sole source of vasopressin and oxytocin in the brain, for destruction of these nuclei is not necessarily followed by disappearance of these peptides from other parts of the neural axis. Cell bodies containing these peptides may be more diffusely located than anticipated (Buijs, De Vries, Van Leeuwen & Swaab, 1983).

Some of the areas supplied with vasopressin- and oxytocin-containing fibres, including the dorsal septum, dorsal hippocampus and the area of the parafascicular nucleus in the posterior thalamus, may be significant in the control of memory processes. In parallel with the anatomical studies, pharmacological experiments involving the administration of neuro-hypophysial peptides, and some analogues of these compounds, drew attention to the possible involvement of vasopressin and oxytocin in memory and learning, and this field of endeavour has since been intensely cultivated, as is described more fully in Chapter 13.

Vasopressin and oxytocin are normal constituents of the cerebrospinal fluid (CSF), with the concentrations being of the same magnitude as that of plasma. The CSF concentrations do not depend upon those in plasma, and can rise above the levels in peripheral blood. There appears to be a daily rhythm in CSF content, with the highest concentrations being evident during the daylight hours (Meisenberg & Simmons, 1983a, b; Doris, 1984). Vasopressin might also be involved in the control mechanisms governing blood pressure, and a case to this effect has been put by Reid & Schwartz (1984), who point out that the peptide is an extremely potent vasoconstrictor that increases total peripheral resistance and causes a redistribution of blood flow at plasma concentrations below those required to produce maximal urine concentration: that is, within the range of normal plasma concentrations. It also potentiates the pressor response to catecholamines and inhibits the secretion of renin.

To complicate the physiological story of the neurohypophysial peptides further, compounds resembling oxytocin and vasopressin have been found in the ovaries of women. They seem to come from the corpus luteum, with oxytocin being the predominant peptide. Oxytocin may be concerned with the local control of corpus luteum function (Wathes *et al.*, 1982).

Control of drinking and water balance

The neural control of water balance provides an elegant example of neuro-endocrine integration, and well illustrates the interactions between hormone production by the brain, renal function, and behaviour. Receptors within the hypothalamus, in or near the supraoptic nucleus, are sensitive to changes in the osmolarity of the extracellular fluid, although osmoreceptors are also to be found outside the brain (Edwards, 1977; Moses, 1980). An increase in osmolarity causes vasopressin secretion, which in turn promotes the conservation of water by increasing the resorption of water in the collecting ducts of the kidney. The osmoreceptors are extremely sensitive, and there is a close correlation between the plasma vasopressin level and osmolarity in healthy adults (Robertson, Shelton & Athar, 1976). The average plasma vasopressin concentration is slightly above 2 pg/ml with a plasma osmolarity of about 287 mOsmol/kg. A 2 per cent increase in total body water suppresses vasopressin secretion, and thirst sets in with about a 2 per cent fall in body water (average plasma osmolarity 294 mOsmol/kg), which increases plasma vasopressin to about 5 pg/ml, a level sufficient for maximal urine concentration.

Vasopressin secretion is readily affected by neural stimuli, with emotional stress and pain being excitatory, and conditioning and hypnosis being inhibitory. Likewise, many drugs of psychiatric significance influence the output of this hormone, with secretion being increased by nicotine, morphine, barbiturates and some of the tricyclic antidepressants, and decreased by chlorpromazine and reserpine (Edwards, 1977). Physical or emotional stress can generate the syndrome of inappropriate vasopressin or antidiuretic hormone secretion, although the syndrome can also arise through the production of vasopressin by diseased lung or other tissue.

In addition to exercising control over water excretion, the hypothalamus also governs water intake. This was signalled in spectacular fashion in the goat by the work of Andersson (1953), who injected hypertonic saline into the hypothalamus, or electrically stimulated that area, and found that avid drinking resulted. Conversely, lesion studies have shown that adipsia can result from damage within the medial forebrain bundle, a fibre tract in the lateral hypothalamus. There is a curious distinction between water and other fluids, in that water is refused by lesioned dogs but nutritive fluids, such as beef broth, accepted. Hypovolaemia, or the reduction of blood volume without affecting the osmolarity of the remaining plasma (by haemorrhage or ligation of the inferior vena cava to reduce the venous return), also readily increases water intake (Epstein, 1982), so that there must be other sensors besides the osmoreceptors in the hypothalamus. For this response to occur, the kidneys must be present, for they produce the hormone renin. Renin is discharged from the kidneys in response to a fall in blood pressure and acts upon a protein in the plasma to release a decapeptide, angiotensin I, which is converted by an enzyme in the lungs and elsewhere to angiotensin II. This latter octapeptide exerts a variety of physiological functions aimed at restoring plasma volume and the concentration of sodium in the blood to normal.

Renin is found in other organs besides the kidneys, as well as in the brain. The renin found in the brain is not necessarily of peripheral origin, for there is no renin in CSF, as might be expected if it had filtered from the plasma, while the distribution of renin in brain tissue does not parallel the vascularity of the tissue. Further, the chemical composition of brain renin differs from that in plasma, and the concentration of brain renin does not fall after bilateral nephrectomy (Ganong, 1984). Although angiotensins do not cross the blood–brain barrier, they can pass through the fenestrated capillaries of the circumventricular organs to act upon neural tissue to increase drinking as well as the secretion of vasopressin. Salt appetite is also affected by angiotensin through a direct action upon the adrenal cortex to promote aldosterone secretion and sodium retention. However, the thresholds for the physiological effects of angiotensin II are considerably below that for the triggering of drinking.

The relationship of angiotensin to drinking is very close, for drinking is the only behavioural response elicited by the peptide. Nevertheless, there is disagreement concerning the involvement of angiotensin with drinking under normal circumstances, for interference with the renin–angiotensin system has not affected drinking, or the rehydration needed after water deprivation, in experimental animals. Neither has blockade of the angiotensin receptors in the brain by the competitive drug, saralasin acetate (Rolls & Rolls, 1982). On the other hand, Epstein (1982) points to observations showing that drinking is promoted by reasonably physiological doses of angiotensin and that challenges to the renin–angiotensin system produce angiotensin levels far above those necessary to cause drinking. Elevations of plasma renin produced in man by several pathological conditions are associated with excessive water intake and complaints of thirst (Brown *et al.*, 1969; Conn *et al.*, 1972). In two patients with chronic kidney disease who were complaining of thirst, removal of the kidneys reduced plasma renin levels and abolished the obsessive desire for water (Rogers & Kurtzman, 1973).

Angiotensin acts directly upon the brain to cause drinking. The injection of antibodies to angiotensin into the brain prevents the response, although endogenously produced angiotensin would not be expected to cross the blood–brain barrier. However, angiotensin appears to act through receptors in the subfornical area which in turn affect drinking (Rolls & Rolls, 1982; Epstein, 1982). The subfornical organ abuts upon the anterior part of the third ventricle and contains neurosecretory cells and neurons. It is a midline specialization of the ependymal lining of the third ventricle which is richly vascularized, in contact over one surface with the CSF, and outside the blood–brain barrier. Lesions of the subfornical area abolish the drinking response to intravenously injected angiotensin. Likewise, the application of saralasin (the competitive inhibitor of angiotensin) to the subfornical organ has suppressed the drinking induced by an intravenous infusion of angiotensin. The subfornical organ is not necessarily the only angiotensin receptor within the brain; arguments have been advanced for the presence of receptors in the preoptic area, lateral hypothalamus and the area postrema in the medulla. Overall, there is anatomical, physiological and pharmacological evidence that a multisynaptic pathway from the medial preoptic area to the globus pallidus is involved in drinking behaviour, although lesions at various locations along the pathway only reduce, and do not abolish, responses to angiotensin II injected into the medial preoptic area (Swanson & Mogensen, 1981).

With regard to the neuropharmacology of thirst, the selective depletion of dopamine, but not of noradrenaline, reduces the dipsogenic effectiveness of intracranial angiotensin without affecting the thirst induced by carbachol. Procedures that increase the amount of dopamine available in the brain favour fluid intake, and accord with the involvement of the catecholaminergic pathways in the midbrain in the control of eating and drinking. Angiotensin has been shown to affect the turnover of acetylcholine and noradrenaline in the brain (Epstein, 1982; Rausch *et al.*, 1982).

3

The anterior pituitary gland and behaviour

The anterior lobe of the pituitary gland, together with the intermediate lobe and pars tuberalis, makes up the adenohypophysis, or so-called glandular division of the pituitary gland. It produces six hormones of established functional significance: adrenocorticotrophin (ACTH), thyrotrophic hormone (TSH), growth or somatotrophic hormone, follicle-stimulating hormone (FSH), luteinizing hormone (LH), and prolactin. Of these, ACTH and prolactin are of direct behavioural significance, for these two hormones can act directly upon the brain to influence behaviour. The other pituitary hormones act indirectly to influence behaviour by controlling the production of target organ hormones and metabolites, such as thyroxine, triiodothyronine and the sex hormones. Adrenocorticotrophic hormone is of especial concern because of a close connection between ACTH, β-lipotrophin and endorphin secretion (p. 31), and from work on learning and memory (Chapter 13), while prolactin is significant as a multifunctional hormone influencing activities ranging from sexual and maternal behaviour to water balance.

The anterior pituitary gland lacks a secretomotor innervation and the functional link with the hypothalamus, through which the brain influences the output of hormones from the pars distalis, is provided by the hypophysial portal vessels. These arise as a plexus of small capillaries in the median eminence of the hypothalamus, which combine to form blood vessels running along the pituitary stalk to join the sinusoids of the anterior lobe. In this way, neurosecretory products released from the hypothalamus into the capillary loops of the primary plexus are conveyed to the pars distalis. Division of the portal vessels, combined with measures to prevent repair and reconnection across the break, effectively deprives the anterior lobe of hypothalamic neurosecretory substances, or releasing factors, and reduces the output of all hormones but one from the gland. The exception is prolactin, the secretion of which is normally *inhibited* by the hypothalamus.

Despite the arguments put forward by a few iconoclasts, it was accepted until recently that the portal vessels provided a one-way conveyor system from the hypothalamus to the hypophysis. However, the idea that some vessels might carry blood in the opposite direction, so exposing the hypothalamus directly to the influence of hypophysial hormones, is gaining support. Anatomical observations pointing in this direction, and involving the visualization of the hypophysial portal vessels in living animals, were published decades ago, but ignored until attempts were made to account for the seemingly poor drainage of the gland.

The relatively high concentrations of pituitary hormones detectable in the hypothalamus, and in blood collected from portal vessels supposedly draining the hypothalamus, were also puzzling. These considerations led Bergland & Page (1978) to re-examine the vascular architecture of the hypothalamo–hypophysial area in sheep and in primates, using modern methacrylate cast techniques and scanning electron microscopy. Their three dimensional visualization of all of the arteries, capillaries and veins connected with the pituitary gland substantially altered the traditional concepts of pituitary vascular relationships, and it is now thought that the pituitary portal veins do not simply separate a primary capillary bed within the median eminence of the hypothalamus from a second within the anterior lobe, but may serve as capillary exit vessels favouring the movement of substances into surrounding tissue, for they possess fenestrated endothelial cells. Put another way, the adenohypophysis and neurohypophysis may be regarded as being united through a common capillary bed and not separated by portal veins. Anatomical routes thus exist for the transport of pituitary hormones from the gland to the brain, as well as the recirculation of hypothalamic releasing factors back to the hypothalamus, but definitive proof that the channels are so used is not available.

The presence of pituitary hormones in the hypothalamus can be explained in other ways, such as the occurrence of local synthesis, on the basis that the concentration of pituitary hormones in the neural tissue does not fall after hypophysectomy, that some hormones are localized within a discrete system (and not diffused through a region), and because hormones akin to those produced by the pituitary gland can be synthesized by brain tissue *in vitro*. Even so, in his thoughtful review of these matters, Page (1982) was content to leave open the question of the physiological significance of any retrograde flow from the pituitary gland to the hypothalamus.

Adrenocorticotrophic hormone

Adrenocorticotrophic hormone is a 39-amino acid peptide with a molecular weight of approximately 4500. The pituitary gland also contains a large molecule known as pro-opiomelanocortin or POMC, which serves as a precursor for other peptides and thus carries a range of hormone residues, such as endorphins, melanocyte-stimulating hormones and β-lipotrophic hormone (β-LPH), within its structure. The physiological role of POMC is not limited to the pituitary gland, for POMC or peptides derived from the precursor have been found in the brain, placenta, reproductive tract, gastrointestinal tract, lymphocytes and lung (Krieger, 1983a). They have also been detected in earthworms, molluscs, insects and protozoa. As might be expected from their wide distribution, the influence of these peptides extends far beyond the pituitary gland, for they can act in a manner akin to neurotransmitters (Chapter 4). Indeed, immunoreactive POMC-related material has been detected in the hypothalamus of the developing rat fetus 4 days before it appeared in the anterior lobe of the pituitary gland. Within the anterior hypophysis the precursor molecule is processed predominantly to ACTH and β-LPH, whereas in the intermediate lobe of experimental animals the ACTH and β-LPH is further broken down to β-MSH and β-endorphin-like derivatives. Thus stimulation of the secretion of ACTH by physiological or pharmacological means may raise the output of a complex of hormones, rather than that of a single molecule.

The plasma level of ACTH oscillates throughout the day, but is commonly below 100 pg/ml. Secretion from the pituitary gland is controlled by the plasma level of corticosteroids, and two modes of negative feedback are operative: fast and delayed. When cortisol is given intravenously, suppression of ACTH secretion is evident within 2 minutes (fast feedback), but a slower response is also demonstrable. The secretion of ACTH shows a circadian periodicity, with the highest blood levels occurring between 0400 and 0800 hours; some 5–10 bursts of ACTH secretion may be generated over each 24-hour period. The circadian mechanism is superimposed upon the negative feedback mechanism, for in patients with Addison's disease suffering damage to the adrenal glands (with a reduction in adrenal steroid secretion and a consequently enhanced release of ACTH from the pituitary gland), the circadian rhythm is retained, and, indeed, exaggerated (Imura *et al.*, 1982). The importance of ACTH in general metabolic processes must not be overlooked, for adult patients with pituitary insufficiency frequently show depressive symptoms and an apathy that may progress to stupor, coma and death. These features flow from the metabolic changes accompanying the condition and can be reversed rapidly by treatment with adrenal hormones (Michael & Gibbons, 1963).

Numerous stimuli provoke the secretion of ACTH, and generally fall under the heading of stresses. These can be systemic, as with infection, the injection of a pyrogen, or insulin-induced hypoglycaemia; neural, and often associated with pain; or psychological. All operate through the hypothalamus and induce discharge of (adreno)corticotrophin-releasing factor (CRF), and, in turn, ACTH. Together with ACTH, the secretion of β-LPH and β-endorphin may also be enhanced.

Much significance has been attached to the increase in adrenal steroid output arising from stressful influences, and the 'general adaptation syndrome' of Selye, discussed earlier, attracted much interest. Selye (1957) predicted that an overproduction of adrenal cortical hormones was an aetiologic factor in the generation of a large number of diseases, including rheumatoid arthritis, and that treatment with ACTH or adrenal hormones would exacerbate the symptoms. In the event the reverse proved to be true, for the glucocorticoids exerted anti-inflammatory actions. But the question of the physiological significance of the rise in adrenal cortical activity with stress remains. Why is so much adrenal hormone produced, and how do the glucocorticoids protect the individual under stressful circumstances? There is no doubt that protection is exercised, for clinicians are well aware of the need to supply patients with increased amounts of glucocorticoid at such times.

One attractive idea is that many fundamentally important glucocorticoid effects do not arise immediately from direct effects of the hormones on the target cells, but arise secondarily through the action of various intercellular mediators that are under glucocorticoid control, for glucocorticoids inhibit the production, and sometimes the actions, of intercellular mediators like the prostaglandins and lymphokines (proteins and peptides secreted in response to stress or tissue damage). Munck, Guyre & Holbrook (1984) argue that the stress-induced increases in glucocorticoid levels do not serve to protect against the source of stress itself, but rather restrain the normal defence reactions that are activated by stress. The glucocorticoids are considered to achieve this end by turning off the defence reactions, and thus preventing them from overshooting and thus threatening homeostasis in a potentially more damaging way. There is much that is appealing in this view.

Adrenocortical dysfunction and behaviour

Ever since the first report of Addison in 1855, mental changes have been known to follow damage to the adrenal glands. Common early symptoms include loss of initiative, fatigue and weakness, with a voice that is weak and whining in character (Smith, Barish, Correa & Williams, 1972; Jefferson & Marshall, 1981). Memory impairment is a major feature in up to three-quarters of cases (Michael & Gibbons, 1963). This observation should be borne in mind in evaluating the current work on the relationship between ACTH-like peptides and memory, for the secretion of ACTH is raised in Addison's disease, although plasma corticosteroids are reduced. However, so many physiological perturbations flow from adrenal insufficiency that it is difficult to isolate the most significant factor. Thus, there are changes in electrolyte, carbohydrate, protein and fat metabolism, as well as in the circulation of blood through the brain. Nevertheless, correction of the disturbed electrolyte balance by treatment with the mineralocorticoid aldosterone does not improve mental function, correct the abnormalities in the EEG or restore the sensory thresholds to normal. Glucocorticoids, as exemplified by cortisol, are necessary.

The majority of patients with an oversecretion of adrenal steroids, or Cushing's syndrome, show mental changes, and a disorder sufficiently severe to be termed psychotic occurs in 5–20 per cent of cases; the incidence of lesser mental changes is much greater (Williams, 1970). Martin, Reichlin & Brown (1977) pointed out that the literature failed to discriminate between the psychic effects of pituitary or hypothalamic origin and those produced directly by adrenal hormones. This distinction can be important in the light of recent work on the direct effects of ACTH-like peptides upon brain function (p. 178), although few of the attempts to account for the mental disturbances resulting from malfunction of the pituitary–adrenal axis have been satisfactory. Numerous possibilities were examined by Quarton, Clark, Cobb & Bauer (1955) on the presumption that changes in the blood level of corticosteroids were responsible. Included among the endocrine mechanisms was the hypothesis that cortisone or ACTH may interfere with the mechanisms of learning or retention in such a way as to lead to mental disorder. As long as thirty years ago this possibility was considered to merit extensive examination.

Several of the endocrine abnormalities in patients with Cushing's disease may be attributed to disorders in hypothalamic regulation (Pepper & Krieger, 1984). These include resistance to the suppression of ACTH secretion by the feedback action of exogenous corticosteroid, an absence of circadian periodicity in ACTH, growth hormone and prolactin secretion, and abnormal sleep EEG patterns characterized by a decrease in the percentage of slow-wave sleep. These changes cannot be accounted for by the excessively high levels of adrenal steroids in the blood and may persist after the reduction of the plasma level of cortisol seen to follow irradiation of the pituitary gland. Treatment of patients with a serotoninergic blocking agent, cyproheptadine, has induced remission in some 60 per cent of cases, so implying the involvement of a neural mechanism. There is thus good reason for applying the term 'Cushing's disease' to hypercorticalism of diencephalic origin, and 'Cushing's syndrome' to hypercorticalism arising from other causes such as adrenal adenoma or ectopic ACTH-producing neoplasms (Carroll, 1976).

The incidence of mental disturbance among cases of Cushing's syndrome is high. Jefferson & Marshall (1981) concluded that approximately 5–24 per cent of patients experience major mental changes, 22–54 per cent experience moderate but significant changes, and in 32–40 per cent the changes are minor. Depending upon the diligence with which disturbances are sought, the overall percentage of patients with mental disturbance ranges from 44–88 per cent. Depression is the most common mental accompaniment of Cushing's disease (Kelly, Checkley, Bender & Mashiter, 1983), and suicidal tendencies may develop. Other symptoms include irritability, difficulty of concentration, insomnia, and paranoid delusions and hallucinations, and these may appear before the physical signs such as obesity, facial mooning and striae are detected.

A number of reports suggest that affective symptoms are associated more with Cushing's disease than with the syndrome, and there are suggestions that the disease be regarded as a psychosomatic disorder (Carroll, 1976). Comparison of a series of 33 cases of Cushing's disease with 20 cases of the syndrome indicated a much higher incidence of depressive symptoms in patients with the disease than in those with the syndrome. An inability to concentrate, drowsiness, restlessness, insomnia, irritability, apprehension and disturbed sleep were all mentioned by Addison in his description of adrenal insufficiency over 100 years ago, and since the secretion of ACTH is high in Cushing's disease, where plasma cortisol is also high, and in Addison's disease, where plasma cortisol is low, the high incidence of depression in both states may be of significance. At first sight, a high blood concentration of ACTH would seem to be responsible for depression, but high plasma levels of this hormone produced by other means do not have this effect. Rather would it appear that a release from inhibition of the diencephalic–limbic mechanisms controlling ACTH secretion and other functions may be of importance. On the other hand, Cohen (1980) found that 25 of 29 consecutive patients with Cushing's syndrome were depressed. The severity of the depression was not related to the plasma cortisol concentration, but when the tumour or the hyperplastic adrenal glands were removed the depression was rapidly relieved–so pointing to the production of some depressive substance by the adrenal glands. However, as Kelly *et al.* (1983) and Pepper & Krieger (1984) showed, reduction of cortisol secretion in various ways, and irrespective of any reduction in ACTH secretion, alleviates the psychiatric symptoms in patients with Cushing's disease or syndrome. On this basis it is natural to conclude that as Cushing's syndrome develops it commonly gives rise to depression.

Behavioural changes also follow the administration of ACTH or corticosteroids for therapeutic purposes, although these have received less attention in recent years. In 1972 the Boston Collaborative Drug Surveillance

Program reported that acute psychiatric reactions occurred in 21 of 676 patients given prednisolone (a synthetic corticosteroid), that is 3.1 per cent. Earlier reports emphasized the improvement in the feelings of well-being and alertness, alongside elation and euphoria, although this could progress to restlessness, insomnia, increased motor activity and talkativeness. However, euphoric patients may also be anxious, emotionally labile, irritable and restless. Depression may also be seen and alternate with periods of elation (Jefferson & Marshall, 1981). A recent survey of steroid-induced psychiatric syndromes established that 5.7 per cent of medical patients suffered mental disturbances, with a maximum incidence in some samples of 50 per cent (Lewis & Smith, 1983). These findings are quite similar to those reported in a review published over twenty years ago and suggest that the incidence of disorders has not changed materially, despite differences in the types of steroid used. Depression was most commonly seen (40 per cent), with mania following in 28 per cent, and usually became evident early in the course of treatment. As yet, it is difficult to predict which patients will show adverse reactions to steroid therapy (Jefferson & Marshall, 1981). There is no relationship between personality features and the duration and severity of the resultant disorders, while the absence of any mental disturbance during steroid therapy does not imply that subsequent neuropsychiatric disorders are unlikely.

Depression

Ever since the work of Gibbons (1964), it has been clear that the secretion of cortisol is increased in depressive illness. But the cause of the rise remains to be understood. As described earlier, the release of ACTH from the pituitary gland shows a circadian rhythm, with more bursts of secretion in the morning than in the evening. In depressed patients the number of episodes of cortisol secretion is increased, the plasma cortisol concentration at the beginning and end of secretory episodes is greatly raised, and cortisol secretion continues actively throughout day and night, and during sleep, and is not reduced by treatment with the tranquillizing drug chlorpromazine (Sachar, 1980). It has often been suggested that the increase in adrenocortical activity is a consequence of the anxiety and dysphoria experienced by the patient, but the findings of increased adrenal activity in apathetic, as well as in anxious, depressives, and the persistence of such increased activity during sleep, when a psychogenic stressful stimulus would be expected to be switched off, argues against this view. Instead the evidence points to a more fundamental disturbance of brain function and some release from a generally prevailing inhibition of ACTH secretion.

Some insight into the mechanism of increase in ACTH secretion is provided by the dexamethasone suppression test. Dexamethasone is a non-endogenous glucocorticoid that does not interfere with the assay of cortisol in plasma samples, so facilitating assessment of the response to treatment. After the administration of dexamethasone, usually 1 mg orally late at night, ACTH and glucocorticoid secretion in normal subjects is suppressed for at least 24 hours, whereas in depressed patients, or patients with Cushing's disease producing excessive amounts of ACTH, there may be a fall in the output of corticosteroids on the following morning, but the inhibition quickly wanes and steroid production may be back to the pretreatment level in the afternoon. The pituitary–adrenal system is said to have escaped from suppression. With increasing severity of depressive illness, the escape from suppression occurs progressively earlier on the post-dexamethasone day. Elevated night-time plasma cortisol levels are also strongly predictive of an abnormal escape from suppression. Such findings are interpreted as indicating a failure of the normal inhibition of the hypothalamo-pituitary–adrenal axis by the limbic system, but more infor-mation is needed on the basis of the disconnection, although interference with neurotransmitter function is likely. Some 30–40 per cent of depressed patients, as opposed to less than 5 per cent of other psychiatric patients, show an early escape from dexamethasone suppression of the adrenal gland, and the test can be valuable in diagnosis. It has distinguished between monopolar depressed patients with depressive neurosis (who respond nor-mally) at a confidence level of 90–100 per cent (Carroll, Curtis & Mendels, 1976a, b). Repetition of a dexamethasone suppression test after one week in drug free depressed patients showed that the results of the first test were reproducible in 17 of 19 subjects, so implying a high degree of reliability (Charles, Wilmotte, Quenon & Mendlewicz, 1982). The test may also have predictive properties, in that patients showing clinical signs of recovery but with retention of an impaired response to dexamethasone are prone to relapse (Greden *et al.*, 1980).

Because of the close biosynthetic connection between ACTH and β-endorphin, it is not surprising that the morning plasma concentration of β-endorphin, like that of ACTH and cortisol, is increased over the night-time level. The secretion of this peptide was also more readily increased in depressed patients by the inhibitor of cholinesterase, physostigmine, which enhances cholinergic neurotransmission, than in controls (Risch, 1982).

Although electroconvulsive therapy (ECT) can be effective in the treat-ment of depression, the mode of action of this procedure remains unknown. As might be expected, the electrical stimulus induces ACTH and cortisol secretion, as well as surges in prolactin, growth hormone and, sometimes, gonadotrophin secretion. There is also a marked increase in vasopressin release, which lasts for about ten minutes, and has been put forward as of therapeutic value (Sørensen, Hammer & Bolwig, 1982; Whalley *et al.*, 1982; Deakin *et al.*, 1983). In view of the amnesia occurring after ECT the neural response to any vasopressin discharged is unlikely to be marked (see Chapter 13), and the endocrine responses to ECT have so far proved useless in predicting the therapeutic value of the treatment.

ACTH and the brain

The classical biological actions of ACTH are, as its name suggests, exerted through the adrenal glands, with maintenance of a high level of functional activity on the part of the adrenal cortex and the promotion of steroidogenesis. In addition, there are direct actions upon the brain. Close study of the structure–activity relationships of the ACTH molecule has proved to be intriguing and enlightening in that the 39-amino acid sequence can be divided into segments with specific functions (Gispen, 1982). The sequence ACTH 1–3 enhances the potency and efficacy of the compound; ACTH 4–10 conveys the significant message and triggers the receptor; the sequence ACTH 11–24 exerts an addressing function and adds cell-specific affinity, while the series ACTH 25–39 provides the species label and is concerned with transport, potentiation and antigen formation. The vital information for the receptors is encoded in ACTH 4–10, and the extensions in the molecular structure on either side of this sequence are necessary for biological activity. It follows that a given receptor may react with one part of the molecule, whereas another different receptor, even on the same cell, may be affected by another peptide sequence within the molecule and at a distance from the first.

Paradoxically, ACTH is not confined to the pituitary gland and, like the closely related pro-opiomelanocortin derivatives β-endorphin and γ-lipo-trophin, is widely distributed in the brain. The highest concentrations are found in the hypothalamus, amygdala, periventricular gray substance, substantia nigra and superior colliculus, in that descending order (Emson *et al.*, 1984). Procedures known to affect the secretion of ACTH, such as adrenalectomy and the administration of ACTH or glucocorticoids, do not significantly alter the hypothalamic or whole brain content of ACTH. Neither do experimental procedures, like immobilization, that are known to enhance ACTH output. Further, the ACTH content of the brain is not reduced by removal of the major source of the hormone, the pituitary gland. All of these observations lead to the conclusion that the ACTH present in the brain is not derived from, or affected by, changes in the level of activity of the pituitary gland. Indeed, ACTH has been detected in the pond snail, the fruit fly and in a protozoan (Krieger, 1983a, b) – again pointing to activities beyond the mere control of adrenocortical function.

Corticotrophin-releasing factor (CRF)

Over the years, much time, effort, and money has been devoted to the isolation and identification of CRF, but only recently has success been achieved–a decade after the isolation of the releasing factors controlling the secretion of thyrotrophic hormone and the gonadotrophins. Thus, in 1981, Vale, Spiess, Rivier & Rivier reported the isolation of a peptide from ovine hypothalami with 41 amino acid residues that had the activity expected of a CRF. Corticotrophin-releasing factor normally increases the secretion only of ACTH and β-endorphin in man; prolactin or growth hormone secretion is not enhanced (Gold *et al.*, 1984), although CRF produces a rise in growth hormone output in depressed patients. It has since become clear that, as with other hypothalamic releasing factors, the function of CRF probably extends far beyond the simple control of ACTH and β-endorphin release, and could provide a key signal for the co-ordination of endocrine and behavioural responses to stressful and other adaptive stimuli.

Corticotrophin-releasing factor has been detected in the smaller cell bodies of the paraventricular nuclei, as well as in other parts of the hypothalamus. Additionally, CRF-stained cells and terminals have been found in the central nucleus of the amygdala in the temporal lobes of the brain, the bed nucleus of the stria terminalis in the septum, the central gray and dorsal vagal complex in the brain stem, and the medial forebrain bundle and periventricular system. The peptide has also been found in the inter-neurons of the cerebral cortex (Vale *et al.*, 1983). The presence of CRF so far from the pituitary gland points to other functions besides that of the control of ACTH release, and this possibility has been tested by intra-cerebroventricular injection of minute amounts of the material. In experimental animals there is an acute and prolonged elevation of plasma catecholamines upon CRF administration, indicative of activation of the sympathetic system, with the rise in adrenaline (but not of noradrenaline) susceptible to blockade by another pituitary hormone controlling factor, growth hormone release-inhibiting factor or somatostatin. There is also a rise in plasma glucagon and glucose, so that the general reaction is similar to that seen with many kinds of stress.

Behavioural changes produced by the intracranial injection of CRF in the rat include increased locomotion and sniffing, grooming, and rearing consistent with a general arousal. Pre-treatment with CRF, before exposure to a novel and presumably aversive environment, elicited responses that were consistent with an increased emotionality or increased sensitivity to the stressful aspects of the situation (Vale *et al.*, 1983). The micro-infusion of CRF into the arcuate–ventromedial area of the hypothalamus, or into the mesencephalic central gray matter, inhibits sexual behaviour in female rats, possibly through the mediation of β-endorphin (Sirinathsinghji, Rees, Rivier & Vale, 1983).

The availability of CRF has favoured detailed studies of the changes in the control of ACTH secretion in mental illness, as well as exploration of the usefulness of the factor in the differential diagnosis of depression and early Cushing's disease. The experimental observations that CRF, given intra-cerebroventricularly, stimulates the locus ceruleus (which gives rise to much of the monoamines present in the brain) as well as exciting the hypothalamo-pituitary–adrenal system, depresses eating and sexual behaviour, causes changes in activity and may induce seizures in the limbic system, suggested to Gold *et al.* (1984) that an excessive secretion of CRF may generate some of the behavioural changes seen clinically in affective disease. For they recalled that depressed subjects often show hypercor-ticalism, significant anxiety (possibly mediated through the locus ceruleus, Chapter 12), anorexia, diminished libido, and hypoactivity or hyperactivity, and that they may respond to limbic system anticonvulsant therapy. It is easy to see why the search is on for antagonists of CRF capable of passage across the blood–brain barrier (and thus effective after intravenous adminis-tration) so that such ideas can be tested. What might be the consequences of selective inhibition of CRF activity within the brain?

Thyrotrophic hormone

As with other target endocrine organs, the secretory activities of the thyroid gland are controlled by another product of the pituitary complex: thyroid-stimulating hormone, thyrotrophic hormone, or TSH. Thyro-trophic hormone is a glycoprotein, and in its absence (as after hypophysec-tomy or pituitary damage) all of the processes in the thyroid gland leading to the synthesis and secretion of the thyroid hormones are slowed. At least three forms of TSH are in circulation in euthyroid individuals (Morley, 1981). They are not equivalent in biological activity, and this fact points to caution in the interpretation of the results of radioimmunoassays, where the antibody used may bind to a molecular species with minimal, or no, thyroid-stimulating activity and so give rise to erroneous conclusions.

The secretion of TSH is influenced by the brain through the anterior hypothalamus, and through the mediation of monoamines, although the literature is confusing (Morley, 1981). Experimentally, a variety of neuropeptides has been shown to alter the release of TSH, but the physio-logical significance of these observations remains to be established.

There are two major thyroid hormones, 3,5,3′,5′-tetraiodo-L-thyronine (thyroxine) and 3,5,3′-triodo-L-thyronine (T3), although other iodo-thyronines are present in blood. Thyroxine is the major secretory product of the thyroid gland, and much of the T3 in circulation is derived from thyroxine by the removal of an atom of iodine in peripheral tissues. Triiodothyronine is several times more active than thyroxine and in numerous circumstances thyroxine is converted to T3 before utilization by a particular organ or tissue. Thyroid hormones are important in the control of the metabolic rate, and, in turn, the secretion of TSH is affected by changes in the environmental temperature. Exposure of experimental animals to cold, or local cooling of the hypothalamus, increases TSH secretion, but the effects of cold in man are less striking; exposure to heat depresses thyroid function in man. Alongside their metabolic functions, thyroid hormones modulate behaviour, and the emotional apathy and intellectual deterioration seen in cases of thyroid insufficiency, or myxoedema, were described more than one hundred years ago. The psychological improvement and personality changes evident upon treatment with sheep thyroid tissue have been known almost as long (Beach, 1981). Yet the incidence of minor thyroid disorder may be unexpectedly high; among a series of acute admissions to psychiatric hospitals the incidence of hyperthyroidism lay between 6 and 8 per cent. The condition was transient, with thyroxine levels returning to normal within a fortnight after hospitalization. True hyperthyroidism was less common and was found in 0.1–1.7 per cent of psychiatric patients (Morley, 1981).

Almost every type of psychiatric reaction has been associated with hypothyroidism, and nearly all patients experience cognitive changes (Jefferson & Marshall, 1981). Early in the illness a progressive slowing of all mental processes predominates; memory for recent events is impaired and significant depressive affect is common. Although many medical descriptions of hypothyroid patients use terms such as flat, somnolent, stuporous or apathetic, psychiatric descriptions highlight a different aspect of patient behaviour. They are frequently seen as anxious, markedly irritable with labile affect, and suffering from insomnia. Many cases of psychosis associated with hypothyroidism have been reported but the correlation is not invariable (Whybrow, Prange & Treadway, 1969; Jain, 1972), and mental symptoms may appear before clinical signs. The usual symptoms consist of a progressive slowing of all mental processes, tiredness unrelieved by sleep, and poor memory, with recent events being quickly forgotten. Normal mental effort cannot be maintained and there is a tendency to drop off to sleep during the day. Comprehension and motor activity are slowed and sexual activity and desire reduced. Of 30 consecutive hypothyroid patients studied by Jain (1972), 10 were anxious, 13 depressed and only 8 psychiatrically normal.

The fact that mental aberrations in hypothyroidism disappear upon replacement therapy provides convincing evidence for their hormonal basis, and has justified many attempts to treat depression by giving thyroid hormone; for depression might ensue from marginal hypothyroidism. Even today it is suggested that use of a tricyclic antidepressant in a depressed patient should not be abandoned as of little benefit until the effects of supplementation with triiodothyronine have been explored (Goodwin *et al.*, 1982).

The typical patient with hyperthyroidism is hyperactive and complains of nervousness and anxiety associated with a generalized fine tremor and a feeling of irritability and emotional lability (Jefferson & Marshall, 1981). There may be episodes of tearfulness although the patients are aware that these are without evident cause. Subtle disturbances of cognitive function, as exemplified by impaired performance in tasks requiring concentration and memory, are also demonstrable (MacCrimmon, Wallace, Goldberg & Streiner, 1979).

Before the immunological basis of Graves' disease, a hyperthyroid condition wrongly believed to be due to excessive secretion of TSII, was discovered, it was believed that emotional stress frequently preceded, and could precipitate, the disorder. Lidz (1949), for example, cites an 1825 report that 'Elizabeth S., aged 21, was thrown out of a wheel chair in coming fast down a hill . . . and was very much frightened though not much hurt. From this time she has been subject to palpitation of the heart and various nervous affections. About a fortnight after she began to observe a swelling of the thyroid gland.' Little attention seems to have been given to the fact that this lady was sufficiently poorly in the first place to be confined to a wheel chair, and by 1897 it was stated 'that sudden emotion or prolonged worry commonly sets in motion the symptoms [of thyroid overactivity] will be so universally conceded as not to demand extensive illustration.'

In more modern times Kleinschmidt, Waxenberg & Cuker (1956) were convinced that emotional problems antedated the clinical signs of disease in 81 of 84 thyrotoxic patients. However, it has always been difficult to prove that the behavioural changes could be a cause, rather than a consequence, of the disease, and in 71 of the cases (85 per cent) the traumatic events were within the realm of usual life experiences, or 'within the range of life's vicissitudes experienced by all'. Until quite recently it seemed obvious that emotional stresses led to an excessive secretion of TSH. Because the secondary rise in thyroid hormone could not inhibit pituitary function, the high level of TSH release was believed to be maintained and to lead to thyrotoxicosis. This view is no longer tenable, and it is accepted that thyrotoxicosis due to an excessively high TSH secretion is rare. Graves' disease is now considered to represent an immune disease, with antibodies binding abnormally to the TSH receptor sites in the thyroid gland and stimulating the organ (Fowler, 1984). As forcibly stated by Morley (1981) 'scientific evidence for stress-induced Graves' disease is non-existent'.

Thought has been given to the possibility that thyrotoxicosis can precipitate manic–depressive psychoses in suitably predisposed individuals, but the incidence of thyrotoxicosis in patients in mental hospitals (less than 1 per cent) is about the same as that in the general population, while the interpretation of the reported prevalence of psychiatric morbidity in series of patients with thyrotoxicosis is hazardous in the absence of standardized diagnostic instruments (Checkley, 1978). There are occasions when an episode of mania coincides with one of thyrotoxicosis (Corn & Checkley, 1983), but a causal relationship has not been established.

Many investigators have noticed the similarity between the signs of hyperthyroidism (tremor, stare, tachycardia and so on) and the signs of β-adrenergic stimulation, while β-adrenergic blockade is of value in attenuating the signs of thyrotoxicosis. There is an increased tissue sensitivity to catecholamines in hyperthyroidism, which may be due to an increased number of β-receptors on cell membranes. Conversely, the number of β-receptors is decreased in hypothyroidism (Heinsimer & Lefkowitz, 1982).

Thyrotrophic hormone-releasing factor (TRF)

There is now much evidence that the activities of this tripeptide extend beyond the control of release of TSH from the pituitary gland. Indeed, TRF is unable to act through the pituitary gland to increase thyroid function in fish and amphibia although it is present in high concentration in the hypothalamus and brain. It is also present in high concentration in amphibian skin, and the concentration in the blood of the frog *Rana pipiens* is some 1000 times more than in mammals. Such observations support the suggestion that the releasing factors initially arose with a neurocrine or paracrine function, and only later in evolution acquired the role of regulating adenohypophysial function (Jackson, 1981). Accordingly, TRF may be concerned with neurotransmission (a neurocrine function) as well as cell-to-cell regulation (a paracrine function) (Morley, 1981; Jackson, 1982).

Thyrotrophin-releasing factor also acts to promote the secretion of prolactin from the hypophysis, but this is not regarded as being of physiological importance. However, inappropriate lactation, occasionally with elevated prolactin levels, can be found in patients with primary hypothyroidism. Interestingly, when the effects of continuous or intermittent administration of TRF to monkeys were compared, it was concluded that intermittent TRF was more effective in elevating serum prolactin concentration, and continuous TRF infusion more effective in raising TSH and thyroxine levels. Thus, the mode of TRF release from the hypothalamus might determine the relative secretion rates of TSH and prolactin (Pavasuthipaisit *et al.*, 1983). Observations of this kind underscore a current dilemma in terminology. Soon after the first releasing factors were identified, and before the wide range of their activities came to be appreciated, efforts were made to accord these substances the status of hormones. Some success was achieved in that TRF is often called thyrotrophin-releasing hormone (TRH). However, this usage accords overmuch emphasis to but one action of the peptide and the more neutral 'factor' is preferred.

In a number of non-thyroidal disorders, including renal failure, starvation and depression, the hypophysial response to an injection of TRF may be blunted, and in the case of depression the blunted response appears to correlate well with a beneficial response to electroconvulsive therapy. On recovery from depression response to TRF becomes normal, but the basis for the change is not understood. Although depressed patients are generally euthyroid, unipolar depressed individuals secrete lower amounts of thyroid-stimulating hormone in response to administration of the releasing factor. Whereas excess cortisol secretion is seen in both unipolar and bipolar depressed patients, a blunted TSH response is considered by some to appear only in unipolar depressed patients, to be correlated with an increase in the CSF content of 5-hydroxyindoleacetic acid, a principal metabolite of serotonin, and to be possibly indicative of a derangement in the metabolism of this neurotransmitter (Freedman & Carter, 1982). The TSH response test could have prognostic value in that Kirkegaard (1981) gave TRF to patients with endogenous depression who were clinically cured after short-term antidepressant therapy. The patients could be divided into two groups, one showing an increase in plasma TSH level of more than $2.0 \mu U$ TSH/ml, and the other with an increase below that value. The first group of patients did well for at least 6 months whereas the patients in the second group relapsed with a median time of 2 months. Predictions concerning the progress of the patients based upon the changes in TSH release were correct in 60 of 66 cases.

Unhappily, this optimistic prospect is not supported by other investigators, although there is agreement that an increased release of TSH on the occasion of the second test is associated with a favourable outcome (Loosen & Prange, 1982). Nevertheless, this procedure is commended for further study, despite the absence of an endocrine explanation for the findings, and interference by such factors as age, nutritional state, chronic renal failure, prior administration of TRF, or exposure to somatostatin, neurotensin, dopamine, thyroid hormones or glucocorticoids.

Loosen & Prange (1982) accepted that blunting of the response to TRF was not specific to depression, for it had also been seen in some patients with mania, anorexia nervosa, and alcoholism, and more recently the suggestion that the TRF stimulation test is of value in identifying depression and differentiating manic and depressed patients from schizophrenics has been challenged (Wolkin *et al.*, 1984). This group reported the occurrence of abnormal TRF responses in schizophrenic as well as in affectively disturbed patients. The absence of blunting in schizophrenic patients suggests that the altered response is not simply a correlate of mental distress. With regard to the pathophysiology of the blunted TSH response these workers are inclined to favour an initial hypersecretion of TSH which subsequently renders the pituitary gland unresponsive, possibly through down-regulation. But the effects of a period of hypersecretion would not be expected to be as long-lasting as predicated by this idea. The high plasma levels of cortisol found in depression may account for the impaired response to TRF, and this possibility is consistent with the suppressed TSH response observed in patients with untreated Cushing's disease, or who are receiving long-term corticosteroid therapy. Other observers are less impressed (Loosen & Prange, 1982).

Immunoreactive TRF has been found in the hypothalamus and median eminence of all mammalian species studied, and demonstrated by immunocytochemistry in the thyrotrophic area of the anterior hypothalamus. It is also present in the posterior pituitary gland of the rat in a high concentration that is depleted after placement of lesions in the hypothalamus. This has led to suggestions of a novel hypothalamo-hypophysial system, alongside evidence that TRF can affect vasopressin secretion in man (Jackson, 1982). Despite the high concentrations of TRF in the hypothalamus, over 70 per cent of total brain TRF is found outside that part of the brain, albeit at a reduced concentration. Networks of TRF-staining nerve terminals have been observed in several motor nuclei of the brainstem and around motor neurons in the spinal cord. The presence of high-affinity TRF-binding receptors in discrete regions of the monkey brain, especially the limbic system and cerebral cortex, suggests that endogenous TRF is physiologically important, particularly as the biosynthesis of TRF by neural tissue has been demonstrated. Serotonin and TRF exist together in nerve terminals in the ventral horn of the grey matter of the spinal cord and treatment with specific serotonin neurotoxins causes loss of both substances.

Before an endogenous compound can be regarded as a neurotransmitter a number of criteria need to be satisfied. These include localization within nerve terminals, release upon nerve stimulation, attachment to specific postsynaptic receptors, induction of biological effects identical to those produced by direct nerve stimulation, termination of effects by inactivating and re-uptake mechanisms, and a capacity on the part of the nerve cell to synthesize the compound in question. Most, but not all, of these requirements have been met by TRF, so that the peptide is a strong candidate for inclusion in the list of neurotransmitters. In some areas of the brain, TRF may function as an orthodox neurotransmitter, and elsewhere may modulate the actions of the monoamine neurotransmitters (Jackson, 1982).

Numerous neural effects have been produced by administration of TRF, even though the peptide crosses the blood–brain barrier poorly (Jackson, 1982). In the rat the narcotic depression induced by barbiturate or ethanol administration is reversed, as is the depression induced pharmacologically in the hypophysectomized mouse given pargyline (a monoamine oxidase inhibitor) and then L-dopa. Such observations provide clear evidence of stimulation of neural activity, and the compound was soon tested in depression. The first patients responded favourably, but others reacted less well, and the therapeutic value of the use of TRF in depression remains controversial (Donovan, 1978b; Hollister, Davis & Davis, 1980). Nevertheless, there does appear to be a responsive subgroup of depressed patients. These are characterized by the severity of the illness, an abnormal response to TRF, an accentuated release of growth hormone and prolactin in response to stress, and clinical improvement with electroconvulsive therapy (Furlong, Brown & Beeching, 1976). With recovery the hypophysial response to TRF is normalized, as mentioned earlier.

Beneficial effects of the peptide in mania, schizophrenia, hyperkinesia and childhood autism have also been reported, but are similarly controversial. The administration of TRF elicits mild euphoria in normal subjects and an increased sense of well-being in the alcohol-withdrawal syndrome (Prange *et al.*, 1979). After intravenous administration there is often a transient rise or fall in blood pressure and a sensation of urinary urgency. In the rat, hyperthermia, suppression of feeding and drinking behaviour and increased contractility of the colon have been described after intra-cerebroventricular administration.

There is no doubt that TRF can directly affect the electrical activity of nerve cells and influence the response to acetylcholine and noradrenaline; it can also modulate the turnover of acetylcholine in certain brain areas. There are numerous correlations between the response to TRF and that to cholinergic drugs, so that TRF appears to stimulate cholinergic neural activity, resulting in a functional elevation of cholinergic tone. The peptide does not act directly as a cholinergic substance, for its excitatory effects in spinal cord ventral roots or in the brain stem reticular formation are not antagonized by antimuscarinic drugs that block the action of acetylcholine

(Yarbrough, 1983). Such observations, and others, have led to the hypothesis (Metcalf & Dettmar, 1981) that TRF forms an endogenous ergotropic or analeptic system in the brain somewhat analogous to that for the endogenous opiates (Chapter 4). Certain behavioural effects of the opioid peptides, but not the analgesia, are antagonized by TRF, which also acts like the opioid antagonist naloxone in improving blood pressure and survival in experimental endotoxic, haemorrhagic or spinal shock in the rat. The possible clinical applications of TRF may well be extended by the knowledge that *in vivo* it is converted to a biologically active cyclized metabolite, histidyl-proline-diketopiperazine (His-Pro-DKP), which is more effective than the parent peptide in antagonizing ethanol narcosis. The metabolite differs from TRF in inhibiting, instead of promoting, prolactin secretion and causing hypo- (instead of hyper-)thermia. Further, His-Pro-DKP is distributed throughout the rat brain in higher concentrations than that of TRF, which conceivably could serve as a prohormone.

The gonadotrophins

Although no behavioural changes have been attributed directly to the actions of the gonadotrophic hormones, follicle-stimulating hormone (FSH) and luteinizing hormone (LH), the secretion of the gonadal hormones lies under their control, so that a brief survey of the factors governing FSH and LH secretion and, in turn, the output of gonadal steroids is in order.

Follicle-stimulating hormone and LH share parts of their molecular structure, may be produced by the same cell in the pituitary gland, and have their discharge from the hypophysis controlled by the hypothalamus through a single gonadotrophin-releasing factor (GnRF), although there are hints that a second factor preferentially influencing the secretion of FSH may exist. The two hormones (FSH and LH) are seldom released alone and there is much synergistic activity. Thus, for ovarian function, FSH causes proliferation of the granulosa cells in the follicles and the production of an aromatizing enzyme that converts androgens to oestradiol. Then, together, FSH and oestrogen encourage follicular development and the appearance of receptors for LH on the granulosal cells which favour the binding of that gonadotrophin and the synthesis of androgen and yet more oestrogen in response to the trophic hormone. Additionally, FSH promotes the development of receptors to prolactin in the granulosa cells (Yen, 1980). Luteinizing hormone is more concerned with the production of steroids by the interstitial cells of the ovaries and testes, and a joint surge of LH and FSH secretion at mid-cycle causes ovulation and corpus luteum formation in women.

Like other pituitary hormones, FSH and LH are released episodically. The oscillations in the plasma concentration of LH are most marked, and exhibit a periodicity of about 90 minutes during the follicular and ovulatory phases of the menstrual cycle, with a reduced frequency during the luteal phase. This probably follows from the action of progesterone, which has been shown to slow the pulse frequency and augment the amplitude of LH secretion in women (Soules *et al.*, 1984). The magnitude of the pulses also varies and is greatest around the time of ovulation. A rhythmic pattern in the secretion of FSH is much less marked (Ferin, 1983). Episodic hormone secretion is also seen in men.

In essence, the episodic release of the gonadotrophins reflects an episodic discharge of GnRF on the part of the hypothalamus, particularly the arcuate nuclear region just behind the optic chiasma (Ferin, 1983). Appropriately, lesions in the arcuate nuclei that destroy cell bodies containing GnRF produce a rapid fall in the plasma concentrations of both FSH and LH, while other work on monkeys has shown that GnRH is released into the hypothalamo-hypophysial portal circulation of females (spayed to increase GnRF output) at intervals of 60–180 minutes. The mechanism generating episodic hormone secretion appears to reside within the arcuate region, for the surgical isolation of this area from the rest of the brain, but not from the pituitary gland, is compatible with continued pulsatile gonadotrophin release. Increases in multi-unit electrical activity in the arcuate region coincident with the initiation of each LH pulse have also been noted.

The episodic release of GnRF is vitally important in the control of gonadotrophin secretion. Before the discovery of this phenomenon, investigators were puzzled by the difficulty experienced in restoring normal gonadotrophin secretion in monkeys deprived of endogenous GnRF by pituitary stalk-section. A continuous infusion of GnRF was ineffective in monkeys, as were similar infusions into amenorrhoeic women. But when the mode of infusion mimicked the endogenous pattern, with brief hourly injections, normal gonadal function was restored in monkeys. There are numerous examples of the restoration of normal menstrual function and ovulation in hypogonadal women provided with battery-driven portable pumps for the episodic administration of GnRF (Leyendecker & Wildt, 1983). Alteration of the frequency of exposure to GnRF can alter the balance between FSH and LH secretion; when the frequency was reduced from one pulse an hour to one pulse in three hours in monkeys there was an increase in FSH secretion. The loss of sensitivity of the pituitary gland to GnRF accompanying continuous stimulation by the releasing factor is an example of 'down-regulation' (Chapter 5), but the mechanism is not understood, particularly as there is evidence that the number of receptors on the cells of the pituitary gland may be increased (Ferin, 1983). Nevertheless, it is now very clear that changes in the frequency of episodic GnRF discharge may underlie a number of gynaecological disorders. Emotional and neural stimuli may well affect gonadotrophin secretion by alteration of the frequency of hormone discharge.

Gonadotrophin-releasing factor (GnRF)

The commonly accepted gonadotrophin-releasing factor is a decapeptide, with a structure that remains constant in mammals. Although the way in which the secretion of the two gonadotrophins (FSH and LH) can be differentially controlled by a single releasing factor is coming to be understood, it remains possible that a distinct FSH-releasing factor may exist (McCann, Mizunuma, Samson & Lumpkin, 1983). As with TRF, the activities of GnRF may extend beyond control of the secretion of the appropriate trophic hormone. Nerve endings containing GnRF are present in dense concentration in the external layer of the median eminence of the hypothalamus but cells containing GnRF are scattered through much of the anterior hypothalamus, and have also been found in the midbrain, cerebellum, brain stem and cerebral cortex. The function of these cells remains unknown, although there are suggestions that GnRF might influence sexual behaviour (Chapter 8). In turn, the release of GnRF may be controlled by the endogenous opiates (Sirinathsinghji, Whittington, Audsley & Fraser, 1983).

Gonadotrophin-releasing factor is not confined to the central nervous system, for it is present in sympathetic ganglia, is released upon stimulation of the pre-ganglionic nerves, and can act directly upon the neurons to cause a depolarization that lasts for minutes. The neuronal response is blocked by analogues of GnRF that inhibit GnRF-induced gonadotrophin release from the pituitary gland (Krieger, 1983b). It is also noteworthy that there is a close similarity between α-factor, a mating pheromone of yeast, and GnRF. Both natural and synthetic preparations of α-factor bind specifically to receptors in the pituitary gland and can cause release of luteinizing hormone. This particular peptide sequence would thus seem to have a special, but as yet unknown, biological significance.

Growth hormone

There is a considerable degree of structural similarity between growth hormone and prolactin, together with some overlap in endocrine activity, and this gives rise to problems in hormone assay. Nevertheless, the two hormones are physiologically distinct. Both are large molecules, containing almost 200 amino acid residues.

Most of the biological actions of growth hormone are of little interest from the behavioural point of view, yet in cases of pituitary gigantism or acromegaly there may be marked changes in personality, consisting largely of a lack of initiative and spontaneity and a change of mood. There may be great swings of mood, but the enlargement of the hypophysis and consequent pressure upon the hypothalamus that often accompanies the disease renders analysis difficult, for not all of the behavioural changes are due to hormonal action. Thus, there may be increased hunger and thirst, and sleepiness attributable to hypothalamic involvement (Bleuler, 1951). The secretion of growth hormone is highly labile and triggered by a variety of neural and metabolic stimuli. Hypoglycaemia, amino acid administration and exercise are all effective, with stair climbing being particularly useful as a provocative test for growth hormone secretion in children. Like other pituitary products, growth hormone is discharged episodically.

Growth hormone secretion is closely associated with sleep (Chapter 6), and is particularly high in adolescent children, being some 7–8 times higher than that of prepubertal individuals and subsiding with maturity. The operation of neural factors in the control of growth hormone secretion is well illustrated in cases of psychosocial dwarfism, depression dwarfism, abuse dwarfism or emotional deprivation, where there is decreased slow-wave sleep and where a variety of normally effective stimuli, including insulin-induced hypoglycaemia, lose their ability to provoke growth hormone secretion. Paradoxically, the stresses generated by the hostile environment do not enhance growth hormone secretion in the affected children, although malnutrition may be a contributory factor (Brown, 1976). Upon transfer to supportive and loving conditions there is a restoration of normal sleep patterns before sleep-associated growth hormone secretion becomes manifest and recovery ensues. It has been suggested that James Barrie, the author of *Peter Pan*, may have been such a case, for he suffered severe maternal deprivation and never grew up (Martin, Reichlin & Brown, 1977). The intelligence quotient may also be impaired in psychosocial dwarfism, but improves with rescue from the adverse situation (Money, Annecillo & Kelley, 1983).

Experimental work with the rat indicates that growth hormone secretion can be inhibited by some parts of the brain (the ventromedial nuclei of the hypothalamus, the preoptic area, and the corticomedial region of the amygdala), while other areas (the hippocampus, basolateral amygdala, interpeduncular nuclei and locus ceruleus) are concerned with increasing growth hormone release (Brown, Seggie, Chambers & Ettigi, 1978). Less detailed research on the primate supports these generalizations. Some areas participate in the control of growth hormone secretion during rest, whereas others are active in stress-induced release.

Quite commonly, stressful stimuli increase the output of both growth hormone and ACTH, but the joint release of the two hormones is not invariable. A metabolic stimulus, such as hypoglycaemia, can enhance cortisol secretion without affecting growth hormone output, while a procedure such as cardiac catheterization reproducibly elicits ACTH discharge without necessarily evoking growth hormone release. The differences between the subjects releasing growth hormone and those not reacting appears to reside in the manner of coping with the stress. Those talking to the investigator and seemingly engaged with the environment showed no growth hormone elevation, while those appearing to be detached nevertheless displayed an increase in growth hormone secretion (Brown *et al.*, 1978).

Superimposed upon the control of growth hormone secretion by hypothalamic neurohumoral agents are the neurotransmitter systems within the brain itself. There appears to be an excitatory input from dopaminergic, noradrenergic and serotoninergic systems, in that the dopaminergic receptor stimulant apomorphine, a noradrenergic agonist clonidine, and the immediate precursor of serotonin (5-hydroxytryptophan) all increase growth hormone secretion. The dopaminergic theory of the causation of schizophrenia has prompted study of the growth hormone response to apomorphine in patients with this disease, but conflicting findings have been reported.

Alterations in the way in which growth hormone secretion is controlled are discernible in depression. Growth hormone is discharged from the hypophysis in response to insulin-induced hypoglycaemia, and since growth hormone secretion can be blocked by the α-noradrenergic antagonist phentolamine, noradrenaline seems to participate in the discharge mechanism. In depressed patients less growth hormone is secreted following the induction of hypoglycaemia by the administration of insulin and this is apparently associated with a reduced turnover of noradrenaline in the brain (Garver, Pandey, Dekirmenjian & Deleon-Jones, 1975). The response to clonidine, an α-adrenergic receptor agonist, is also impaired although the hypotensive and sedative effects seem to be normal (Checkley, Slade & Shur, 1981).

The basal level of secretion of growth hormone in schizophrenia, and the response to a variety of provocative stimuli, has been studied on numerous occasions, but few consistent results of a positive character have emerged. Particular attention has been given to the changes resulting from interference with neurotransmission because of the evidence that dopaminergic, serotoninergic and α-adrenergic neurons enhance and β-adrenergic neurons inhibit release of the hormone (Brown *et al.*, 1983). However, interpretation of the conflicting results is complicated by factors such as the heterogeneity of brain dopamine systems, the lack of dose–response information on challenge tests, the natural course of the disease, the effects of concomitant drug treatment and the possible heterogeneity of the disorder.

The participation of many other hormones, or endocrine conditions, in the genesis of schizophrenia has been examined in detail, but with a disappointing outcome. Thus, Brambilla & Penati (1978) reviewed a vast number of papers dealing with the adrenal, thyroid, parathyroid and pineal glands, the gonads, hypophysis and glucose metabolism, without reaching any positive conclusions. This effort is reminiscent of that of Bleuler (1954), almost a quarter of a century earlier.

Two peptide factors produced by the hypothalamus seem to be involved in the control of the secretion of growth hormone, with one agent being excitatory and the other inhibitory, and both interacting together. Overall, the hypothalamus exercises a primarily excitatory role over the secretion of growth hormone in man, for transection of the pituitary stalk depresses growth hormone release. Under pathological conditions, as in acromegaly or renal failure, growth hormone secretion can be induced by TRF. Other neuropeptides reported to increase growth hormone secretion include ACTH, α-MSH, β-endorphin, the enkephalins, neurotensin, and vasopressin.

Growth hormone release-inhibiting factor, or somatostatin

Rather in the fashion of TRF, somatostatin shows many behavioural activities alongside that of the inhibition of growth hormone secretion (Donovan, 1978a). From the physiological point of view, somatostatin blocks the secretion of growth hormone expected in response to exercise, arginine administration, or the induction of hypoglycaemia by an injection of insulin. In clinical conditions where growth hormone secretion is elevated, as in acromegaly and diabetes mellitus, an infusion of somatostatin immediately arrests the discharge of growth hormone. The secretion of TSH is also inhibited by somatostatin, and there are suggestions that somatostatin may serve as a physiological inhibitor of TSH release (Morley, 1981).

Somatostatin is present in the neural lobe of the pituitary gland, limbic system, brain stem and spinal cord. The principal source of somatostatin-containing fibres projecting to the median eminence is a layer several cells thick located in the anterior periventricular region of the hypothalamus immediately beneath the ependymal lining (Reichlin, 1983). Additionally, somatostatin is found in the pancreatic islets (producing insulin and glucagon) and elsewhere in the gastrointestinal tract, and can inhibit the secretion of insulin and glucagon, as well as the secretion of a wide variety of other gastrointestinal hormones. Forms of somatostatin larger than the decapeptide molecule exist and may be released from the cells producing them. The different sizes of somatostatin may elicit distinct biological effects in that somatostatin-14 is a more potent inhibitor of glucagon secretion than somatostatin-28, whereas the reverse holds true in the case of insulin (Fenoglio & King, 1983). Somatostatin is ubiquitous in that the immunoreactive peptide has been detected in every vertebrate class and in primitive invertebrates, including a protozoan. The conservation of this molecular structure across the evolutionary scale would seem to point to some special significance of somatostatin, quite apart from its activities in the control of pituitary function (Reichlin, 1983).

In the somatostatinergic neuronal systems studied in detail the peptide is located in secretory granules in nerve endings, and is released in response to a variety of depolarizing stimuli. Numerous neurotransmitters and neuropeptides can cause somatostatin release, and a variety of behavioural changes stem from intra-cerebroventricular injection. There is a general arousal effect in lessening slow-wave and paradoxical sleep, and often an increased excitability of the cerebral cortex, but the severity and duration of strychnine-induced seizures is reduced (Reichlin, 1983). In rats, some of the behavioural patterns observed, such as freezing, piloerection, arched tail and hypersensitivity to tactile stimuli, suggest activation of the limbic system. A dose-related biphasic effect upon behaviour and motor control is also apparent, for low doses of somatostatin produce behavioural and motor activation after an initial period of freezing while higher doses lead to rigidity, loss of motor control and inco-ordination, with the animals tending to remain motionless. The sleep–wake cycle is also profoundly altered, with reductions in REM sleep, slow-wave sleep and total sleep occurring in a dose-related fashion after intra-ventricular, hippocampal or cortical application (Rubinow *et al.*, 1984).

The turnover of several neurotransmitters, noradrenaline, dopamine, serotonin, and acetylcholine, is affected by somatostatin, although the changes are not all in the same direction and seem to be influenced by the preparation used for study. In turn, the release of somatostatin is stimulated by noradrenaline and dopamine, and inhibited by acetylcholine and γ-aminobutyric acid. Such observations have led to studies of the concentration of somatostatin in the CSF of depressed patients, when medication-free depressed patients showed significantly lower levels than detected in CSF collected from normal volunteers, or from patients in an improved condition. However, it is not clear whether these changes arise from alterations in the metabolism of neurotransmitters within the brain, or from changes in the circadian rhythm of somatostatin metabolism (Rubinow *et al.*, 1983).

Growth hormone-releasing factor (GRF), or somatocrinin

This hypothalamic factor was first isolated, late in 1982, from two pancreatic islet cell tumours from patients showing signs of acromegaly, rather than from brain tissue. One tumour was collected in France, the other in the United States, and both were processed at the Salk Institute in California, though the work was done in separate laboratories by different teams and the results published on the opposite sides of the Atlantic (Guillemin *et al.*, 1982; Rivier, Spiess, Thorner & Vale, 1982). Neurons containing immunoreactive GRF are present in the ventromedial and arcuate nuclei of the hypothalamus, with processes extending to the hypophysial portal vessels. There are homologies in the sequence of amino acids in somatocrinin and in several peptides of gut origin of the secretin and glucagon family, but, unlike somatostatin, no GRF has been found in the normal pancreas of monkey or man. Nor does somatocrinin appear to affect the secretion of insulin or glucagon. There is an antagonism between the effects of somatostatin and somatocrinin, for somatostatin inhibits the secretion of growth hormone induced by GRF. Thus far, somatocrinin appears only to increase the secretion of growth hormone; GRF at any dose tested has no effect on the secretion of any pituitary hormone other than growth hormone (Guillemin, 1983).

The administration of somatocrinin causes no marked behavioural change in man, and neither does somatostatin. But, in the light of current knowledge concerning the multiplicity of peptides produced in the gut (Chapter 4), it is worth recalling that almost twenty years ago Fras, Litin & Pearson (1967) showed that 76 per cent of a series of 46 consecutive patients with carcinoma of the pancreas had symptoms of anxiety, depression and premonitions of serious illness, and in nearly half, the psychiatric symptoms appeared before any other signs of disease. They commented that others reported almost forty years earlier that nervousness and mental symptoms preceded the clinical diagnosis.

Prolactin

Prolactin is a large protein hormone, with almost 200 amino acid residues. There are similarities in the structures of prolactin and growth hormone and overlap in some of the actions of the two hormones, but it is now accepted that prolactin and growth hormone exist as separate entities. Like growth hormone, various molecular forms of prolactin have been isolated, but their physiological significance has not been established. Prolactin is concerned with the induction and maintenance of lactation in women, with some aspects of gonadal function and with maternal behaviour in animals, but the latter aspect of its activity in women has not been well studied.

An over-secretion of prolactin is probably the most common pituitary disorder, and an elevated level of this hormone is an important marker of hypothalamic or pituitary disease. Hyperprolactinaemia, arising from tumours of the pituitary gland or psychotropic drug therapy, is often accompanied by amenorrhoea and the cessation of cyclic ovarian function, while in men prolactin excess is associated with hypospermatogenesis and loss of libido (Franks, Jacobs, Martin & Nabarro, 1978; Carter *et al.*, 1978; Schwartz, Bauman & Masters, 1982). Depression of prolactin secretion in men by radiotherapy in the case of pituitary tumours, or by treatment with the dopamine agonist bromocriptine, sometimes improves potency.

Unlike other pituitary hormones, the release of prolactin is tonically inhibited by the hypothalamus, with dopamine acting as the prolactin release-inhibiting factor. There is a strong element of self-regulation in the control of prolactin secretion, in that prolactin directly influences the turnover of dopamine in the hypothalamus. With an increased blood level of prolactin the amount of dopamine reaching the pituitary gland is increased, and the degree of inhibition of prolactin secretion produced by dopamine enhanced. This action of prolactin is specific, in that the secretion of other pituitary hormones is not depressed. Despite the emphasis on the activities of dopamine, there still remains a case for the existence of a peptidic prolactin-inhibiting factor (McCann *et al.*, 1984). Other factors can increase prolactin secretion, such as oestrogens and TRF, while the vaso-active intestinal peptide (Chapter 4) is exceedingly active in this regard and has been detected in hypophysial portal vessel blood. Morphine has long been known to stimulate prolactin release, and this action is shared by the opioid peptides. Treatment with naloxone, an opioid receptor blocker, depresses prolactin secretion under a variety of circumstances (McCann *et al.*, 1984). Psychic and physical stresses increase prolactin secretion, and the response of women is greater than that of men (Bohnet & McNeilly, 1979). More prolactin is present in the circulation of women than of men but the function of the hormone in men is not known.

Suckling or breast stimulation increases the secretion of prolactin, as can disturbance of the neural pathways between the chest and hypothalamus produced by surgery, trauma, herpes zoster, and tight-fitting garments. Extension of the nursing period, by prolonged breast feeding, maintains prolactin secretion and delays the return of normal menstrual cycles (Boyd, Spare, Bower & Reichlin, 1978).

Because of the link between dopamine production by the hypothalamus and prolactin secretion (Snyder, 1982), efforts have been made to determine whether measurement of prolactin would serve as an indicator of value in schizophrenia, for there are suggestions that the dopaminergic systems in the brain may be overactive in this condition. Here, the presumption is that any change in the dopaminergic links between the midbrain and limbic system significant in the genesis of schizophrenia would also be evident in the hypothalamo-pituitary system. Sadly these hopes have not been realized (Meltzer, Sachar & Frantz, 1974; Snyder, 1982), and might be taken as evidence against the theory that a derangement of dopamine metabolism is involved in the genesis of the disorder. However, the relative clinical potency of a neuroleptic is directly related to its ability to block postsynaptic dopamine receptors and to bind to high-affinity dopamine binding sites. Some workers have found a correlation between the clinical response to neuroleptics and a rise in plasma prolactin, but others have not, although there can be a connection between plasma prolactin concentrations and the development of extrapyramidal symptoms (Brown *et al.*, 1983). One problem is that the maximal change in plasma prolactin in response to neuroleptic drugs occurs below the dose level required for clinical treatment, so that the high dosages given obliterate any subtle change in prolactin secretion. At low dosage a good correlation between prolactin response and dopamine blockade emerges.

As an alternative to dopaminergic involvement in the development of schizophrenia, some derangement in the opioid systems in the brain might be responsible. Suggestive evidence for this idea has been forthcoming (van Ree & De Wied, 1981), but the observations are confusing in that both an endorphin excess and an endorphin deficiency have been postulated in this condition. In part, the differing concepts may be reconciled on the basis of involvement of various endorphin derivatives, so that it is the balance of α-, β- and γ-endorphins that may be important. Treatment with endorphin can enhance prolactin secretion, while naloxone inhibits prolactin release.

Ectopic hormone production

Although not of significance in normal bodily function, it is as well to note that hormones can be produced by cells not commonly regarded as endocrine. Such 'ectopic' hormone production is illustrated by the observations that tumours of several kinds produce peptides of the pro-opiomelanocortin family, and can generate the signs of ACTH excess seen in Cushing's syndrome. Indeed, it has been suggested that ectopic ACTH production causes 10–15 per cent of cases of adrenal hyperplasia in adults (Dunlop & Chalmers, 1984). Antidiuretic hormone and parathyroid hormone are also produced by carcinomas of the lung and it seems that all of the hormones thus far known to be produced ectopically are peptides (Pullan, 1984). This might be anticipated from the widespread synthesis of peptides prominent in information transmission, as will be enlarged upon in the next chapter.

4

Neurotransmitters, neuromodulators and endocrine function

Neurons communicate with one another chemically, with a neurotransmitter or other substance being released at a nerve ending to cause depolarization or hyperpolarization of an area of the contiguous cell membrane across a synaptic cleft. The many synaptic inputs to a cell can be variously excitatory (depolarizing) or inhibitory (hyperpolarizing), and the innumerable opportunities for interaction between neurons results in a broad span in firing rate. Direct electrical communication between cells occurs, but is utilized rarely.

Neurotransmitters

Some neurotransmitters, such as acetylcholine, dopamine and noradrenaline, have been known for many years, while other familiar substances exerting very similar actions (adrenaline, serotonin, and histamine) have yet to be fully acknowledged as neurotransmitters. This is because certain criteria held to be critical in the recognition of a substance as a neurotransmitter have not been fully met. The criteria in question are that the substance must be synthesized in the neuron; that the substance must be present in the synaptic ending and released in amounts sufficient to affect the contiguous nerve membrane; that the application of the candidate substance to a suitable test tissue should reproduce the effects of endogenously released material; and that a special mechanism should exist for locally inactivating or rapidly destroying the substance after use to ensure short-lived and speedy repetitive effects. These criteria were drawn up before it was realised that neuropeptides might also serve as neurotransmitters, and thus could require revision since mechanisms inactivating peptides in the synaptic cleft may not exist. If that is so, then the criteria will need to be modified to encompass these additional features. Adjustment of the criteria to allow the recognition of neuropeptides as neurotransmitters would vastly extend the list of such agents, for there are some 30 neuropeptides that could function in this way (Iversen, 1984).

There are problems in regarding peptides as neurotransmitters. Unlike the monoamines, such as noradrenaline and dopamine, which are synthesized in nerve terminals, peptides are formed only in cell bodies, where the ribosomes necessary for peptide bond formation are available. They are then transported down the axon for release at the nerve ending. Probably because of the lack of specific and rapid mechanisms for the termination of their action, peptides are effective in much lower concentration than the customary neurotransmitters, and act for much longer. Additionally, peptides coexist in neurons with the more classical neurotransmitters. Thus, acetylcholine can be present in a neuron alongside vasoactive intestinal peptide; noradrenaline together with somatostatin, enkephalin or neurotensin; and dopamine with cholecystokinin or enkephalin. The possibilities for interaction, and the fine tuning of a neuronal response as the outcome of competing neurohumoral systems, are magnified accordingly.

In an effort to distinguish between the archetypal neurotransmitters of the acetylcholine and monoamine mould, and peptide action, some have classified the peptides as neuromodulators. Neuromodulators would then be differentiated from neurotransmitters in that the former may not generate post-synaptic spike discharges, but rather modify the release of the primary neurotransmitter, or adjust the receptivity or sensitivity of the postsynaptic elements to the primary neurotransmitter. However, as Frederickson & Geary (1982) point out, monoamines could be acting as neuromodulators and peptides as neurotransmitters. The action of monoamines is relatively weak and their onset of action is somewhat slow, as is the recovery of the receptors from their effects. By contrast, opiate peptides can act quickly and transiently.

Monoamines

Together with the involvement of the monoamines noradrenaline, adrenaline and dopamine in neurotransmission (with correlations between the level of monoamine function and depressive disorders), there is a strong connection with endocrine activity. The release of hypophysial hormones is in part influenced by monoaminergic systems so that, in turn, disturbances in hormone release may be indicative of a disorder in monoamine metabolism. Further, one facet of hormone action upon the brain is modulation of monoamine turnover. Happily, the introduction of sensitive techniques for the localization and assay of catecholamines has led to such progress that we now have more information on the anatomy, chemistry and pharmacology of these systems in the brain than for any other neuronal system (Moore, 1982), although advances in understanding have not matched the accretion of facts. It should also be borne in mind that the catecholamine systems represent less than 1 per cent of the total neuronal population of any mammalian brain, even when the neocortex is excluded from the comparison. The total number of catecholaminergic neurons in the brain of the rat, for example, is remarkably low and is approximately matched by the number of cells in the small suprachiasmatic nucleus of the hypothalamus. Even so, each cell body may generate an enormous number of nerve endings and each makes many connections with other cells: each dopaminergic neuron in the substantia nigra of the rat is estimated to have about 500 000 terminal boutons in the neostriatum, and in the human the figure may rise to 5 000 000 (McGeer & McGeer, 1980).

There are three groups of catecholaminergic neurons, preferentially synthesizing dopamine, noradrenaline and adrenaline. The cells producing dopamine are most numerous, and three prominent collections of long dopaminergic neurons can be made out: the nigrostriatal, the mesolimbic, and the mesocortical systems, as well as two smaller systems within the hypothalamus (the tuberoinfundibular and the incerto-hypothalamic) (Muller *et al.*, 1981). There is little doubt that this subdivision of the dopaminergic system reflects different functional activities. The cells in the substantia nigra are associated with the automatic execution of learned motor acts, the cells in the interpeduncular nucleus may be involved in the control of emotional and complex behaviour, while the cells in the hypothalamus are probably concerned with the control of prolactin and growth hormone secretion. This range of functions poses clinical problems, for pharmacological interference with the action of dopamine, by the administration of neuroleptic drugs valuable in the treatment of schizo-phrenia, generates undesirable side-effects such as tardive dyskinesia. Fortunately, it now seems that selective interference with the activity of one or other set of dopaminergic nuclei is becoming possible and that dopamine can be visualized by positron emission tomography atraumatically (Chiodo & Bunney, 1983; White & Wang, 1983; Garnett, Firnau & Nahmias, 1983).

The neurons producing noradrenaline are located largely in the pons and medulla, and project widely to other areas, while little is known about the adrenaline-producing neurons, which are very few and partly overlap with the noradrenaline neurons. The noradrenergic neurons can be divided into two systems, depending upon the location of the cell bodies and their pattern of projection (Moore, 1982). The largest group is located in a single nucleus, the locus ceruleus, with the remainder being found in scattered groups in the lateral tegmentum, from the caudal medulla to the rostral pons. These neurons give rise to axons with ascending and descending branches and many collaterals that supply wide areas. The locus ceruleus is comprised almost entirely of neurons projecting primarily to the cerebellum and cerebral cortex, although the dorsal thalamus, the ventral horn of the spinal cord, brain stem sensory nuclei, a few hypothalamic nuclei and basal forebrain areas are also supplied. This widespread distribution is provided by a cell population within the locus ceruleus of some 16 000 neurons or less (McGeer & McGeer, 1980; Foote, Bloom & Aston-Jones, 1983). Axon terminals from the locus ceruleus reach the cerebral cortex early in brain differentiation and may be influential in cortical development, particularly in the regulation of synapse formation and synaptic plasticity. The extensive subdivision of noradrenergic axons and the development of collaterals has been taken to imply a role in general state-dependent actions such as autonomic and neuroendocrine regulation and the control of behavioural arousal.

The distribution of serotoninergic, or 5-hydroxytryptaminergic, neurons and fibres in the brain has been less intensively studied than that of noradrenaline or dopamine. In the rat, the serotoninergic neurons are located in the nuclei of the raphe system situated dorsally in the brain stem near the midline, with some cell groups located more laterally. Some ascending fibres to the forebrain travel in the medial forebrain bundle, and among the structures supplied by serotoninergic fibres may be listed the reticular formation, lateral geniculate nuclei, preoptic area, hypothalamus, amygdala, pallidal system, hippocampus and cortex (Iversen & Iversen, 1981).

Histamine is a further substance emerging from the shadows to claim attention as a neurotransmitter involved in hypothalamic and neuro-endocrine function. The highest concentrations of this compound in the brain occur in the hypothalamus, although some may be contained in the ubiquitous mast cells. Most functional evidence points to involvement of histamine in the control of prolactin secretion, the control of water intake, and pressor responses, but more information is needed to delineate the precise sites of action, the receptors involved, and the relative roles of endogenous and exogenous histamine (Roberts & Calcutt, 1983).

Amino acid neurotransmitters

Some amino acids may act as neurotransmitters (Fagg & Foster, 1983). These are γ-aminobutyric acid (GABA), glutamate, aspartate and glycine. In addition to their involvement in afferent and local circuit systems, they appear to serve important functions as transmitters released from a wide variety of corticofugal projection neurons.

GABA is produced from glutamate by carboxylation and is regarded as the most common inhibitory or hyperpolarizing transmitter in the brain; it may serve as a neurotransmitter in one-third of all synapses (Iversen & Iversen, 1981). High concentrations of GABA are present in the hypothalamus and median eminence, and the actions of GABA can be blocked with the drug bicuculline. The receptors for GABA on target neurons appear to act by opening chloride ion channels, which serves to stabilize the membrane potential of the cell at or near the chloride equilibrium potential, and the barbiturates and minor tranquillizers of the benzodiazepine class act upon this mechanism to enhance the effect of GABA. Barbiturates potentiate GABA activity by prolonging the duration of opening of ion channels, whereas the benzodiazepines act by increasing the frequency of channel openings in response to GABA. Other GABA receptors are known which differ from the preceding type in that they are blocked by other drugs, and do not necessarily influence chloride channels. They seem to be located largely presynaptically on monoaminergic neurons (Iversen, 1984).

Despite the obvious difficulties in studying GABA metabolism in the human brain, there is increasing evidence that derangements of the metabolism of this amino acid are associated with psychiatric illness: the problem lies in determining the manner in which the disturbance arises and whether it is a cause of the illness or one consequence. In any event, some effort is being devoted to the assay of the plasma levels of GABA in psychiatric patients of various kinds with a view to determining the diagnostic value of these measures (Petty & Sherman, 1984).

In parallel with the effects of GABA, but in the opposite sense, glutamate may itself serve as the universal excitatory transmitter used by afferent inputs and interneurons in the central nervous system, and act by rapidly opening sodium channels. Definitive proof has been difficult to obtain because drugs active in blocking the effects of glutamate were not available until recently. Already, subcategories of glutamate receptors have been distinguished (Iversen, 1984).

Glycine is another amino acid that has been proposed to act as an inhibitory neurotransmitter in a number of brain regions, including pathways from the cortex to the hypothalamus.

Neuropeptides

Once immunocytochemical procedures permitted the localization and estimation of peptides in brain tissue, exploration was extended to other tissues, and the existence of what might be termed the brain–gut axis became apparent. Essentially, those peptides first identified in the brain were detected in the gut and peptides thought to be specific products of the gut were found in the brain. Although efforts have been made to attach physiological significance to such parallelism, the occurrence of peptides common to both systems rather seems simply to reflect the wide distribution of the regulatory peptides. Indeed, it now appears that peptides common to the central nervous system and gut have a history extending back over more than 500 million years of vertebrate evolution (Barrington, 1982). A molecule similar to human calcitonin (a calcium-mobilizing hormone) has been found in the nervous system of amphioxus, ascidians and *Myxine*, while neurons in the brain of the blowfly contain a material with biological and immunological properties similar to bovine insulin. Further, there is immunocytochemical evidence for the occurrence of at least 15 peptides in the nervous system of the pond-snail, *Lymnaea stagnalis*, that are biologically active in vertebrates.

Simple unicellular organisms produce molecules that are exceedingly similar to the hormonal peptides of vertebrates. Material similar to insulin has been detected in a species of protozoan, two species of fungi, and three strains of *Escherichia coli*. Compounds similar to somatostatin and ACTH(1–39), as well as β-endorphin, have been detected in protozoa, and material similar to human chorionic gonadotrophin found in extracts of bacteria. Roth *et al.* (1982) feel that these hormone-like materials are similar to their counterparts in vertebrates, especially in the conservation of the three dimensional regions needed for recognition by specific receptors in vertebrates and by specific antibodies. Neurotransmitters (catecholamines, serotonin and acetylcholine), as well as steroids and steroid-like molecules closely resembling their vertebrate counterparts, have also been reported in unicellular organisms. Adrenaline stimulates adenylate cyclase in protozoa, with its action being blocked by propanolol, and opioid peptides alter the feeding behaviour of the amoeba, with the response being blocked by the antagonist naloxone.

The origin of neurotransmitters and hormones may well be traced to local tissue factors acting upon secretory cells and their neighbours, so that with evolutionary progress a subset of the messenger molecules acquired a wider role. The finding that some classical hormones (insulin, glucagon, somatostatin) and neurotransmitters also serve physiologically as paracrine agents and local tissue factors supports this idea. In this vein, Roth *et al.* (1982) point out that in vertebrates exocrine and endocrine secretory cells are remarkably similar in appearance, in the preparation of protein for export, and in their mechanisms of secretion. And this similarity could provide an explanation for the finding that many humoral messenger molecules, such as epidermal growth factor, nerve growth factor and prostaglandins, as well as somatostatin, GnRH, gastrin and prolactin, are present in exocrine fluids like saliva, intestinal secretions, milk and semen. Further, the production of hormonal peptides need not be confined to glands, nerves or cancerous tissue. Material indistinguishable from human chorionic gonadotrophin is present in the urine of prepubertal children and in extracts from many tissues collected from individuals lacking a tumour or a placenta; the difference in activity between placenta, tumour and normal cells may be purely quantitative. Similarly, ACTH is found not only in the anterior lobe of the pituitary gland, brain and tumours, but also in the adrenal medulla, the fetal lung and normal tissues. Insulin, or a substance exceedingly like insulin, has been detected in brain tissue, the peripheral nerves and cultured cells of both neural and extraneural origin.

Thyrotrophin-releasing factor is found in the nervous systems of all vertebrate species, but, in contrast to mammals, is unable to activate TSH secretion in amphibians or fish, despite being present in the brain in concentrations that far exceed those in mammals (Jackson, 1982). Observations of this kind suggest that in evolutionary terms TRF was first concerned with neural function and was later co-opted by the hypothalamus and hypophysis to serve as a releasing hormone for TSH secretion. As has been seen, many peptides directly excite or inhibit neuronal activity, depending upon the cells studied. Additionally, for many peptides the 4–8 amino acid sequence critical for their activity as a hormone and secretogogue is also essential for their influence on the firing rate of neurons (Kelly, 1982).

Some of the difficulties arising from a premature attempt to fix the nomenclature of the releasing factors have been alluded to earlier in connection with TRF, and here an important general principle to arise from peptide research is that a peptide will rarely, if ever, be found to serve only a single biological function. The same chemical may be used as a hormone, a paracrine factor, a neuroendocrine releasing factor, a neuromodulator or as a neurotransmitter in various parts of the body, or in different species. Within the nervous system an individual peptide may be involved in many different functions. As Iversen (1983) wrote, this should come as no surprise, as we have long been accustomed to thinking of acetylcholine and other monoamines in this way, but somehow the neuropeptides were first regarded as more specialized in their likely neural functions.

To some extent, the custom of naming peptides after the functional activity through which they were first discovered may retard progress. This point is well made by Kastin, Banks, Zadina & Graf (1983), who recall that melanocyte-stimulating hormone (MSH) is named for its action in darkening the skin of lower vertebrates and was found in the intermediate lobe of the pituitary gland. Now it has been detected in brain tissue and CSF, but not in the blood, of adult humans lacking a separate pars intermedia. The pigmentary actions of MSH in man are evident only under pathological circumstances, but the peptide has behavioural effects in facilitating attention. There are several peptides that inhibit the release of MSH from the hypophysis of experimental animals, but this action may be artefactual; one such factor (MIF-1) may alleviate Parkinson's disease and serve as an opiate antagonist. Further, all of the hypothalamic peptides identified on the basis of their influence on the secretion of pituitary hormones have been shown to have extra-endocrine actions, as discussed elsewhere, and peptides found in the gastro-intestinal tract act upon the brain. Cholecystokinin, named for its effects upon the gall bladder, and bombesin, labelled after the frog from whose skin it was first isolated, are present in both gut and brain, and both peptides suppress feeding. Vasoactive intestinal peptide has potent vasodilator and hypotensive properties and is found in the hypothalamus as well as the gut. It stimulates the release of prolactin, growth hormone and luteinizing hormone, increases drinking, and decreases motor activity. Clearly, the name given to a newly discovered hormone may prove to be more misleading than informative.

Endogenous opiates

Ever since the identification of two pentapeptides with potent opiate agonist activity, methionine- and leucine-enkephalin (Hughes *et al.*, 1975), there have been suggestions that metabolic abnormalities in the production or metabolism of these agents can disrupt behaviour. These opiate peptides possess a common tetrapeptide sequence: Try–Gly–Gly–Phe, and when methionine is added to the phenylalanine residue the pentapeptide methionine-enkephalin results. When leucine is used instead of methionine the product is leucine-enkephalin, and both enkephalins are of major physiological and behavioural significance.

The term 'endogenous opioid' refers to a substance occurring naturally in the brain and elsewhere that has pharmacological properties similar to those of the opiate alkaloid morphine. In turn, 'endorphin' is a contraction of 'endogenous morphine'. The further realization that the pituitary gland produces pro-opiomelanocortin (Chapter 3), which can serve as a precursor molecule for β-endorphin, met-enkephalin, ACTH and MSH in man, and the observations indicating that endogenous opiates may participate in the mechanisms controlling pituitary function, made such considerations the concern of endocrinologists. Appropriately, ACTH, β-LPH and β-endorphin appear to be secreted concomitantly in man, but the presence of common amino acid sequences (residues 59–89) in β-endorphin and β-LPH has complicated assay of the smaller opiate peptide, particularly as β-LPH can yield β-endorphin in plasma (Rees & Smith, 1982; Krieger, 1983a, b).

The administration of corticotrophin-releasing factor causes a parallel discharge of all three peptides, while dexamethasone serves to inhibit the release of all three substances. After adrenalectomy, when ACTH secretion is expected to increase, the output of β-LPH and β-endorphin also rises. Likewise, stress increases the blood levels of all three members of the trio. Strenuous exercise leads to a marked increase in plasma β-endorphin, alongside a rise in plasma ACTH. The increased activity of β-endorphin could be responsible for the so-called 'runner's high', although it is necessary to presume that more endogenous opiate is produced within the brain to account for the state than is detected in the blood, for the rise in plasma β-endorphin in elated runners is not as high as expected (Frederickson & Geary, 1982). There are numerous reports of stress-induced analgesia in runners, including cases of myocardial infarction where vigorous exercise continued despite the appearance of cardiac ischaemia. The sensitivity to pain is reduced following intense exercise, while administration of the opiate antagonist naloxone has reduced some analgesic effects as well as the post-run feelings of joy and euphoria (Janal, Colt, Clark & Glusman, 1984).

β-Endorphin is present in cerebrospinal fluid, and since the concentration does not fall after hypophysectomy and can vary independently of plasma levels, the brain itself seems to be able to synthesize the material. Neurons containing β-endorphin-immunoreactivity can be found throughout the brain and be distinguished from those reacting with antisera to met-enkephalin. The distributions of met-enkephalin and β-endorphin differ in that most met-enkephalin is present in the globus pallidus, putamen, caudate nucleus and substantia nigra, whilst most β-endorphin-immunoreactivity is to be found in the anterior and posterior hypothalamus, with smaller amounts in the periaqueductal grey matter and the pineal gland.

Although β-endorphin contains the peptide sequence of the enkephalins within its structure, no physiological processing of β-endorphin to enkephalin has been demonstrated (Frederickson & Geary, 1982). Enkephalins are synthesized in neurons and in the adrenal gland, and, for the neurons, a precursor is synthesized in the cell body on ribosomes and transported in secretory vesicles to the nerve terminals. During transport, numerous met-enkephalin and leu-enkephalin molecules are produced by proteolytic cleavage from the precursor protein. One precursor may serve for the formation of both met-enkephalin and leu-enkephalin, in that a protein with multiple copies of met-enkephalin and single copies of leu-enkephalin has been isolated. This may explain the ratio of 4–7:1 for met- to leu-enkephalin observed in the adrenal medulla and brain regions. However, there are also separate populations of met-enkephalin and leu-enkephalin-containing neurons. Enkephalins, as befits their nature as peptides, are broken down by a variety of peptidases, although it is not clear whether such peptidases are important in the physiological degradation of enkephalins at synapses. Inhibitors of aminopeptidase (puromycin, bacitracin) can potentiate some actions of enkephalins, and can produce a naloxone-reversible analgesia.

Currently, the superfamily endorphin includes all endogenous peptides whose sequences include an enkephalin pentapeptide (either met-enkephalin or leu-enkephalin) and share some common actions at presumptive opiate receptors as defined by naloxone antagonism (Bloom, 1983). There are at least three major branches of the endorphin family: the pro-opiomelanocortins, the enkephalins, and the C-terminally extended leu-enkephalin peptides, dynorphin, α-neoendorphin and β-neoendorphin, all of which contain an N-terminal leu-enkephalin sequence followed by two or more basic amino acids with further C-terminal extensions of different lengths. All three are potent opioid agonists in bioassays without cleavage to the pentapeptide. β-Endorphin is the major endorphin agonist derived from pro-opiomelanocortin, and is the 31-amino acid C-terminal sequence of β-lipotrophin. Shorter cleavage products, α-endorphin and γ-endorphin, have also been isolated. The pro-opiomelanocortin precursor is processed to different end products at three locations–to ACTH and β-LPH in the anterior lobe of the hypophysis, to α-MSH and β-endorphin in the intermediate lobe of the pituitary gland, and to α-MSH and β-endorphin as well as to acetylated, and inactive, forms of β-endorphin in the brain. The predominant effect of the endorphins in virtually all brain regions is depression of spontaneous neural activity, which is associated in some cases with a hyperpolarization and an increased conductance of the cell membrane.

Viewed another way, the brain (of the rat, at least) contains three opioid peptide systems: the enkephalin, dynorphin and β-endorphin systems. This has been shown by immunocytochemical procedures using highly specific antisera. The main cell group producing peptides of the pro-opiomelanocortin class is located in the region of the arcuate nucleus of the medial basal hypothalamus, with fibres projecting widely to many areas of the limbic system and brain stem. A second group of cells producing these peptides lies in the nucleus of the solitary tract and nucleus commissuralis. The enkephalin and dynorphin systems share representation in a number of areas (caudate–putamen, nucleus accumbens, globus pallidus, hippocampus, amygdala, periaqueductal central grey matter, locus ceruleus, nucleus of the tractus solitarius and spinal cord), but the enkephalin system is represented separately from the dynorphin system in other regions (habenular nuclei, interpeduncular nucleus, and cingulate and pyriform cortex).

The magnocellular nuclei of the hypothalamus and the pars reticulata of the substantia nigra, by contrast, contain dynorphin but not enkephalin (Watson *et al.*, 1982).

Not only is there a variety of endogenous opiate peptides, but also a range of opiate receptors. Some appreciation of the differences between the various kinds is desirable in order to understand the range of responses to seemingly similar opiate agonists and antagonists. Originally, three basic types were defined: a μ or morphine receptor, a κ or ketocyclazine receptor, and a σ or SKF 10047 receptor, with κ receptor activation being differentiated from μ activation by absence of the bradycardia expected with an acute dose of μ activator and by a failure to either precipitate or suppress withdrawal symptoms in morphine-dependent dogs. Activation of σ receptors, as with an acute injection of SKF 10047, produces a general activation of the CNS, including pupillary dilatation, tachypnoea, tachycardia, and mania.

Now enkephalin or δ receptors, and β-endorphin or ϵ receptors must be added to the list. Work aimed at the selective demonstration of particular opiate receptors in the brain suggests that μ receptors predominate in several hypothalamic and thalamic nuclei, the periaqueductal grey matter, the interpeduncular nucleus, inferior colliculus, and the median raphe nucleus, while δ binding appears to be relatively greater in the amygdala, nucleus accumbens, olfactory tubercle and the pontine nuclei. In the cerebral cortex, μ sites show striking laminar heterogeneity across regions, and are densest in the limbic cortex, while δ sites show a much more laminar and regional distribution (Akil *et al.*, 1984). The significance of such observations has yet to be realized, but they point to a major and selective role of the different opiates in brain function.

Dynorphin injected into the brain produces a wide range of motor and behavioural effects that differ significantly from those produced by alkaloid narcotics or other enkephalin-containing endorphins. Further, many of the dramatic motor and behavioural changes produced by dynorphin cannot be prevented by naloxone. Rats treated with dynorphin show unusual contorted postures, which may be accompanied by marked changes in the EEG, including a flattening of the hippocampal EEG (Walker *et al.*, 1982). Cells containing dynorphin are present in the suprachiasmatic nuclei, and the concentrations of immunoreactive dynorphin are higher during the night than in the day. Deprivation of food and water, or of water alone, increases the day-time concentration of dynorphin in the hypothalamus. Such information implicates dynorphin in the control of circadian rhythms and of water balance (Przewlocki *et al.*, 1983).

The availability of opiate antagonists, effective against the endogenous compounds as well as narcotic drugs, has greatly accelerated progress. Much work has been done with naloxone, and the responses observed have suggested a potential role for endorphins in nociception, respiration, sexual behaviour, neuroendocrinology, cardiovascular physiology, digestion and psychopathology (Frederickson & Geary, 1982). By themselves, moderate doses of opiate antagonists have very few direct effects in man, other than perhaps causing a slight increase in anxiety. However, with high doses of naloxone (up to 4 mg/kg), normal volunteers showed dysphoric changes in various measures of mood, such as tension–anxiety, anger–hostility, confusion–bewilderment, depression–dejection, vigour–activity, and fatigue–inertia. There was also a deterioration in tests of memory, as well as an increase in plasma cortisol and growth hormone levels (Cohen *et al.*, 1983). Naloxone can cause hyperalgesia in man, but the response depends upon the subject. Stress-induced analgesia is antagonized, as is that produced by acupuncture. One complication here is that the endogenous opiates are not the only peptides involved in the response to noxious stimuli or nociception. Some, such as bradykinin and substance P, lower the sensitivity to pain when injected into the brain or spinal cord, whereas others, such as cholecystokinin and somatostatin, share some of the properties of the opiates, with the effects being reversed by naloxone. The latter peptides may induce the release of opiates or may interact with opiate receptors (Luttinger, Hernandez, Nemeroff & Prange, 1984).

Claims have been made that naloxone may be beneficial in schizophrenic patients experiencing auditory hallucinations, but these have not been generally accepted (Verebey, Volavka & Clouet, 1978). If naloxone were effective, then it would appear that opioid activity is excessive in schizophrenia. However, there are also suggestions that an opioid deficiency may be involved in this disease state.

Addiction to opiates impairs or abolishes sexual behaviour in man (Hollister, 1975), so that information concerning the response to opioid antagonists, such as naloxone, is highly desirable. Observations on laboratory animals are conflicting, in that sexual behaviour can be enhanced or impaired. In one study, the opiate antagonists naloxone and naltrexone inhibited sexual behaviour in male rhesus monkeys, but retching and vomiting were induced simultaneously (Abbott *et al.*, 1984). It is worth making the point that some opioid activity could be exercised at the lower level of the spinal cord. Studies in the rat indicate that the application of morphine to the spinal cord inhibits sexual receptivity, while naloxone has the opposite effect. In male rats, local treatment of the lumbo-sacral region of the spinal cord with morphine extended the number of intromissions required before ejaculation occurred, whereas naloxone facilitated ejaculation (Wiesenfeld-Hallin & Södersten, 1984).

Sex steroids are known to influence the concentration of β-endorphin in the brain (Wardlaw, Thoron & Frantz, 1982), so that there is an endocrine basis for steroid–opiate interaction on neural tissue. Further, the β-endorphin content of hypophysial portal vessel blood of monkeys fluctuates in phase with the menstrual cycle and is highest during the luteal phase. At times when ovarian steroid concentrations are low, as at menstruation or after ovariectomy, β-endorphin is lacking in portal vessel blood (Wehrenberg, Wardlaw, Frantz & Ferin, 1982). The infusion of naloxone into normal women increases the frequency of LH pulses and raises the blood level of the hormone, as does naloxone given orally (Morley, 1983). The responsiveness of LH secretion to naloxone administration varies during the menstrual cycle, with little effect being evident during the early follicular phase and marked changes being demonstrable by the late follicular and during the mid-luteal phases. Naloxone seems to influence gonadotrophin secretion at the hypothalamic level and above. In women with hyperprolactinaemia and amenorrhoea the infusion of high doses of naloxone induced a marked rise in serum FSH and LH, without affecting prolactin secretion (Grossman *et al.*, 1982).

Overall, these observations leave little doubt concerning the participation of opiatergic mechanisms in the control of sexual function, although much important information is missing, and it may be noted that the performance of sexually inactive rhesus monkey males did not improve upon treatment with naloxone (Glick, Baughman, Jensen & Phoenix, 1982). It should be added that the opiates do not seem to be affecting the release of GnRF directly, but rather through the mediation of a noradrenergic step. Thus, the surge of LH secretion that can be precipitated in ovariectomized rats treated with oestrogen and progesterone can be prevented by either naloxone or clonidine, a noradrenergic agonist, and the advancement of LH secretion produced by naloxone can be blocked by inhibition of noradrenergic activity. This observation also illustrates the general point that the opioid peptides, or any other peptides for that matter, do not function in isolation from the more classical chemical mediators of neuronal activity. Thus, analgesic doses of β-endorphin, given intraventricularly, decrease the turnover of acetylcholine in a number of brain areas; the turnover of dopamine is also affected but the precise kind of response depends upon the neurotransmitter and the structure in question (Oliverio, Castellano & Puglisi-Allegra, 1984).

Endogenous opiate activity may be of particular significance during development (Sandman, Kastin & Schally, 1981), for β-endorphin in the amniotic fluid is increased during fetal distress. Intra-uterine exposure of rats to β-endorphin, by treatment of the mother, subsequently delayed eye opening, depressed motor activity and caused a more rapid gain in weight. The animals were less sensitive to environmental stimuli, and more sensitive to analgesic doses of morphine, than controls. When rats were given β-endorphin between the 2nd and 7th days of life and then left undisturbed until testing at three months of age, the threshold to thermal pain was increased.

In the human situation, tumours arising away from the hypophysis, such as pancreatic islet-cell, thymic and lung carcinoid tumours, may produce β-endorphin, and the opioid peptides released from the growths might alter mood and behaviour, as well as reducing pain. Rees & Smith (1982) point out that psychiatric symptoms in patients of this kind have resolved after resection of the growths, that depressive illness may precede other clinical features of malignancy by many years, and that some tumours, particularly peptide-producing tumours like medullary carcinoma of the thyroid, are associated with a high incidence of depression before tumour recognition. This correlation has been encountered earlier (Chapter 3).

Control of anterior pituitary hormone secretion

Morphine has long been known to block ovulation and cause the release of ACTH and prolactin from the pituitary gland, and these effects are reproduced by treatment with endogenous opiates. The secretion of three hormones, ACTH, growth hormone and prolactin, is increased by opiates and that of another three, FSH, LH and TSH, inhibited. However, less is known about the locus of action of the peptides within the brain, for commonly they have been given by intra-cerebroventricular injection, when diffusion and distribution of the material is widespread. The results of studies involving the local application of endorphin to the arcuate nuclei indicate that this area may be involved in the control of ACTH and prolactin release (McCann, 1982).

As is the case for the gonadotrophins, opioid peptides probably influence the secretion of other hormones through changes in monoaminergic systems (McCann, 1982). Dopamine turnover can be reduced and that of serotonin, and possibly noradrenaline, increased. In the case of growth hormone, the increased blood level produced by opiates may be generated through central noradrenergic neurons acting through α receptors, since a variety of inhibitors of noradrenaline synthesis and of α, but not β, receptor-blocking drugs prevent the growth hormone-releasing action of morphine.

Many of the peptides in the brain can alter the secretion of pituitary hormones: the problem lies in deciding whether the effect is physiological or pharmacological. Two, cholecystokinin and bombesin, are extremely potent and active at nanogram doses when given intra-ventricularly, whereas the others need to be given in microgram amounts. Only two compounds, vasoactive intestinal peptide and substance P, stimulate discharge of gonadotrophin-releasing hormone; the others usually inhibit LH release, and effects upon the secretion of FSH have seldom been seen. Growth hormone release can be provoked by most peptides, although bradykinin provides one exception and inhibits growth hormone secretion. Some peptides can act directly upon the pituitary gland and possibly represent new hypothalamic releasing or inhibiting factors. Thus, vasoactive intestinal peptide stimulates prolactin secretion and has been found in hypophysial portal vessel blood, as well as in the hypophysis. Neurotensin and substance P stimulate prolactin release and neurotensin inhibits TSH secretion (McCann, 1982).

Substance P
Substance P merits a little more attention, even though understanding of its physiological role is limited. The material is concentrated in certain neurons of the dorsal root ganglia, basal ganglia, hypothalamus and cerebral cortex, although more than thirty different groups of substance P-containing neurons have been described in the rat brain, and the list is steadily being lengthened. The finding that substance P terminals are particularly concentrated in regions containing the cell bodies of noradrenergic (locus ceruleus) and dopaminergic (substantia nigra and ventral tegmentum) neurons suggests that this peptide may be concerned with the control of central adrenergic systems. Microinfusions of substance P into the region of the dopaminergic neurons in the ventral tegmentum of the rat elicit an amphetamine-like hyperactivity response.

Substance P has also been proposed as a mediator in the action of primary afferent sensory fibres from the dorsal root ganglia projecting into the substantia gelatinosa of the spinal cord and conveying the sense of pain. It could also be involved in the striato-nigral system in the modulation of motor movement. The finding that the neurotoxin capsaicin, the pungent factor contained in red peppers, could damage or destroy substance P-containing sensory fibres, and that it caused a decreased sensitivity to pain, appeared at first to support the involvement of substance P in pain mechanisms. But subsequent work has shown that capsaicin causes indiscriminate damage to all unmyelinated sensory fibres, and some small diameter myelinated fibres, though not to small diameter unmyelinated fibres in the autonomic nervous system (Iversen, 1983).

Cholecystokinin

Cholecystokinin-like peptides are present in the central nervous system in concentrations that exceed those of most other peptides (Iversen, 1983). The principal form is the C-terminal octapeptide fragment CCK-8, but smaller fragments may also occur. Radioimmunoassay indicates that cholecystokinin-like peptides are most concentrated in the cerebral cortex, hippocampus, amygdala and hypothalamus. The concentration in the cortex is the highest of all other neuropeptides, with cholecystokinin being present in interneurons with large radially oriented processes.

Alongside influences upon food intake, catecholamine metabolism and hypophysial function, cholecystokinin may serve as an opiate antagonist. Food intake decreases after intraperitoneal or intraventricular administration of cholecystokinin, and increases when morphine or β-endorphin is given. Stress-induced feeding is mediated by endogenous opiates and blocked by cholecystokinin, which could be regarded as a satiety factor were it not for the fact that the anorexic effects of the peptide are abolished by vagotomy. Thus the action seems to be peripheral and may involve the activation of visceral afferent fibres. Nevertheless, the amounts of cholecystokinin depressing food intake when given intra-cerebrally are much less than those active peripherally, so that the likelihood of a central role remains (Chapter 11).

Dopamine turnover in some brain areas is decreased by cholecystokinin, but increased by morphine. The peptide also powerfully antagonizes the opiate-mediated analgesia produced by foot shock in rats, and appears to act through spinal mechanisms. It is present in the dorsal horn of the spinal cord, and is effective when given intra-thecally. Cholecystokinin given intra-ventricularly lowers the plasma concentrations of LH and TSH, but raises that of growth hormone (McCann, 1982; Faris, Komisaruk, Watkins & Mayer, 1983). A start has been made upon clinical correlations in that the concentration of cholecystokinin immunoreactivity in the CSF collected from patients with bipolar manic–depressive illness and untreated schizophrenia is significantly decreased (Verbanck *et al.*, 1984).

Neurotensin

Neurotensin is a widely distributed peptide with a broad spectrum of biological activity (Brown & Miller, 1982). It is found throughout the brain, with the highest concentrations being located in the limbic system, hypothalamus, substantia nigra and brain stem. The peptide may well serve as a neurotransmitter, for it is released upon depolarization of nerve cells, interacts with specific binding sites on nerve cells, induces depolarization of neurons, and is destroyed by peptidases in the brain. Besides inducing hypothermia, neurotensin affects hormone release when applied to the brain. Somatostatin production is increased and that of growth hormone reduced.

Neurotensin is present in various parts of the brain concerned with pain perception and exerts an anti-nociceptive effect when injected into the cisterna magna. The potency of neurotensin in this regard is surpassed only by β-endorphin and is greater on a molar basis than that of morphine or the enkephalins.

There are suggestions that neurotensin alters the activity of dopamine-containing neural pathways and possesses properties in common with the neuroleptics. Neurotensin and neurotensin receptors are strategically located in high density in the nuclei giving rise to catecholaminergic pathways in the locus ceruleus, ventral tegmentum and substantia nigra, and the loss of substantial numbers of neurotensin binding sites from the rat substantia nigra after 6-hydroxydopamine-induced lesions suggests that neurotensin receptors may be located in part on the catecholaminergic neurons, so facilitating interaction between neurotensin and the central dopamine receptors (Iversen, 1983).

Bombesin

Bombesin is a tetradecapeptide, and is present in highest concentration in the hypothalamus. When injected into the brain it alters body temperature and produces hypothermia or hyperthermia depending upon the ambient temperature: hyperthermia when the animal is exposed to a high environmental temperature and hypothermia upon transfer to a cold place. The effect is rapid in onset, long-lasting and exerted through the anterior hypothalamic–preoptic area, without the mediation of dopaminergic, catecholaminergic or cholinergic pathways. Bombesin increases the blood sugar level upon intra-cranial injection, probably through an increase in the activity of the sympathetic system which induces a rise in plasma adrenaline and glucagon. An intriguing finding is the prevention of stress-induced gastric ulcers by the injection of bombesin into the cerebral ventricles. There is a marked reduction in the volume of gastric secretion, an inhibition of gastric acid secretion and of that of pepsin, and the effect is again long-lasting, reversible, specific and dose-dependent. However, the way in which these changes are brought about is not clear (Taché & Brown, 1982).

Vasoactive intestinal peptide

Once again, the confusions inherent in present neuropeptide terminology are illustrated by vasoactive intestinal peptide (VIP), for this compound was detected in brain tissue almost as soon as a radioimmunoassay method for the peptide became available. But the name has stuck. The immunoreactive material in the brain appears to correspond to the 28 amino acid peptide originally characterized in gut extracts, and there is no evidence for the molecular heterogeneity found in the gastrin/cholecystokinin family of peptides (Iversen, 1983). Most VIP is present in the neocortex, but VIP-containing interneurons are found in all regions of the cerebral cortex and the hippocampus. There are also VIP-containing terminals in the hypothalamus, amygdala, bed nucleus of the stria terminalis, and the periaqueductal grey matter. Although VIP is present in hypophysial portal vessel blood, and might serve as a releasing factor for pituitary hormones, there are no strong links with any behavioural pattern.

Alongside the vasodilatory action of VIP, peripheral administration of the peptide can relax non-vascular smooth muscle, stimulate intestinal secretion, stimulate pancreatic bicarbonate secretion and bile flow, inhibit gastric acid secretion, induce hyperglycaemia, stimulate adenylate cyclase activity and lipolysis, and stimulate the release of several hormones, including insulin, glucagon, somatostatin, growth hormone, prolactin and LH. In patients with a pancreatic islet cell tumour, or a tumour of neural origin producing excessive amounts of VIP, there is a profuse watery diarrhoea due to massive intestinal secretion (Buchanan, 1982). But any behavioural changes are not remarkable.

Brain peptides and schizophrenia

The possibility that abnormalities in the activity of brain peptides may be involved in the genesis of schizophrenia has been raised, as indicated by a comparison of the peptide distribution in the brains of normal and schizophrenic individuals (Roberts *et al.*, 1983). The highest levels of cholecystokinin, somatostatin and VIP were found in the cerebral cortex, amygdala and hippocampus, with moderate to low levels in the striatum, and the lowest levels in the thalamus. By contrast, most substance P and neurotensin was found in the basal ganglia, with moderate to low levels in the amygdala and hippocampus. Least was present in the cortex and thalamus. The schizophrenic patients were divided into two groups: a Type I syndrome characterized by positive symptoms–delusions, thought disorder and hallucinations–that were reversible with neuroleptic drugs and not associated with intellectual impairment, and a Type II syndrome characterized by negative symptoms–affective flattening and poverty of speech– that were not drug reversible and could be associated with intellectual impairment and possibly structural changes in the brain. In the limbic lobe the VIP content of the amygdala was significantly increased, and was significantly higher in the Type I group, when compared to Type II.

Substance P was elevated in the hippocampus and cholecystokinin decreased in the temporal cortex when compared to controls, as well as being significantly decreased in the hippocampal and amygdaloid tissue collected from the Type II patients. Somatostatin was increased in the lateral thalamus of the schizophrenic patients, and it was suggested that the fact that amygdaloid VIP and hippocampal substance P was increased in Type II subjects was consistent with the appearance of positive symptoms. Others have found low concentrations of TRF in two frontal cortical regions, reduced somatostatin levels in one frontal cortical area and increased neurotensin levels in one frontal cortical area of psychiatric patients (Nemeroff *et al.*, 1983). While it is far too early to guess at the significance of these changes, which are unlikely to be post-mortem artefacts, these observations signpost the direction of future research endeavours, for many more studies of this type can be expected.

The therapeutic value of vasopressin in schizophrenic patients has been explored and the hormone has been shown to be beneficial in some. Upon long-continued daily treatment with large doses of the peptide increased sleeping time, reduced psychomotor activity and increased awareness have been described, as well as improvements in anxiety, emotional withdrawal and depression. There is the suggestion that vasopressin mainly affects emotional withdrawal, anergia and blunted affect (Legros & Lancranjan, 1983).

The possible function of TRF as a neurotransmitter or neuromodulator has prompted the treatment of schizophrenics with this peptide, but the results have been discouraging (Lindstrom, Gunne, Ost & Persson, 1977). Other hormonal studies indicate that chronic schizophrenic patients as a group may show low blood levels of FSH and LH, with reduced spontaneous fluctuations in LH, but normal levels of growth hormone, prolactin, thyroid hormones and gonadal steroids. The hormonal response to the administration of hypothalamic releasing factors was disturbed in that there was a reduced FSH response to GnRF and a reduced prolactin response to TRF, as well as increases in growth hormone secretion in a number of patients after GnRF and TRF. It is important to note that these patients had been free from any drug treatment (though not from pre-medication prior to anaesthesia) for at least a year (Ferrier, Johnstone, Crow & Rincon-Rodriguez, 1983), so that there is little likelihood of any drug-induced change, but the biological basis of these altered responses remains obscure. Even so, these observations may point to the only definite endocrine abnormality yet established in schizophrenia.

Although there may be some increase in the plasma cortisol concentration coincidentally with periods of emotional arousal, schizophrenic patients do not show the resistance to dexamethasone suppression of ACTH secretion evident in cases of depression–a point that supports the specificity of the response in that particular disease.

Blood–brain barrier

In any consideration of the effects of endogenous peptides upon brain function the question of access of the peptides to neural tissue becomes of great significance. For unlike the capillaries of other organs, the capillaries within the brain are characterized by high-resistance tight junctions that essentially cement brain endothelia together (Pardridge, 1983). This blood–brain barrier prevents all water-soluble substances in the blood from entering the brain interstitium and has all the properties of a cell membrane. Compounds can gain access to neural tissue by lipid mediation or free diffusion through the endothelial cell membrane–when the degree of lipid solubility becomes a determining factor–and by carrier-mediation or transport via specific enzyme-like carriers located within the capillary endothelium. The steroid molecules traverse the blood–brain barrier by lipid mediation, while the movement of thyroid hormones, glucose, amino acids, choline, purine and ketone bodies employs carrier mediation. As yet, carrier-mediated transport of the neuropeptides remains to be established. Pardridge (1983) considers that the most promising, but least evaluated, strategy for increasing the delivery of peptides to the brain is latentiation, or the chemical conversion of a water-soluble compound to a lipid-soluble molecule, for this can produce 'log order' increases in the ability to permeate the blood–brain barrier. The chemical change should be reversible, so that the active peptide is regenerated once it enters the brain. Apparently, the classical example of drug latentiation is morphine. When the two hydroxyl groups in morphine are acetylated heroin is formed, and this crosses the blood–brain barrier at a very much faster rate than that of morphine. Once inside the brain, heroin is transferred back into morphine by pseudocholinesterase hydroxylation of the acetyl groups.

There are gaps in the blood–brain barrier. These adjoin the cerebral ventricles and include the choroid plexus, the median eminence and organum vasculosum of the lamina terminalis, the subfornical organ at the roof of the third ventricle, and the area postrema at the base of the fourth ventricle. At these locations, collectively grouped together as the circumventricular organs, the walls of the capillaries are fenestrated and porous and the ependyma of the ventricles has low-resistance tight junctions. Circulating peptides can penetrate the blood–brain barrier at these places and reach the plasma membrane of neighbouring nerve endings. Indeed, there is evidence for the existence of receptors for peptides such as insulin, prolactin, angiotensin, calcitonin, and ACTH in nerve endings in the median eminence. Additionally, peptides can diffuse through the circumventricular organs to reach the CSF for wider distribution, although entry into the brain through this non-specific route can be very slow, with a half-time of the order of several hours.

The endothelium of brain capillaries does not serve merely as a mechanical barrier to the movement of neuropeptides into the brain, but functions actively in the degradation of neuroactive substances (Pardridge, 1983). Monoamines are inactivated by monoamine oxidase and acetylcholine by cholinesterase. Brain capillaries also possess aminopeptidase activity, and this can serve to degrade enkephalins.

In their consideration of the role of the blood–brain barrier in controlling the entry of circulating peptides into the brain, Meisenberg & Simmons (1983b) concluded that its properties can be altered by an action of the peptides upon vascular receptors to affect the supply of nutrients, or by releasing a second messenger to affect the brain. Polypeptide hormones may act directly upon receptors in the circumventricular organs, as we have seen for angiotensin, insulin and calcitonin, while the entry of peptides into the CSF may take place through the openings provided by the choroid plexuses or circumventricular organs. Blood-borne substances may also be taken up and retrogradely transported to the cell body by axon collaterals terminating in the circumventricular organs.

5

Cellular mechanisms of hormone action

There are three broad classes of hormone: polypeptides, steroids and tyrosine derivatives. The polypeptide hormones, like insulin, glucagon, the products of the pituitary gland, and the hypothalamic releasing factors bind to receptors on the surface of the target cell. Steroid hormones, such as oestradiol, progesterone, the androgens and the corticosteroids, have their receptors located within the cell, in the cytoplasm or nucleus. And, lastly, the tyrosine derivatives form a mixed category, with some receptors, e.g. adrenergic, being present on the cell surface, and others, as those for the thyroid hormones, being found in the nucleus (Levey & Robinson, 1982).

Steroid hormones are carried in the blood in two fractions, one bound to plasma proteins and the other, much smaller, dissolved and free. Only the free hormone is available for action and it diffuses into cells to bind, where appropriate, to specific cytoplasmic receptors. In turn, the hormone–receptor complex is translocated to the nucleus where it interacts with DNA through an acceptor protein, when new messenger RNA is generated. Finally, the messenger RNA moves to the cytoplasm where it influences the translational process producing new proteins.

The brain contains receptors for all classes of steroid hormones (oestrogens, progestins, androgens, glucocorticoids and mineralocorticoids), and the receptors are similar to those found elsewhere in the body. When the effects of steroids upon neural tissue are examined closely a variety of responses emerge, from the regulation of progestin receptors in the hypothalamus by oestrogen to the regulation of specific proteins in glia and neurons by glucocorticoids (McEwen et al., 1982). For example, oestrogen induces an increase in acetyltransferase activity in the preoptic area of female, but not of male, rats–an effect possibly linked to the control of sexual behaviour. Adrenalectomy increases, and glucocorticoids suppress, high affinity GABA uptake in the hippocampus, but not in the cerebral cortex or cerebellum. These effects of glucocorticoids upon the metabolism of GABA are probably mediated through the genome, but other changes wrought by steroids appear to involve the cell surface. Thus, rapid changes in the discharge rate of neurons in the hypothalamic area follow the application of oestradiol 17β-succinate; the α-enantiomer is ineffective. Directly applied cortisol also affects neuronal activity in the hypothalamus.

Gonadal steroids

Gonadal steroids produce changes in the electrical activity of neurons. Changes in the basal firing rate of cells, in the absolute refractory period, and alterations in the magnitude or direction of the responses to sensory stimulation have been observed, alongside decreases in the threshold for activation of specific neural pathways in the brain (as from the preoptic area to the hypothalamus). The direct application of gonadal steroids to neurons in the hypothalamus by micropipette and iontophoresis can also modify the firing rate within milliseconds. There is a considerable degree of stereospecificity in the response, in that, as mentioned earlier, the natural 17β-epimer is effective, and the 17α-epimer is not (McEwen & Parsons, 1982).

The location of neurons that bind gonadal steroids has been mapped extensively with the aid of autoradiographic techniques, and there appears to be a common plan among the vertebrates (McEwen, 1981). Cells binding oestrogens are found predominantly in the medial preoptic area, the tuberal hypothalamus, in specific brain regions such as the amygdala, and in a region of the midbrain deep to the tectum. The distribution of neurons concentrating tritiated testosterone is similar to that of oestrogen, though not identical, but interpretation is complicated by the fact that testosterone is extensively converted to oestradiol in the brain, as well as to 5α-dihydrotestosterone. The aromatizing enzyme systems that convert testosterone to oestradiol are concentrated in those areas that have oestrogen receptor sites, including the amygdala, hypothalamus and preoptic area, but mammalian species differ in the degree to which these metabolic pathways are utilized in the sexual differentiation of behaviour. The matter is further complicated in that it is argued that there are three categories of receptor for androgen in the brain. One class preferentially binds testosterone, while a second has a greater affinity for dihydrotestosterone. The receptors in these categories are in equilibrium between nucleus and cytoplasm, and can be activated and transformed by steroid for concentration in the nucleus. A third class of receptor may bind both steroids with the same relative affinity, but can only be activated by steroid with no transfer to the nucleus. On this basis testosterone can be conceived to act on a few discrete populations of neurons in the brain, whereas dihydrotestosterone would have a very diffuse action (Sheridan, 1983).

Sex differences in the distribution of receptors for sex hormones are few, with the spread of testosterone- and oestradiol-binding neurons being similar. However, close analysis is bringing some other sex differences to light in that the spinal cord of the male rat contains a group of androgen-concentrating neurons innervating the striated muscles of the penis that are lacking in the female. Other sex differences in the nervous system will be described later on.

In rodents, the discharge rate of hypothalamic neurons alters during the oestrous cycle of the female, with the firing rate being raised in the arcuate–ventromedial nuclear area in phase with the triggering of an increase in gonadotrophin secretion necessary for ovulation. Similar changes occur in islands of hypothalamic tissue and are probably due to a direct action of gonadal steroids upon the nerve cells. In ovariectomized rats, oestrogen increases the rate of the resting neuronal discharge in the anterior basomedial hypothalamus. The neurons concerned appear to fire slowly, or may show no resting discharge. Appropriately, stimulation of this region of the hypothalamus at a slow rate facilitates sexual behaviour, whereas stimulation of the preoptic area is inhibitory. For the preoptic area, treatment with oestrogen decreases the resting firing rate of nerve cells. There are also oestrogen receptors in the ventromedial portion of the ventromedial nucleus, and here the local application of oestradiol in nanogram quantity facilitates sexual behaviour in the ovariectomized rat; the application of a protein synthesis inhibitor, anisomycin, to the same area blocks the action of oestradiol. In turn, the hypothalamus probably controls sexual behaviour through projections to the dorsal midbrain, which is another region affected by oestrogen (Pfaff & McEwen, 1983). The synthesis of protein, and the transport of protein away from the cell and down the axon, could result from the action of oestrogen, in that blockade of axonal transport by the injection of colchicine into the medial hypothalamus has delayed the onset of the lordotic (sexually receptive) behavioural response to oestrogen.

At the metabolic level other changes in brain function in response to oestrogen are known. Oestrogen increases the turnover of dopamine in the corpus striatum, and this response may be reversed by progesterone. Contrariwise, gonadal steroids decrease the turnover of noradrenaline (McEwen & Parsons, 1982), and may depress the response to a noradrenergic stimulus. In other words, the influence of a noradrenergic system upon a particular physiological or behavioural mechanism could be depressed or abolished by oestrogen. One way in which this effect could be brought about is by change in the level of activity of monoamine oxidase, an enzyme involved in the degradation of noradrenaline, dopamine and serotonin. Other effects upon neurotransmission may be indicated by observations that the activity of glutamic acid decarboxylase (and, in turn, possibly the efficiency of the GABA mechanism) is decreased by oestrogen, while the density of muscarinic cholinergic receptor sites in the ventromedial nuclei is increased (Pfaff & McEwen, 1983).

Progesterone also modulates neuronal function and, as for oestrogen, most information is based upon studies in the rat. In this species the initial facilitation of sexual behaviour produced by the steroid can be blocked by inhibition of protein synthesis with anisomycin. The local implantation of progesterone into the ventromedial nuclei, but not elsewhere, promotes sexual behaviour; it is interesting that oestrogen-primed castrated male rats, which fail to manifest sexual behaviour upon treatment with progesterone, show relatively few progesterone receptors in the ventromedial nuclei, by comparison with females, although the number of receptors in the arcuate nucleus is not reduced (Pfaff & McEwen, 1983).

Adrenal steroids

Like the gonadal steroids, adrenal glucocorticoids bind to neurons in the brain, but the pattern of labelled cells differs markedly, in that there is a high degree of labelling in the hippocampus and septum and very little accumulation of steroid in the preoptic area and medial hypothalamus (Pfaff & McEwen, 1983). Corticosteroid binding sites are most numerous in the hippocampus, particularly in the large pyramidal cells of Ammon's horn, the amygdala, septum and cerebral cortex. Remarkably, a synthetic glucocorticoid that effectively inhibits ACTH secretion, dexamethasone, differs from native corticosteroids in binding strongly to cells in the pituitary gland. While this finding may account for the potent effect of dexamethasone upon ACTH release, it also points to caution in the use of this steroid in experimental studies, for its mode of action may not be the same as that of endogenous hormone (McEwen, 1980). (Dexamethasone has already been mentioned (Chapter 3) in terms of its importance in clinical work on depression.) Most commonly, when dexamethasone is applied to single neurons in the hypothalamus there is an inhibition of activity, although many cells remain unaffected. The response is often instantaneous and may linger for 5–100 seconds after the steroid is withdrawn. Chronic systemic treatment with glucocorticoid has increased the resting potential of motor neurons in cats by more than 4 mV, but this indication of a decreased excitability is countered by the finding that the depolarizing current needed to trigger an action potential is lessened, perhaps because of selective changes in the impulse-generating initial segment of the axon (Hall, 1982).

Glucocorticoids alter neurotransmitter function, although the changes are not straightforward. The synthesis of serotonin in various brain regions is increased by glucocorticoid and has been related to an acute enhancement of tryptophan uptake by synaptosomes alongside a slower induction of trytophan hydroxylase. Implantation of cortisol into the hypothalamus of the rat increases the concentration of noradrenaline, although with chronic treatment no changes in brain noradrenaline may be evident, perhaps because of a reduced availability of tyrosine for catecholamine synthesis. Adrenalectomized animals have reduced brain levels of GABA, which, in the light of the generally inhibitory actions of this amino acid, would accord with the lower seizure threshold and increased central excitability that ensues. Chronic treatment with cortisol can also decrease the brain seizure threshold, together with depression of the brain GABA concentration (Hall, 1982).

Brain excitability

Several steroid hormones, including desoxycorticosterone and pro-gesterone, produce anaesthesia when given in large doses, so that it is to be expected that steroid hormones can influence general brain excitability, as assessed by the response to electric shock (Vernadakis & Culver, 1982). In the case of desoxycorticosterone the effect seems to follow from changes in electrolyte metabolism, but the mode of action of other steroids is unclear. The brain of the female rat is more sensitive to the induction of seizures by electric shock than that of the male, and the excitability varies in phase with the oestrous cycle. Seizures are most readily induced at the time of ovulation. The seizure activity may be quite localized, as in the hippocampus and amygdala (where that in the dorsal hippocampus and medial part of the amygdala is significantly decreased near oestrus, while that of the lateral part of the amygdala is increased). The intraventricular injection of cortisol into various subcortical regions in cats enhances electrical activity ranging from the appearance of localized spikes in the hippocampus and lateral hypothalamus to generalized convulsive activity. There is an overall slowing in the electrical activity of the cerebral cortex and subcortical structures in adrenal insufficiency.

The preceding observations would be of largely theoretical interest only, were it not for the fact that the incidence of convulsions in epileptic women is highest around the time of onset of the menses. One study concluded that 72 per cent of over 33 000 seizures took place at this period. Because there were relatively few seizures during the luteal phase of the cycle, and the rise in frequency coincides with the decline in plasma progesterone concentration, it is suggested that this steroid exercises a protective action against the provocative influence of oestrogen, and that the ratio of oestrogen to progesterone can be important in these circumstances. Epileptiform activity has been artificially induced in patients given conjugated oestrogens intravenously, and these set in between 30 seconds to 20 minutes after injection. Movement disorders can be potentiated by increases in the sex steroid concentrations of the blood, and the occurrence of chorea during pregnancy has long been known. As indicated by its name, chorea gravidum is rarely permanent and subsides after delivery or therapeutic abortion, although the high percentage of patients having a previous history of rheumatic fever or cardiac pathology suggests that the development of chorea is related to earlier damage suffered by the basal ganglia. Chorea may appear in women taking oral contraceptives and could again be linked with the presence of subclinical damage to the basal ganglia (Cogen & Zimmerman, 1979).

Steroid–neurotransmitter interaction

Most, if not all, of the brain areas that selectively concentrate steroid hormones contain catecholaminergic neural elements, and steroids are to be found in the nuclei of many catecholamine-containing cell bodies. Steroid effects upon the enzymes involved in catecholamine synthesis and degradation, on catecholamine release and re-uptake, and on the postsynaptic sensitivity to catecholamines have been demonstrated, and other neurotransmitter systems are probably affected in comparable ways. Conversely, neurotransmitter activity can affect steroid production by influencing the release of the appropriate trophic hormones from the pituitary gland. Thus, steroids affect neurotransmission and neurotransmitters affect steroid activity. Additionally, the actions of steroids within the target tissues themselves can be modulated by neurotransmitters (Nock & Feder, 1981). Adrenal steroids regulate the activity of the β-adrenergic receptor–adenylate cyclase system in a variety of tissues, as well as influencing the number of β-adrenergic receptors on cells, but the mechanisms of action are not understood and the basis of tissue and species differences in the response to steroids remains a mystery (Davies & Lefkowitz, 1984).

In the female guinea-pig, sequential treatment with oestradiol and progesterone is followed by the development of lordosis (a posture facilitating copulation) in response to light pressure at the base of the spine. Drugs that interfere with noradrenergic transmission block the induction of lordosis by steroids, while a drug that enhances noradrenergic transmission potentiates lordotic behaviour (Nock & Feder, 1981). These actions are exerted at the level of the hypothalamus, and it seems that changes in noradrenergic transmission alter the action of oestrogen in some way, with that of progesterone being affected secondarily.

Oestrogens also reduce dopamine receptor sensitivity, although not all reports are concordant. Most of the evidence suggests that oestrogens act upon dopaminergic systems like weak neuroleptics and share some properties with antidepressants (Holsboer, 1983).

Thyroid hormones

Thyroid hormones act in a similar way to steroids, in that bound and free fractions exist in the blood, and only hormone from the free fraction enters cells. However, thyroid hormones bind to a protein in the nuclear chromatin and induce the synthesis of new messenger RNA without prior linkage to a cytoplasmic receptor. The messenger RNA promotes the synthesis of a number of structural and enzymatic proteins, such as sodium potassium adenosine triphosphatase which influences oxygen consumption.

Much is known about the cellular receptors for thyroid hormone, largely because of the ease of labelling the hormonal ligand. Both thyroxine (T4) and 3,5,3'-triiodothyronine (T3) enter the cell and probably bind to mitochondria and cytosol proteins to facilitate transport of the hormone among the organelles (Ramsden & Hoffenberg, 1983), but the prime target is the nucleus. Triiodothyronine binds to the nucleus more avidly than does T4, in accordance with the relative biological potencies of the hormones. Further, T3 represents about 85 per cent of the bound triiodothyronines, so that T4 appears to exert little action upon the nucleus. Triiodothyronine is largely formed by the deiodination of T4 in peripheral tissues. However, so far as the brain is concerned, 80 per cent of the T3 occupying the receptors in neural tissue is generated from T4 locally. Tissues like the testis and spleen, which are unresponsive to thyroid hormones, show no nuclear binding of these hormones.

Some of the neural effects of thyroid hormone are mediated by the nucleus and others by actions on synaptosomes, which may contain considerable quantities of T3 (Mashio *et al.*, 1982). The number of nuclear binding sites in the brain of the neonatal rat increases at the time when thyroid hormone is critically important in the development of the cerebral cortex (Chapter 7). Eventually, binding of thyroid hormone by the nucleus leads to changes in the rate of synthesis of specific proteins mediating the effects of the hormone. These proteins may be retained within the cell, as in the case of α-glucose phosphate dehydrogenase (α-GPD), malic enzyme and sodium potassium adenosinetriphosphatase, or exported like growth hormone (Ramsden & Hoffenberg, 1983). Cells differ in their specific response to thyroid hormone, in that, for example, α-GPD is affected in rat liver, but not in brain or human liver.

The actions of thyroid hormones are similar in some respects to those of adrenaline and noradrenaline, and in hyperthyroid animals there is an increase in β-adrenergic receptors. There are also suggestions that thyroid hormones may enter into the biosynthetic pathways of adrenergic neuro-transmitters (Sterling, 1979). Thyroid hormones, by increasing β-adrenergic receptor activity, may promote the action of catecholamines, and especially that of noradrenaline, at central adrenoceptor sites. In depression the provision of additional thyroid hormone could enhance β-adrenergic receptor function, promote transmission in central noradrenergic pathways and accelerate recovery (Whybrow & Prange, 1981). But in bipolar, manic–depressive illness the promotion of noradrenergic transmission while favouring recovery from depression may precipitate mania.

Polypeptide hormones

Polypeptide hormones act upon cells in a different way from steroids or thyroid hormone, for they do not need to approach the nucleus but bind to specific receptors on the surface of the cell. It is the nature of the receptor on the surface of the target cell that gives specificity to the action of particular hormones. The large glycoproteins, follicle-stimulating hormone, luteinizing hormone and thyrotrophic hormone, are of similar structure in that each is a combination of two parts–an α and a β subunit. The α units are common to all three hormones, but the β subunits differ in their ability to bind to the cell surface and stimulate adenylate cyclase, the common effector in the cell. Adenylate cyclase converts ATP to cyclic AMP, which acts as a second messenger to cause protein synthesis, glycogenolysis, lipolysis and so on. However, not all polypeptide hormones alter adenylate cyclase activity: growth hormone and insulin are exceptions.

Characteristically, the binding of peptide hormones to their receptors on the target cells exhibits high specificity and high affinity, with high specificity favouring the selective uptake of the relevant ligand molecules from among the vast pool of peptides in the extracellular fluid, and high affinity needed to extract the hormonal ligands existing in very minute concentration (often about 10^{-10} M) in the circulation (Catt & Dufau, 1983). Despite these features, hormone receptors are highly mobile within the plasma membrane and are subject to changes of conformation upon binding with a hormone–which leads to the expression of hormone action. Similar changes can be produced by hormonal agonists, or by antibodies to receptors. The binding of certain thyroid-stimulating antibodies to TSH receptors provokes TSH release and thyroid hormone secretion (Graves' disease), whereas the release of destructive antibodies results in the loss of thyroid cells and Hashimoto's disease. In other circumstances, the binding of antibodies to insulin receptors causes glucose uptake hypoglycaemia, the binding of antibodies to catecholamine receptors activates adenylate cyclase, and the binding of antibodies to prolactin receptors results in the synthesis of casein in the mammary gland. This list of responses, together with a corresponding increase in the understanding of disease states, can be expected to grow rapidly.

The number of receptors on the surface of target cells is far from static and appears to be related to the prevailing circulatory levels of trophic hormone, or the ambient concentration of ligand. Here, the mobility of the receptors and the ability of the cell to ingest the hormone–receptor complex by means of endocytosis becomes significant. Thus for the gonadotrophin receptors on Leydig cells each receptor site might be occupied only once and then degraded and reprocessed (Catt & Dufau, 1983). Direct visualization of the process of internalization by the use of fluorescent analogues of insulin and gonadotrophin-releasing hormone with cultured cells has demonstrated that the hormone–receptor complexes are initially distributed uniformly on the cell membrane, but then rapidly become aggregated into patches that are ingested as endocytotic vesicles within the cytoplasm.

Two features of hormone–receptor interaction are of special importance in understanding the response to hormone administration. These are called 'down-regulation' and 'up-regulation', mentioned previously. The first concerns the situation where a chronic elevation in the blood level of a particular hormone results in a decrease in the number of receptors for that hormone, and, in turn, to a loss of sensitivity to that hormone. Conversely, 'up-regulation' covers the increase in the number of specific hormone receptors in response to chronically decreased levels of a particular hormone. Occasionally, elevated levels of a trophic hormone can increase the number of receptors for that hormone, as occurs upon exposure of the Leydig cells of the testis of the fetus or neonate to human chorionic gonadotrophin.

In the past, down-regulation has been referred to as tachyphyllaxis, desensitization, or refractoriness. At the receptor level it may involve structural modification or inactivation of the binding sites, persistent occupancy of the binding sites by bound hormone, and internalization and degradation of the sites (Catt & Dufau, 1983). Thus the pituitary gland soon becomes refractory to the action of gonadotrophin-releasing factor upon continuous or excessively frequent exposure to this peptide. In obesity with chronic hyperinsulinism and glucose intolerance there is a reduced number of insulin receptors, and this accounts in large part for the insulin resistance seen in this condition. To take another example, only 10–20 per cent of diabetic patients totally lack insulin and require this hormone to sustain life.

Most retain endogenous insulin secretion, which is often at a high level, but the number or concentration of insulin receptors is reduced. Accordingly, current therapeutic policy is aimed at relieving the insulin resistance and increasing the number of insulin receptors. Changes in the number of insulin receptors are seen in other circumstances, as in acromegaly, where patients may show moderate insulin resistance and a fall in receptor concentration. By contrast, there are a few patients with extreme resistance to the action of insulin who possess antibodies to insulin receptors that are detectable in the blood. Here the antibody presumably binds to the receptors and blocks the access of insulin (Roth & Taylor, 1982).

The biochemical basis for the fall in responsiveness of a target cell to further stimulation after the initial reaction is currently the subject of intensive research. Where cyclic AMP is involved in the hormonal response it seems that exposure to a stimulating hormone causes an initial surge in cyclic AMP formation, followed by a fall towards the basal level and a loss of responsiveness to further stimulation, possibly through deactivation of a nucleotide-regulating protein or of a catalytic enzyme unit. As set out by Catt & Dufau (1983), the peptide and transmitter ligands that influence adenylate cyclase are believed to act through a common regulatory protein that binds guanyl nucleotides and couples receptor occupancy to activation of adenyl cyclase, with release of cyclic AMP into the cytoplasm. The nucleotide regulatory (N) protein is converted by guanyl triphosphate binding into an active form that associates with the enzyme catalytic unit, stimulating the conversion of ATP to cyclic AMP. Calcium is a particularly important intermediary in hormone action, for in many instances the binding of a hormone to its receptor leads to an influx of calcium into the cell, and a redistribution of intracellular calcium. This activates calcium-dependent enzymes, including phosphodiesterase and adenylate cyclase, with calmodulin (a calcium receptor) being involved in these events. Thyrotrophin-releasing factor, GnRF, and angiotensin II are calcium-dependent hormones.

After hormone–receptor binding and activation of the adenylate cyclase system, the hormone–receptor complex may undergo a conformational change that disconnects it from the adenylate cyclase system. As a result, the cell may become refractory to further activation. The period of refractoriness may be transient, as in the case of the β-adrenergic receptors, or more lengthy, as for gonadotrophin–gonadal interaction, where the initial period of refractoriness is followed by a pronounced loss of LH receptors due to internalization and degradation of the hormone–receptor complexes (Catt & Dufau, 1983).

There are other ways for hormones to affect target cells, with the signal responsible in some cases for eliciting target cell responses remaining unknown (Catt & Dufau, 1983). The signals mediating the reactions to insulin, growth hormone, prolactin and the growth factors have not been identified, but a peptide derived from the plasma membrane could mediate changes in intracellular enzyme activity, as for insulin. In hepatocytes, this hormone promotes the formation of a low molecular weight factor that stimulates nuclear RNA synthesis, while prolactin promotes the formation of a plasma-membrane factor enhancing casein messenger RNA formation in the mammary gland.

While discussion of the physiology of receptors has been focussed upon the responses to hormones, the principles outlined have a much wider application, for they cover neurotransmission as a whole and are of major clinical significance in relation to the effects of psychotropic drugs. As shown many years ago, after deprivation of a neurotransmitter, usually from degeneration of the axon terminals after denervation, the appropriate receptors become supersensitive. Thus, broadly in this fashion, increased activity of dopaminergic neurons may arise in Parkinsonism and in syndromes resulting from the prolonged administration of dopamine blocking agents. Chronic administration of blocking agents, or the chronic inhibition of dopamine synthesis, results in an increase in the number of central dopamine receptors, so that a greater than normal response occurs when the drug is withdrawn, and neurotransmitter release allowed (Friedhoff & Miller, 1983). Sometimes the supersensitivity developing with chronic drug administration may overcome the effects of the drug, so producing signs of neurotransmitter excess. Further, receptor sensitivity modification has been utilized in the treatment of conditions believed to be responsive to a reduction in dopaminergic activity, such as tardive dyskinesia, schizophrenia and the Gilles de la Tourette syndrome. To this end, an initial increase in dopaminergic activity was induced by the administration of a dopaminergic agonist or agonist precursor to cause a secondary down-regulation of dopamine receptors and a net reduction in dopaminergic activity upon withdrawal of the agonist or precursor. The difficulties arising from the initial exacerbation of the condition and the temporary nature of the final beneficial phase will be evident.

Morphological changes

Hormones do not simply affect the functional activity of the nervous system; they can produce distinctive structural changes as well.

Thyroid hormones

When thyroid deficiency occurs early in human life it results in mental retardation, as well as other dramatic somatic effects. The anatomical changes associated with cretinism include a reduction in brain weight, a reduction in the size of the cells in the cerebral cortex, malformed convolutions of the cortical layers, axonal degeneration and delayed myelination (Cramer & Ford, 1982). Similar changes occur in the brain of the rat deprived of thyroid hormone, and this species has been used extensively in research in this area. The effects of hypothyroidism upon the cerebral cortex of the rat include an increase in the size of the blood vessels and a decrease in the number of capillaries, a decrease in the size of pyramidal perikarya, a decrease in the amount of neuropil, a significant decrease in the number of spines per unit length of the apical shaft of the pyramidal cells, an impairment of the migration of glial cells from the subependymal zone, and a reduced deposition of myelin. Neonatal hyperthyroidism has equally detrimental consequences associated with a decrease in postnatal cell formation. The cerebellum is also affected. In adult rats, thyroidectomy reduces the size of the nucleus in neurons in the hypothalamus, while the administration of thyroxine enlarges the cell nuclei.

Adrenocortical hormones

In contrast to the effects of thyroid hormone, the adrenal steroid cortisol appears to slow down the development of the brain. Experimental studies indicate that DNA synthesis and cell division are inhibited in the cerebrum and cerebellum. There is also a decrease in the number and size of the dendrites. Differential effects on the nuclei of cell groups within the mature hypothalamus have been observed in that after adrenalectomy of the rat there was an increase in nuclear volume in the anterior medial cell group of the ventromedial nuclei and in the arcuate nuclei, and a reduction in nuclear volume in the cells of the anterior ventromedial and ventral premammillary nuclei (Cramer & Ford, 1982). The significance of these changes is not understood, although they point to a functional subdivision of the cell groups concerned.

Sex hormones

Because of the importance of gonadal hormones in controlling the sexual differentiation of the brain of the rat (Donovan, 1980), considerable attention has been given to sexual dimorphism in the brain of this species. The findings include larger neuronal nuclear size in the ventromedial, arcuate, suprachiasmatic, paraventricular and supraoptic nuclei of young females, when compared to young males, ultrastructural differences in axon terminals in the arcuate nucleus, and a greater number of synapses of non-amygdalar origin on dendritic spines in the preoptic area of the female than in the male (Cramer & Ford, 1982). Concordant changes are produced after gonadectomy and replacement therapy, and regular changes in the nuclear size of neurons in the hypothalamus have been seen in phase with cyclic variations in reproductive activity. Increases in the amount of rough endoplasmic reticulum in cells of the ventromedial nuclei under the influence of oestrogen, and indicative of an increase in protein synthesis, have also been seen (Pfaff & McEwen, 1983).

The administration or deprivation of sex hormones during early development also affects nuclear size, myelination and synaptic connections within the hypothalamus, as well as the number of preganglionic neurons in the spinal cord. The nuclei of neurons in the medial and central parts of the amygdala are larger in females, but can be reduced to the size seen in males by treatment with androgen soon after birth. Paradoxically, the nuclei in the amygdala of male squirrel monkeys are bigger than in females. In more general terms, sex differences in cortical development, neuronal nuclear or nucleolar size, neuronal number, neuronal connectivity and regional nuclear volume have all been demonstrated, so that, as Gorski (1983) emphasizes, it is no longer tenable to view the brain functionally or structurally as independent of the sexual or hormonal status of the individual.

Under organ culture conditions, both oestradiol and testosterone enhance the proliferation of neuronal processes in fragments of hypothalamic tissue collected from new-born mice, and this effect is particularly evident in explants of the preoptic–anterior hypothalamic area. Treatment of cultures with serum containing antibodies to oestradiol retarded and reduced the outgrowth of processes. Other studies in rats indicate that neonatal oestrogenization accelerates synapse formation (Toran-Allerand, 1978).

Sexual differences in the anatomy of the nervous system are not confined to the preoptic area or limbic system. There is a prominent dimorphism in a motor nucleus of the rat spinal cord, the spinal nucleus of the bulbo-cavernosus muscles of the penis. This is identified by injecting horseradish peroxidase into the penile muscles, killing the animals 20 hours later, and staining the retrogradely transported enzyme in the spinal cord. Differentiation of the paired nuclei appears to depend upon androgen, for they are absent in males with the testicular feminization syndrome in which the number of androgen receptors is markedly reduced. The cells in the nuclei bind androgen (Breedlove & Arnold, 1980).

Growth hormone

In clinical cases of infantile growth hormone deficiency intellectual deficits have been reported, although others have found normal intelligence and school performance. Efforts to resolve this uncertainty by study of the influence of growth hormone upon the structure of the developing nervous system have not proved rewarding, although most studies support an effect which may be indirect (Donovan, 1980; Cramer & Ford, 1982).

Insulin

In humans, the neurological change most frequently described in association with diabetes mellitus involves the peripheral nerves and nerve roots. But myelopathy, with degeneration of the long tracts, demyelination, gliosis and microinfarcts, and encephalopathy, including cell damage, demyelination, gliosis and severe angiopathy, may also ensue (Cramer & Ford, 1982).

6

Patterns in hormone secretion

Biological clocks

Many biological processes are rhythmic in character. There are well-defined rhythms in body temperature, hormone secretion, food-seeking behaviour and activity, and even the reaction time of men and women to visual or auditory signals is longer in the morning than in the late afternoon. The mortality rate of mice given constant amounts of toxic drugs, such as $E.$ $coli$ endotoxin, ouabain or barbiturate, varies according to the time of day of administration. On this basis it has often been argued that as much attention should be given to the timing of drug treatment as to the size of the dose. Repetitive phenomena of this kind frequently recur on a daily basis and are termed circadian rhythms, for under constant conditions, as with a subject living deeply underground and deprived of time cues, the length of a 'free-running' cycle approximates to that of a day (Aschoff, 1980), although the circadian period changes from 24 hours to a mean of about 25 hours. The exogenous free-running period has been shown to persist throughout the life span of an animal and is remarkably stable in most species. Few chemical agents influence the free-running period, although there are some striking exceptions: gonadal steroids, lithium and possibly the tricyclic antidepressants (Moore-Ede, Czeisler & Richardson, 1983).

Human beings have a free-running period of approximately 25 hours, so that if their circadian pacemakers were not regularly reset then their endogenous rhythms would drift away from clock time by an hour each day. Animal studies indicate that for environmental cues to be effective they should be applied at times near the transition between night and day. Single short pulses of light applied early in the dark period may lengthen a cycle (cause a phase delay), and when applied late in the night shorten the cycle (cause a phase advance). Phase relationships concern the relative position in time to the environmental day–night cycle. Shifts in phase can be brought about by chemical means, and it is notable that the methylxanthines including the theophylline and caffeine of coffee are effective in this regard. Moore-Ede *et al.* (1983) highlight the fact that the typical range of entrainment of approximately 23.5 to 26.5 hours easily accommodates normal synchronization to the 24-hour period of rotation of the earth, but allows in any one daily cycle a phase advance with respect to environmental time of only an additional half-hour, while permitting a phase delay of 2.5 hours. This may explain why adaptation after long flights is more rapid in most people after westbound travel (requiring a phase delay) than after eastbound journeys (requiring a phase advance). During the process of readjustment the endogenous circadian rhythms in sleep, alertness, gastro-intestinal function and mood are not synchronized with the new time zone and symptoms of malaise and fatigue appear. These are popularly known as signs of 'jet lag'.

Other physiological timing expressions frequently encountered in discussions of rhythmic processes include *ultradian*, with periodicities of much less than a day, and *infradian*, which are much longer rhythms of monthly, seasonal or yearly extent. Examples of ultradian rhythms are the patterns seen in the electrocardiogram, electroencephalogram (EEG), and the rapid eye movement–non-rapid eye movement (REM–NREM) sequences in sleep, as well as those connected with respiration. Infradian rhythms are exemplified by menstrual cycles and the longer-term rhythms of breeding. The external triggers or factors that induce synchronization of the internal rhythms with changes in the external environment are referred to as *zeitgebers*. Light is an important *zeitgeber*.

While it is natural to assume that the occurrence of a circadian rhythm in a biological function is indicative of the involvement of the central nervous system, this is not always the case. Adrenal tissue cultured under *in vitro* conditions still continues to secrete corticosteroids in a rhythmic fashion, while in monkeys, episodes of cortisol secretion can be maintained in the face of an infusion of ACTH at a constant rate. Other tissues supported *in vitro*, such as heart, gut, and liver cell suspensions, can continue to show circadian rhythmicity, so that the existence of a variety of other circadian oscillators, besides those located in the nervous system, is likely (Moore-Ede, 1983).

The possibility that extra-terrestrial factors might influence biological rhythms has often been mooted, although there is little hard information concerning their nature (Tromp, 1975). Some observers have been impressed by the occurrence of periodicities in seemingly random events. E. R. Dewey, a psychologist, once analysed the incidence of international battles and civil war conflicts between 600 BC and AD 1943 as an index of aggressiveness. Eight highly significant cycles emerged, of 6, $9\frac{2}{3}$, $11\frac{1}{4}$, $12\frac{1}{3}$, $17\frac{3}{4}$, 22, 143 and 164 years. If random numbers instead of battle dates were used, no cycles were found. The relationship between the month of birth and conviction for ill-treatment, manslaughter and murder was examined in a group of about 3400 subjects in Amsterdam. Agressive behaviour was most common among people born in February and least frequent in those delivered in September. Monthly changes in the sedimentation rate of blood cells have been followed in the Netherlands for many years and short-term and long-term fluctuations recorded, while similarities in the trends from data collected in Sweden, Austria and South Africa suggested the operation of a world-wide, possibly extra-terrestrial, cause. Whatever might be the basis of such synchrony, systematic investigation of seasonal fluctuations in biochemical variables has shown unimodal annual rhythms in platelet serotonin uptake and dopamine-β-hydroxylase activity, bimodal seasonal rhythms in plasma free and total tryptophan, melatonin and platelet serotonin, and significant fluctuations of higher frequency in platelet monoamine oxidase activity and protein. The seasonal changes were often greater than the differences previously found between depressive patients and controls (Wirz-Justice & Richter, 1979).

As part of the rostral projection of the brainstem reticular activating system, the hypothalamus is involved in the control of sleeping and waking (Plum & van Uitert, 1978). Lesions in the anterior hypothalamus induce wakefulness, probably by interfering with an inhibition exercised over the reticular activating system, while damage to the posterior hypothalamus precipitates a drowsiness, stupor or coma that may last for weeks. On this basis, normal sleep–wake cycles are believed to originate as the outcome of interaction between the anterior and posterior hypothalamic areas, although slowly developing lesions may become large and invade all regions of the hypothalamus without disturbing consciousness or sleep–wake patterns. That a desynchronization of circadian rhythms can occur in a variety of disease states is well known (Aschoff, 1980; Wehr *et al.*, 1983). In manic–depressive illness, when episodes of mania are succeeded by phases of depression, and then reversion to mania, the episodes are often irregular but consistent cycles are sometimes seen. Several clinical features of manic–depressive illness lead to the conclusion that disturbances in timing or in the phase-position of circadian rhythms could be important (Wehr *et al.*, 1983), and this view has been referred to as the phase-advance hypothesis of depression. There are the observations that early morning awakening may occur and be associated with depressive symptoms that wane during the course of the day. Then there is the possibility that cyclicity in emotional illness could arise if a component in the circadian system became free-running and subsequently went in and out of phase with other periodicities that remained entrained. There is also some association of manic and depressive episodes with the seasons of the year, and evidence that several days of exposure to an artificially lengthened photoperiod may trigger clinical changes in patients with seasonal manic–depressive cycles.

The fairly drastic measure of imposing acute sleep deprivation has a mild to moderate antidepressive effect in some endogenously depressed patients (Gerner, Post, Gillin & Bunney, 1979; Gillin *et al.*, 1984); however the effect is transient, lasting only 24–48 hours and evident in about 30–60 per cent of medication-free patients. No difference in the response of unipolar versus bipolar patients, and no correlation with sex or length of illness, was observed, although endogenous depressives have benefited more than patients with non-endogenous depression. The selective deprivation of rapid eye movement (REM) sleep, and partial sleep deprivation (forced early awakening) has worked, as well as total sleep deprivation (Rubin & Poland, 1982). In one elaborate study, endogenously depressed patients were deprived of REM sleep on consecutive nights until the subject had been awakened 30 times in a single night or until the end of 6 consecutive nights of sleep deprivation, over a period of 3–9 weeks. After the criterion was reached each patient was allowed one night of uninterrupted sleep, and the overall antidepressive response was similar to that produced by imipramine and greater than that of non-selective sleep deprivation (Vogel *et al.*, 1975).

Depressive illness has been influenced by the less drastic procedure of altering the sleep–wake pattern. The results were promising in that a manic–depressive woman was twice brought out of depression for two weeks by advancing her sleep period so that she went to sleep and arose 6 hours earlier than usual. The anti-depressant effect of this procedure was similar in duration to the circadian desynchronization induced by jet lag in healthy subjects (Wehr *et al.*, 1979). These workers later summarized their views on the genesis of depression by shifts in the phase of a circadian rhythm (Wehr *et al.*, 1982), but the evidence is more suggestive than convincing. For them, the phase-position of a circadian rhythm oscillator appears to be abnormal or advanced in depression, so that adjustment of the timing and amount of sleep sometimes induces clinical remission. In manic–depressives, the disturbance in the circadian rhythm could arise from an abnormal sensitivity to light acting as a *zeitgeber*, for such patients may show an enhanced depression of nocturnal melatonin secretion upon exposure to light. Accordingly, two monoamine oxidase inhibiting anti-depressant drugs (clorgyline and pargyline) could function by slowing the intrinsic rhythm of circadian pacemakers and desensitizing the circadian system to light.

Support for this idea comes from animal studies, where the circadian rest–activity cycle of hamsters has been lengthened by the chronic adminis- tration of clorgyline. Treatment with clorgyline or the tricyclic antidepress- ant drug imipramine also led to a dissociation between various components of the activity pattern, such as a lengthening of the morning period of running (Wirz-Justice & Campbell, 1982). Lithium salts, often effective in the treatment of depression, markedly lengthen the period of the rhythm of body temperature change in healthy subjects and would be expected to have the same effect as the transient phase advances produced by alterations in environmental lighting (Moore-Ede, Czeisler & Richardson, 1983). Addi- tional support for these ideas can be drawn from experiments in which the therapeutic benefit of exposure to bright white light was tested by waking depressed patients at about 5 a.m., two hours before the usual time, and exposing them for an hour to intense warm white fluorescent light or to dim red light. White light was superior to red in producing a small but rapid decrease in depressive symptoms (Kripke, Risch & Janowsky, 1983). Others have applied bright light late in the evening or early in the morning (Rosenthal *et al.*, 1984).

Close study of circadian rhythmicity in persons isolated from external time cues has shown that some rhythms can drift apart, with, for example, the rest–activity cycle settling to a period of approximately 33 hours and the body temperature rhythm stabilizing at a periodicity of 24.5 hours (Moore- Ede *et al.*, 1983). When such internal desynchronization occurs, the various behavioural and physiological variables cluster into two groups, tracking either with the rest–activity cycle or with the body temperature rhythm. This separation has been taken to indicate the operation of two pacemakers referred to as 'X' (body temperature driving) and 'Y' (concerned with the rest–activity and other cycles). Normally the circadian rhythm of a particu- lar function emerges as the net result of signals from both sources, but under free-running conditions dissociation of the two systems and their associated functions can occur. Thus slow-wave sleep and growth hormone secretion follow the Y pacemaker, while the propensity for rapid eye movement sleep and cortisol secretion follows the X pacemaker. Because both the X and the Y rhythms change their periods under free-running conditions there must be some mutual coupling between the two pacemakers, and because one deviates more from the internally synchronized period than the other it is suggested that the X pacemaker must exert much more influence upon the Y pacemaker than the other way around, with a ratio of coupling strengths of about 4 : 1 being postulated (Moore-Ede, 1983).

As alluded to earlier, the anatomical basis of circadian rhythms is located in the hypothalamus, and centres upon the suprachiasmatic nuclei. The firing rate of neurons in these nuclei exhibits a circadian rhythm regardless of environmental lighting conditions, and the rhythm persists after isolation of the nuclei from adjacent hypothalamic tissue. When the suprachiasmatic nuclei were destroyed in squirrel monkeys the behavioural rhythms of activity, feeding and drinking were disrupted, but that for body temperature persisted. This dichotomy in effect suggests that the Y pacemaker, responsible for rest–activity, lies within the suprachiasmatic nuclei and was destroyed, while the X pacemaker, governing body temperature, lies elsewhere. In rhesus monkeys destruction of the same nuclei is compatible with persistence of a circadian rhythm in the cortisol concentration of cerebrospinal fluid – an X-driven variable (Moore-Ede, 1983).

The suprachiasmatic nuclei receive a monosynaptic input from the retina through the retino-hypothalamic tract; damage to this pathway interferes with entrainment to light–dark cycles, and circadian rhythms free-run. There are other connections between the optic chiasma and the suprachiasmatic nuclei, as well as projections to these nuclei from the lateral geniculate bodies of the classical visual pathway. The suprachiasmatic nuclei project to, and receive input from, the anterior hypothalamic area, the retrochiasmal area and several nuclei of the tuberal hypothalamus, particularly the ventromedial nuclei. An additional retino-hypothalamic projection has been identified, with terminals of retinal origin making synaptic contacts on dendrites of lateral hypothalamic neurons, primarily in pockets of neuropil located in the optic chiasma.

Although the suprachiasmatic nuclei are very small, their structure is complex. Three subdivisions of the rat nucleus have been distinguished: a small rostral component and a larger caudal area, which contains a dorsomedial and a ventrolateral division. Retinal afferents are confined almost exclusively to the ventrolateral region. Three groups of peptidergic neurons can also be made out, for vasopressin-containing neurons are present in the rostral and dorsomedial regions and form a dense axonal plexus, which also innervates the ventrolateral region. Vasoactive intestinal peptide-containing neurons are found in the ventrolateral parts of the suprachiasmatic nuclei, while somatostatin-containing cell bodies and axons are present throughout the structure. Each of the paired suprachiasmatic nuclei is interconnected with its partner by a series of highly topographically organized projections. The anterior ventral division on one side projects to and receives projections from the same area on the opposite side, and so on through the nucleus (Moore, 1983).

Many cells in the suprachiasmatic nuclei change their firing rate when the retina is exposed to light. Observations based on the cat and rat indicate that the change can occur in either of two ways: most cells increase their rate of discharge when the luminance is increased to a higher level (light-activated cells), whereas a smaller proportion reacts in the opposite way (light-suppressed cells). It seems that the suprachiasmatic nuclei are primarily sensitive to the large ambient luminance changes that occur between day and night, and are relatively unaffected by different intensities of moonlight (Groos, Mason & Meijer, 1983).

Sleep and hormonal rhythms

Sleep provides a fine example of a circadian rhythm recurring once every 24 hours. Closer examination shows that the phenomenon known as sleep can be divided into two stages, rapid eye movement (REM) sleep, and non-rapid eye movement (non-REM) sleep. During REM sleep the EEG loses the high-amplitude, synchronized pattern typical of deep (slow-wave) sleep and this is replaced by low amplitude, desynchronized activity resembling that of the waking state. Muscle tone is reduced and dreaming may occur. Normally, individuals may become progressively more deeply asleep over the first one or two hours of rest; a short REM episode then occurs and throughout the rest of the night REM and non-REM sleep alternate rhythmically (Rubin & Poland, 1982). As sleep progresses, slow-wave sleep occurs less and less often while REM sleep becomes more prominent. Under normal conditions, the relative amount of time spent in the various stages of sleep is rather constant from night to night and from subject to subject. Infants show relatively large amounts of REM sleep, while young adults devote some 25 per cent of sleep time to the REM variety.

The classical neurotransmitters participate in the mechanisms controlling sleep, although the contribution of any particular neurotransmitter is not well understood. In general terms it appears that brain serotonin concentrations are directly correlated with REM sleep, and that brain catecholamine concentrations correlate inversely with this sleep stage (Rubin & Poland, 1982). Because of the involvement of neurotransmitters in the control of the secretion of pituitary hormones it might be expected that the output of hormone would fluctuate according to the stage of sleep, and that, in turn, study of the patterns of hormone secretion might provide some insight into neurotransmitter activity within the brain, and in particular the hypothalamus. The realization that neuropeptides can also influence hormone secretion has reduced the likelihood of any simple correlation between neurotransmitter activity, sleep stage and hormone release, but study of the endocrinology of sleep has become increasingly important, especially in relation to psychiatric disease.

The secretion of several pituitary hormones is linked to the sleep–wake cycle (Rubin & Poland, 1982). Adrenocorticotrophic hormone has a prominent circadian rhythm, with the peak levels occurring near the time of wakening and the nadir during the early hours of the sleep period. Serial study of individuals has shown remarkable reproducibility in the fluctuations plotted, with a curve obtained on one occasion being almost superimposable upon that derived from blood samples collected two months later (James *et al.*, 1978). Thus there appears to be considerable inertia in the system and the individual episodes of ACTH secretion do not accord well with those of REM sleep. The release of β-LPH appears to be similar to that of ACTH.

Growth hormone is released soon after sleep onset and is closely associated with slow-wave sleep. Alteration of the sleep schedule readily alters the release of growth hormone, when it is secreted anew in phase with the shifted timing of slow-wave sleep. Analysis of the effects of time shifts, whether caused by jet lag or by sleep deprivation in the laboratory, points to two effects upon growth hormone secretion (Golstein *et al.*, 1983). First, a marked increase in the release of growth hormone due to an increase in the magnitude, rather than the number, of secretory spikes, was evident. Return to basal levels was slower after westward than eastward travel and took at least 11 days. Later, one day after travelling from Chicago to Brussels or after 33 hours of sleep deprivation, the major growth hormone surge normally occurring early in sleep was shifted to late sleep. While the occurrence of surges of growth hormone secretion was significantly linked with slow-wave sleep, the total amount of growth hormone produced was determined by the degree of REM–non-REM oscillation.

Little rhythmic periodicity is evident in the secretion of follicle-stimulating and luteinizing hormone secretion. The prominent episodes of LH release in adults are randomly distributed throughout the day and night, and the episodes of FSH release appear to occur independently of those of LH. At ovulation the mid-cycle surge of LH may begin in sleep, or around the time of wakening. For prolactin, there is a prominent circadian rhythm, with blood levels beginning to increase with sleep and rising to maximal values an hour or two before wakening. Early wakening interrupts prolactin secretion, and the pattern of prolactin release changes upon re-arrangement of a sleep schedule. Peaks of prolactin secretion occur during non-REM sleep, and release is low at the time of rapid eye movement. The circadian rhythm in TSH secretion is again different, with the highest blood levels being seen during the late evening, just before sleep. Since TSH secretion at that time is prolonged by sleep deprivation it seems that sleep may inhibit TSH release.

The rise in ACTH secretion in cases of depression has been mentioned earlier. There is an overall shift upwards in the circadian pattern of adrenal activity and some indication that the morning increase in cortisol secretion occurs several hours earlier than usual. In accord with the increased output of adrenal steroids, which fails to exert a normal negative feedback action upon ACTH secretion, the secretion of ACTH is less readily suppressed by dexamethasone in depressed patients than in others. Patients suffering from manic–depressive illness may change or switch rapidly from depression to mania. The switch may occur during sleep and the rhythm of sleep–waking may be accelerated without change in those oscillations concerning temperature, mood or cortisol secretion (Gillin *et al.*, 1984). Thus the link between sleep and ACTH secretion is not immutable, and the separation of the rhythms implies the operation of separate oscillators.

The secretion of growth hormone is reduced in depression, possibly as a result of the accompanying sleep disturbance lowering the amount of slow-wave and REM sleep, and extending the time between lights out and sleep onset. Tests on the release of growth hormone in response to a variety of provocative stimuli, such as insulin-induced hypoglycaemia, amphetamine, the α-adrenergic agonist clonidine, or the tricyclic antidepressant desmethylimipramine, have shown a reduced or blunted response (Rubin & Poland, 1982). Although thyrotrophic hormone-releasing factor does not ordinarily affect growth hormone release, an abnormal secretion of this hormone has been observed in anorexia nervosa, schizophrenia and depression, and attributed to changes in the neural control of release of the pituitary factor. An alternative explanation is that the increased sensitivity of the pituitary gland to TRF in disease states reflects disturbance of the normal circadian rhythm, for Caroff, Winokur, Snyder & Amsterdam (1984) have shown in healthy young men that the amount of growth hormone secreted after a standard dose of TRF was significantly greater in the evening than in the morning, and that reversal of the rest–activity cycle abolished the rise in growth hormone secretion expected after the administration of TRF at 2000 hours.

Prolactin secretion, like that of growth hormone, is related to sleep and, again like growth hormone, the limited information available indicates that the output of prolactin is modestly reduced in depressive illness. Comparisons of the plasma levels of prolactin at half-hourly or hourly intervals over 24-hour periods in patients with unipolar or bipolar depression have pointed to a difference in secretion that could be of diagnostic value, in that less prolactin was produced in bipolar depression, probably as one result of a lessened nocturnal discharge (Mendlewicz *et al.*, 1980). Because of the lack of any pattern in the secretions of FSH and LH, changes in the release of these hormones in depression have proved difficult to trace. The information available suggests a slight diminution in the plasma levels of LH, testosterone and possibly FSH in men, and reduced LH but increased oestradiol and testosterone in circulation in women (Rubin & Poland, 1982).

Depressed patients complain of disturbances of sleep, and the reports linking changes in hormone output with sleep disruption are substantiated by electrophysiological studies (Gillin *et al.*, 1984). Insomnia is reported most often, but some patients will sleep longer than normal. The amount of slow-wave sleep is reduced, the interval between sleep onset and the first period of REM sleep is cut from 70–90 minutes to about half that time, and rapid eye movement activity is increased. Endogenously depressed patients can be distinguished from others by the use of such parameters, and Rubin & Poland (1982) cite work indicating that patients with primary depression could be separated from others with depression following major psychiatric or medical illness with an accuracy of some 80 per cent. The latency to the onset of REM activity and the degree of REM activity were the measures of greatest value, although a hastening of REM sleep has been seen in other psychiatric conditions. It is unlikely that the changes in sleep generate depressive illness directly, for similar changes in sleep patterns may occur in the absence of psychiatric disturbance. The latency to REM sleep can be shortened in normal volunteers by REM sleep deprivation, by phase-shift experiments or under free-running conditions, without producing depression. A short latency to REM sleep may occur naturally in some individuals, while some depressed patients sleep normally.

When the connection between sleep and hormone secretion is put alongside the therapeutic effect of a shift in sleeping time, or sleep deprivation, in cases of depression the question arises whether the benefit results from changes in hormone secretion. There seems to be an additional increase in the plasma cortisol levels in patients benefiting from the loss of a night's sleep and some suggestion that patients improving with sleep deprivation showed normalization of their TSH response to TRF (Rubin & Poland, 1982), but the studies are few and many more are needed.

Episodic hormone secretion

The circadian patterns of hormone secretion are superimposed upon an episodic mode of hormonal discharge. This complicates efforts to map the course of a circadian rhythm by collecting serial blood samples, for if too few samples are taken then the coincidence of a secretory surge with a blood sample can lead to erroneous conclusions being drawn from the high hormone concentration measured in that sample. Fairly soon after the occurrence and significance of episodic hormone secretion came to be appreciated, it was evident that for the reliable assessment of the secretory pattern of a pituitary hormone blood samples needed to be drawn at frequent intervals over some hours. Thus for LH, samples collected at 20-minute intervals for at least three hours were needed in order for the mean level of LH to be estimated with 95 per cent confidence limits of ± 18 per cent. Alternatively, 9 consecutive daily samples were needed to provide 95 per cent confidence limits of less than ± 25 per cent (Santen & Bardin, 1973). Despite certain obvious practical difficulties this is not a counsel of perfection but eminently sound advice. Current work indicates that in order to map a pattern of hormone secretion with precision even more frequent blood collection is desirable. When blood samples are obtained at 5-minute intervals, or less, a variety of small peaks and wave patterns is revealed.

The pineal gland

The pineal gland has been regarded as significant in neuroendocrine mechanisms for many years, but proof of this belief has been hard to find. Early work was particularly concerned with the control of sexual function, for damage to the pineal gland appeared to result in precocious puberty in children (Donovan & van der Werff ten Bosch, 1965). In rodents, the pineal gland can depress reproductive activity (Reiter, 1983), but for many the prime function of the organ is as a neuroendocrine transducer. To the enthusiast the pineal gland is an active functioning neuroendocrine organ that responds primarily to photic stimuli, exhibits circadian rhythms, and influences the metabolic activity of a host of endocrine glands. Secretions from the pineal gland are believed to participate in the control of gonadal, adrenal and thyroid function, sleep, and in various other biological rhythms. In some species, changes in reproductive function related to the length of the day can be effected by pineal ablation or denervation. In hamsters, for example, exposure to short photoperiods induces marked falls in the weights of the testes and accessory organs, and the gonadal collapse induced by any light period of less than 12.5 hours daily can be prevented by removal of the pineal gland, or by disconnecting it from its central sympathetic innervation (Cardinali, 1983; Reiter, 1983). However, in man the functions of the pineal gland have proved to be much more difficult to discern.

The major product of the pineal gland is melatonin, or N-acetyl-5-methoxytryptamine. This is an indoleamine which is derived from serotonin by acetylation to N-acetylserotonin and then O-methylated by hydroxyindole-O-methyltransferase (HIOMT) to form melatonin. The activity of the pineal gland enzyme HIOMT is greatest during darkness, and most melatonin is synthesized then. Other products of the pineal gland are 5-methoxytryptophol and 5-methoxytryptamine. Light acutely suppresses the night-time secretion of melatonin; the light–dark cycle controls or entrains the circadian pattern of melatonin production, and the light–dark cycle or the changing length of day throughout the year regulates the seasonal changes in the duration and timing of melatonin secretion. The secretion of this indoleamine does not appear to be affected by stress, locomotor activity, diet, the stages of sleep, sleep deprivation or acute changes in the rest–activity cycle. Light is the only variable known to affect the timing of melatonin secretion and for this reason the assay of plasma melatonin is regarded as advantageous as a marker for the endogenous pacemaker. Recent observations point to a powerful influence of sunlight or bright artificial light upon melatonin secretion; ordinary room light seems to be of much less significance (Lewy, 1984a).

Light influences HIOMT activity and melatonin production through a remarkably indirect pathway involving an excursion from the eyes down the spinal cord and back up the sympathetic system to the pineal gland. From the retina, the stimulus of light traverses the optic nerves, the suprachiasmatic nuclei, the medial forebrain bundle, the brain stem reticular formation, the intermediolateral column of the spinal cord, and the outflow to the superior cervical ganglia and post-ganglionic pathways to β-adrenergic receptors on cells in the pineal gland. Other fibres may run in the inferior accessory optic tract. Stimulation of the β-adrenergic receptors by nor-adrenaline increases melatonin synthesis and secretion, but stresses causing the release of catecholamines do not appear to increase melatonin levels. The β-adrenergic receptors of the pineal gland are outside the blood–brain barrier and accessible to blockade by a β-adrenergic agonist like propanolol. This drug blocks the night-time increase in plasma melatonin concentration (Lewy, 1984b).

In man, treatment with melatonin induces drowsiness with rapid eye movement. This has led to the experimental use of melatonin in the treatment of various psychiatric disorders, but with disappointing results (Smith, 1983).

7

Hormones and brain development

Although the sequence of developmental processes in the brain is probably common to all mammals, the timing of the changes in various species can be very different, and can never be neglected in comparing experimental observations. Growth of the human brain is most rapid between the middle of gestation until around two years after birth, whereas that of the rat is maximal around 10 days after delivery; most of the development of the brain of the guinea-pig occurs during gestation. Expressed in another way, the brain of the new-born rat or rabbit may be regarded as equivalent in developmental terms to that of a 5-month human fetus, and that of a guinea-pig to a 2- or 3-year-old child.

The brain is not uniformly susceptible to the effects of hormones during development. Alongside the differential responses of various parts of the brain, the sensitivity of any particular structure changes with time and may be permanently affected only when a hormone is given at a particular phase of development, or critical period. Thus, sex hormones are most effective in influencing the pattern of sexual differentiation of the brain of the rat when given during the first few days after birth (p. 104), although the sensitivity of the brain to steroid extends from the 18th day of gestation to the 11th post-natal day. The concept of a critical period has a long history and wide applicability through the behavioural sciences (Scott, Stewart & de Ghett, 1974). It was largely developed on the basis of work on the primary socialization of dogs, or the process of forming attachments to other dogs, other animals including man, or to particular places. Many critical periods can be discerned and may overlap or be widely separated in time, depending upon the function or process studied. Naturally, the anatomical or physiological basis of a critical period varies, but often may simply represent the phase in development during which the organization of a particular system is proceeding most rapidly and consequently most readily subject to disruption. If an organizational process continues at a uniform rate throughout life then no critical period exists, so that the presence of a critical period implies that significant changes are taking place within the system studied.

Gonadal hormones

Gonadal hormones act upon the brain during fetal life to imprint functional patterns that are of great significance at maturity. The bulk of the information available is derived from work with rats, guinea-pigs and monkeys and much may not be appropriate to the human situation. Nevertheless, the experimental studies have profoundly influenced considerations of the biological basis of human sexual behaviour and cannot be neglected.

The simplest generalization is that the androgen produced by the testis of the male fetus acts upon the brain to impose a masculine pattern upon a mechanism that is fundamentally female. This view can be traced back to classical studies of the hormonal control of differentiation of the genital tract, and was elaborated by Phoenix, Goy, Gerall & Young (1959) on the basis of an analysis of the effects of exposure to testosterone during intra-uterine life upon the subsequent sexual behaviour of female guinea-pigs. When pregnant guinea-pigs were injected with androgen the female offspring showed masculinization of the genitalia and, later, an increase in male mounting behaviour and aggressiveness. There was also a reduction in the expression of lordosis after treatment with oestrogen and progesterone. As mentioned earlier, lordosis refers to the attitude adopted by the sexually receptive female in contact with a male; she remains still and, with her back flattened and pelvis elevated, presents the vagina to the male. These changes were never seen when adult females were treated with androgen and so pointed to a specific action of testosterone upon the brain of the fetus.

Subsequently, most studies of the sexual differentiation of the brain have employed the rat, for the actions of androgen in this species are exerted over the first few days of post-natal life and experimental intervention is facilitated accordingly. Castration of neonatal male rats, or treatment with an antiandrogenic drug, especially very soon after birth, promotes the later expression of lordosis after priming with oestrogen and progesterone. Lordosis is much less common in similarly treated intact males, or males castrated when adult and then primed with female sex hormones. However, males castrated neonatally retain some capacity for masculine mounting behaviour which is much more than that of comparable ovariectomized females but less than that of males castrated in adult life.

Bisexuality in mammals appears generally to be more common among females than among males. Goy & Goldfoot (1975) suggested that there may be an inverse relationship between the sexes in this regard in that for a given species, the greater the bisexuality of the female the less that of the male, and *vice versa*. The situation is exemplified by the rhesus monkey, where males show a conspicuous bisexuality throughout early development and to some extent during adult life, whereas among females male behaviour is rare during infancy and not favoured by treatment of the adult female with testosterone. Exposure of the female fetus to androgen, which produces masculinization of the genitalia and pseudohermaphroditism, leads to significantly more rough-and-tumble play, or 'tomboy' and dominance behaviour, than shown by normal females of the same age, and suggests a shift in behavioural pattern toward that of the male. The onset of menstrual cycles may be delayed, but once initiated, cycles are normal. Neonatal castration does not inhibit the expression of normal male behaviour in infancy, but any effect of androgen upon brain development could have been exercised earlier (Resko, 1975).

Despite the hazards of generalization, the temptation to regard conclusions based upon work in one species as applicable to another can prove irresistible. Dörner (1979), for example, took particular note of the fact that the effect of androgen upon the brain of the neonatal rat is graded in character, so that near the threshold a dose–response relationship can be made out. The higher the androgen level during this phase of hypothalamic differentiation, the stronger the masculine and the weaker the feminine behaviour manifest during adult life, regardless of the genetic sex. This led him to the view that a neuroendocrine predisposition for primary hypo-, bi-, and homosexuality might be based upon different degrees of androgen deficiency in males and androgen excess in females at a critical period in brain development. Thus sexual deviation in man could be based, at least in part, upon discrepancies between the genetic sex and the levels of the appropriate hormones in circulation at that time. Therefore, Dörner argued, suitably timed hormonal prophylaxis might prevent such discrepancies. But proof that the hypothalamus of the human male is masculinized during fetal life in a manner similar to that of the rat is still awaited.

The evidence for a role of gonadal hormones in influencing psychosexual differentiation in man is necessarily indirect but can be related to four areas of behaviour (Ehrhardt & Meyer-Bahlburg, 1981). These are (i) gender identity, which refers to the primary identification of an individual with one sex or the other; (ii) gender-role or sexually dimorphic behaviour, covering those aspects of behaviour in which normal boys and girls differ from one another in a particular society; (iii) sexual orientation, dealing with the erotic responsiveness of one individual to others of the same or opposite sex and being homo-, hetero-, or bisexual; and (iv) intelligence and cognitive differences, such as the strengths and weaknesses of various aspects of mental ability linked with sex.

Gender identity is a peculiarly human characteristic and could be influenced substantially by upbringing or learning. This point was well made by Ellis (1945), who surveyed 84 cases of hermaphroditism and noted that only two exhibited bisexual behaviour. None of the individuals reared as boys had adopted a female sex role and only 7 of the 45 individuals reared as girls had adopted a male gender identity. On this basis Ellis (1945) concluded that sex role is destined primarily by the sex of rearing, particularly as 87 per cent of the hermaphrodites reared as boys were heterosexual, as were 73 per cent of those reared as girls. His comparisons with normal populations showed that the psychosexual orientation of hermaphrodites was not significantly different, and hence that physiological factors, like hormones, did not exert any direct effect.

Money, Hampson & Hampson (1955) gave considerable attention to patients in whom the biological sex differed from the sex of rearing, largely because of ambiguities in the structure of the external genitalia, and postulated that gender identity is established during the first $2\frac{1}{2}$ years of infancy, with gender identity typically depending upon the sex of rearing. This would seem to be illustrated very clearly by a pair of twins, where one boy lost his penis at 7 months as the result of a surgical accident at circumcision. After tremendous agonizing on the part of the parents, and with strong pressure from their professional advisors, the sex was re-assigned at 17 months of age and orchidectomy and genital reconstruction undertaken (Money & Ehrhardt, 1972; Money, 1975a). After six years the transformation appeared to be quite successful, with the child adopting a feminine role and demonstrating a clear preference for dresses over slacks, and for long hair. By comparison with the twin brother, the child took much greater pride in being neat and clean, was glad to assist in housework, and preferred girls' toys. The publication of a detailed description of the case (Money & Ehrhardt, 1972) attracted considerable attention in the popular press and greatly fostered the contention that it is basically nurture, and not nature, that determines sexual identity as male or female and the adoption of the appropriate gender role. Up to the time of puberty all seemed to be well with the child, but more recent information forces some re-evaluation of the findings. Instead of a successful switch to life as a female the twin, when seen by a new set of psychiatrists at 13 years of age, was said to be beset with problems (Diamond, 1982). The psychiatrists are quoted as saying that the adolescent refused to draw female figures, but would draw a man, that the youngster had a masculine gait, looked masculine, and was regarded by others as not particularly feminine. The 'girl' was said to aspire to masculine occupations, to want to be a mechanic, and to have difficulty in making friends, besides being ambivalent about her status. It was not clear whether the adolescent knew of her true status, or had any recollections of being born a male, for the psychiatrists would not reveal the truth to the patient or raise the issue with her. Evidently the question of the predominance of nurture over nature in relation to sexual orientation is not as simple as once appeared.

The conclusions of Ellis (1945) and Money, Hampson & Hampson (1955) have not escaped challenge on other grounds. They have been attacked on the basis of the possibly unrepresentative nature of the data, and over the interpretation. Cappon, Ezrin & Lynes (1959) objected to the idea that gender identification was based upon sex assignment and rearing and found in their series of 17 cases of hermaphroditism that somatic variables (gonads, genitalia and endocrine status) were better predictors of gender role than the sex of rearing. This correlation was supported by Diamond (1965) who, like Zuger (1970), cited cases in which a change in gender role was achieved successfully at later ages than seemed likely to Money and his colleagues. Diamond (1965) describes the case of an unambiguous male who was reared from birth as a female. Despite vigorous attempts on the part of the parents to make this child a girl the infant refused to be comfortable in the assigned sex or sex of rearing. At the age of 14 the patient was found to be a genetically and endocrinologically normal male and transformed himself into a boy extremely quickly. The heat generated in the debate over the biological basis of gender role determination is well illustrated by an exchange of views between Money and Zuger (Zuger, 1970).

There is a remarkable series of cases of genetic male pseudohermaphrodites who were reared as girls, accommodated to this role and then shifted to a male gender role at puberty. The cause of the pseudohermaphroditism lay in a deficiency of the enzyme 5α-reductase, which is needed for the transformation of testosterone to the active metabolite, 5α-dihydrotestosterone (Imperato-McGinley, Guerrero, Gautier & Peterson, 1974). Since testosterone is available during fetal life, the vas deferens, epididymis and seminal vesicles develop normally, whereas the penis and scrotum appear as a clitoris and associated labia, presumably because these structures require dihydrotestosterone for differentiation. The infants were reared as girls, but at puberty the phallus grew and the scrotum became rugated and hyperpigmented, with the testes descending into the scrotum in most subjects. The voice deepened, and the subjects developed a muscular habitus. Erections and intromission became possible but, because of the position of the urethra, insemination was not possible.

The condition is inherited as an autosomal recessive trait, and 38 male pseudohermaphrodites were found in 23 interrelated families spanning four generations in three rural villages in the Dominican Republic (Imperato-McGinley, Peterson, Gautier & Sturla, 1979). Nineteen of 33 surviving subjects had been unambiguously raised as girls and adequate postpubertal psychosexual data was available from 18. Of these, 17 had successfully changed to a male gender identity and 16 to a male gender role. The 17 subjects who changed to a male gender identity began to realize that they were different from other girls in the village some time between 7 and 12 years of age, when they did not develop breasts, when their bodies began to develop in a masculine direction, and when masses were noted in the inguinal canal or scrotum. A male gender identity gradually evolved over several years as the subjects passed through stages of no longer feeling like girls, to feeling like men, and, finally, to the conscious awareness that they were indeed men.

The change to a male gender role occurred either during puberty, or in the postpubertal period, at an average age of 16, with a range of 14 to 24 years. It was not necessarily trouble free, for the individuals viewed themselves as incomplete persons because of the appearance of their genitalia, and feared ridicule by the members of the opposite sex. However, 15 of the 16 subjects who changed to a male gender role lived with women, worked as farmers, miners or woodsmen and enjoyed their role as head of the household.

Parental attitudes during the change in gender role reflected amazement, confusion, and, finally, acceptance rather than prevention. Social pressures caused the boys anxiety but were not strong enough to prevent change. Circumstances may be different in the affected villages now that the parents are aware of the problem, for the pseudohermaphrodites are raised as boys from birth, reared as boys as soon as the problem is recognized in childhood, or reared ambiguously as girls. Indeed, the affected children and adults sometimes become the object of derision.

Four other cases of 5α-reductase deficiency are described by Green (1982), who relates that from their earliest memories, although being raised as girls, they felt that something was wrong: they felt like boys. They rejected the toys, games and activities of girls and secretly harboured the fantasy that some day they would become men. With the onset of adolescence they became aware of sexual attraction to women and underwent virilization. Family pressures forced them to live as women, although feeling like men, until they became aware of appropriate medical facilities outside their community; at this point they fled, their condition was diagnosed and they thenceforth pursued lives as men.

The study of Imperato-McGinley and her colleagues has been discussed at some length because their conclusion that hormonal effects on gender identity are demonstrable conflicts with the view that, while prenatal hormones specifically affect gender role behaviour, gender identity is profoundly influenced by the processes of rearing. The view holds that nurture can overcome nature so that the development of gender identity and gender role behaviour is similar to imprinting, beginning at 12 months, reaching a critical period at 18 months and being relatively well established by $2\frac{1}{2}$ years. This is the concept developed by Money, Hampson & Hampson (1955) and its impact has been outlined. In turn, the inferences of Imperato-McGinley and her co-workers have been questioned by Rubin, Reinisch & Haskett (1981) and Meyer-Bahlburg (1982), who remain unconvinced that the individuals concerned were really brought up unambiguously as females (for the condition is well known among the affected villagers in the Dominican Republic) and whether a full male gender identity was developed. It is argued that, because of the lack of individual privacy in village society, any physical abnormality of a hermaphroditic individual would be noticed by many, result in some confusion in gender identity during childhood, and foster a shift in gender identity later in life. The fact that a male gender identity gradually evolved over several years as the individuals passed through stages of no longer feeling like girls, to feeling like men and finally to the conscious awareness that they were indeed men is regarded as being too slow for a neuroendocrine mechanism and an experiential–cognitive explanation was preferred. This adopts the view that by comparison with their normal female peers, the affected villagers experience a progressive decline in their physical femininity, become increasingly unattractive and have little hope of acquiring a mate. The prospect of childlessness in their agricultural society would also loom large. Simultaneously, however, the potential of these youngsters for life as a male rapidly improves with the development of an attractive male physique, muscular strength and masculine genitalia, so that the pressure toward a change in sexual identity becomes almost irresistible.

Gender role, or sexually dimorphic behaviour, is of interest in connection with the changes that result from exposure *in utero* to unusual amounts of androgens, oestrogens or progestogens, either through treatment of the mother or a congenital defect in the fetus. There are a variety of aspects: energy expenditure, as illustrated by a liking for active outdoor games and athletic skills in humans and rough-and-tumble play in monkeys; social aggression, covering physical and verbal fighting in childhood and adolescence; parenting rehearsal, or doll play or participating in infant care in girls in contrast to the playing with cars or aeroplanes of boys; peer contact and group interaction, reflecting the sex of the playmates preferred; gender role labelling, derived from the terms applied to the child by peers, such as 'tomboy' or 'sissy'; and grooming behaviour (Ehrhardt & Meyer-Bahlburg, 1981). The last category is fast becoming unsatisfactory, with the blurring of sexual preferences in clothing and the increased use of adornments by boys.

With the aid of such discriminatory criteria studies of children with the adrenogenital syndrome can provide information of great value. Because of a defect in the synthesis of cortisol the genesis of adrenal steroids is arrested at the preceding step and excessive amounts of androgen are produced alongside enlargement of the adrenal glands (congenital adrenal hyperplasia, CAH). Once diagnosed, the condition is treated by replacement therapy with corticosteroids to reduce the secretion of adrenocorticotrophic hormone and suppress the production of androgen. If the fetus is male little structural harm results, although untreated boys typically show sexual development in infancy. In females, however, the genitalia become masculinized and surgical feminization is necessary, but with appropriate corticosteroid treatment pubertal development is undisturbed and normal heterosexual interests set in. During childhood girls with CAH fully identify themselves with the female gender, but some differences from control girls or siblings are evident (Ehrhardt & Meyer-Bahlburg, 1981). They typically demonstrate (i) a combination of intense active outdoor play, increased association with male peers, and long-term identification as a 'tomboy' by self and others; and (ii) decreased parenting rehearsal such as doll play and baby care, and a greater concern for a career than for wifely or maternal activities. An increase in aggressive behaviour has been suspected but not established.

Similar conclusions have been derived from girls unwittingly exposed during fetal life to the masculinizing effect of excessive amounts of progestational agents possessing androgenic properties (Money & Lewis, 1966; Lev-Ran, 1974; Baker, 1980; Ehrhardt & Meyer-Bahlburg, 1981). In these children endocrinological normality is restored after delivery, although masculinization of the phallus may require correction. Nevertheless, many girls exhibited high athletic interests and skills, as well as preferences for male rather than female playmates, for utilitarian and functional rather than traditional feminine clothing, for toy cars and guns rather than dolls, and for a career rather than motherhood. Other progestational agents lack androgenic side-effects and the information available on the consequences of prenatal exposure to these drugs points toward the expression of femininity, although the results are not conclusive. A recent follow-up study of twelve young women of 12 to 27 years exposed to progestins prenatally indicates that stereotypically feminine behaviour prevails (Money & Mathews, 1982). There is some suggestion that progesterone itself may serve as an androgen antagonist.

Very little information is available on the effects of oestrogen on human brain development, although the feminine gender identity of individuals with Turner's syndrome (in which the lack of a normal X chromosome is associated with gonadal dysgenesis and a deficiency of gonadal hormones) argues against an essential role for oestrogen in the psychosexual development of women. Gonads are lacking in these cases and they develop phenotypically as females. However, despite a lack of oestrogen they are feminine in appearance and psychosexual outlook. Oestrogens are now rarely given in pregnancy, unless in combination with progestogens, so that there is little information on the consequences of inadvertent overdosage. Studies on animals have led to paradoxical conclusions in that oestrogens tend to masculinize females and to demasculinize males. In one study of boys delivered of diabetic mothers given oestrogen and progesterone to sustain pregnancy there was evidence of less rough-and-tumble, less aggressive and less athletic behaviour than controls, although the differences may have been related to changes in the maternal behaviour of the sick mothers (Yalom, Green & Fisk, 1973). In a more extensive study (Reinisch & Karow, 1977) the effects of treatment with various preparations of oestrogen and progestins upon the offspring of mothers treated for threatened pregnancy were assessed and the children compared with siblings born of uncomplicated pregnancies. When the subjects were classified on the basis of the ratio of oestrogen to progesterone, those given least oestrogen were more independent, individualistic, self-assured, self-sufficient and sensitive, whereas those given most oestrogen and least progestin were more group oriented, more group dependent, less sensitive and less self-assured. These observations, though inconclusive, correspond with others obtained more recently (Ehrhardt & Meyer-Bahlburg, 1981).

Lack of gonadal hormone action in genetic males during fetal life occurs in the androgen insensitivity or testicular feminization syndrome, where the tissues lack receptors for androgen and are thus insensitive to steroids of this type, although testosterone production by the testes is normal. The external genitalia are female in appearance but there is no uterus and only a short, blind, vagina. Breast development occurs as a consequence of the oestrogen produced by the testes, or in response to oestrogen therapy, for the gonads are commonly removed for fear of malignancy. Gender identity and sexual orientation are typically female (Baker, 1980; Ehrhardt & Meyer-Bahlburg, 1981), and show no hint of masculinization. As children, affected individuals play primarily with dolls and girls' toys and are interested in infant care; as adults, there is a preference for homecraft and no hint of anything other than purely feminine sexual behaviour (Vague, 1983).

A particularly intriguing finding in studies of patients with the adrenogenital syndrome has been the increased incidence of patients with a high IQ, so pointing to a possible effect of androgen upon cognitive development. Money & Lewis (1966) were impressed by the frequent incidence of high IQ's in their patients, and since unusually high IQ's were later found in a group of progestin-induced pseudohermaphrodites the effect seemed to result from the operation of hormonal rather than genetic factors. This effect was also noted in the Soviet Union (Lev-Ran, 1974), and a similar conclusion drawn from studies of children born of hormone-treated pregnancies (Dalton, 1979). However, it now appears that the parents and siblings of adrenogenital patients also show high IQ's, and the view that the recessive gene underlying the syndrome is possibly linked to another favouring intellectual development is gaining ground (Ehrhardt & Meyer-Bahlburg, 1981). The existence of any connection between maternal treatment with progestogens and a high IQ on the part of the offspring has been discounted (Lynch & Mychalkiw, 1978; Lynch, Mychalkiw & Hutt, 1978), although it is well known that verbal ability tends to be higher in females and spatial perception appreciably greater in males, with the difference being accentuated at puberty.

It is frustrating that years of effort have so far failed to establish a sound case for, or against, the participation of gonadal hormones in the genesis of psychological sex differences. This view is perhaps over cautious, for there is much suggestive information, but there is a great need for double-blind studies and appropriate controls. Hines (1982) refers to studies of females exposed prenatally to androgenic hormones that suggest subsequent dissatisfaction with the female sex role and diminished interest in marriage, motherhood, or the presentation of a feminine appearance and an enhanced tendency to boyish play. Here, parental awareness of genital masculinity at birth may have led to rearing practices that produced behaviour with masculine elements, or the awareness of an endocrine problem on the part of the child may have restrained a natural tendency to fantasize or verbalize about marriage and motherhood. Studies of individuals who were exposed to unusual hormones prenatally, but who were born without abnormalities, have yielded little evidence of diminished maternal interest or masculinized play, in contrast to that derived from somatically androgenized girls, but it can be reasoned that the levels of hormone in circulation were below the necessary threshold, or that the period of exposure was too short. There are also studies of people in which the genitalia were unaffected by prenatal exposure to steroids and in which the subjects grew up, in most cases, unaware of any possible hormonal effect. In one, an analysis of men exposed prenatally to oestrogens and progestins implied a relationship between these hormones and feminine gender identity as assessed by paper and pencil inventories; in another, enhanced aggression was indicated in a group of children exposed to progestins, while in a third a study of women exposed to diethylstilboestrol suggested a shift toward masculinized patterns of lateralization for verbal stimuli (Hines, 1982).

Possible mechanisms of action

Some ways in which gonadal steroids act upon the brain have been described earlier (Chapter 5), but there is surprisingly little understanding of the mechanisms of action of androgen in influencing brain development. One view is that this steroid interferes with the normal development of oestrogen receptor proteins in the brain, and with the accumulation of oestrogen by the appropriate neurons. Such oestrogen-sensitive neurons might then become desensitized and functionally unresponsive to endogenous fluctuations in blood oestrogen concentration (Flerkó, 1974). In accord with this concept, there are many reports that the responsiveness of peripheral target organs such as the uterus and vagina to oestradiol is reduced in animals treated with androgen early in life. There are sex differences in the oxygen usage of the hypothalamus, with consumption by the male hypothalamus being greater.

Another view of the process of sexual differentiation of the brain is that it is a consequence, not of the action of androgen alone, but of an interaction of androgen with progesterone, which is acting in this case as an anti-androgen (Resko, 1975). In the male primate fetus testosterone levels are high and progesterone levels low and androgenization occurs, whereas in the female not only are blood androgen levels low, but the relatively high concentration of progesterone prevents the action of even the small amounts of male hormone in circulation. Progesterone is known to prevent the masculinizing action of testosterone in neonatal rats, but proof of this supposition in the primate is awaited.

The hypothalamus is affected locally by androgens during development. Female rats can be rendered acyclic and anovulatory by the local application of micropellets of testosterone to the hypothalamus, with the most effective region being the ventromedial–arcuate nuclear area (Nadler, 1973). There appear to be specific sites where implantation of testosterone or oestradiol produces masculinization of the patterns of gonadotrophic hormone secretion, or of the patterns of sexual behaviour (Christensen & Gorski, 1978). Implants of gonadal steroid into the dorsal preoptic area perinatally increase the amount of masculine sexual behaviour displayed by adults. On the other hand, the ventromedial hypothalamus is the only area where neonatal implants of steroid hormone produce acyclic gonadotrophic hormone secretion in adults. Sexually dimorphic variations in the synaptic connections of the preoptic area of the hypothalamus are also known in that the number of non-amygdaloid synapses on the spines of dendrites in that region is greater in female rats than in males (Raisman & Field, 1973). One intriguing observation concerns a unilateral effect of oestrogen in determining sexual orientation in rats. When oestrogen pellets were placed in either the right or left hypothalamus of new-born female rats so that only one half of the hypothalamus was exposed to the influence of the hormone, the effects upon gonadotrophin secretion and reproductive behaviour varied. Exposure of the left hypothalamus to oestrogen decreased subsequent female sexual behaviour and eliminated the positive feedback action of oestrogen in adults exposed to oestradiol. Exposure of the right hypothalamus to oestrogen increased the later expression of male patterns of sexual behaviour (Nordeen & Yahr, 1982).

The relationship of hormones to asymmetries in the brain has been given prominence in another context, for there are other differences between the brains of men and women that are not directly connected with endocrine function. There is, for example, a sex difference in the shape and surface area of the corpus callosum, where the caudal portion or splenium is more bulbous and larger in women. The splenium is involved in the transfer of visual information from one hemisphere to the other, and the sex difference may suggest that more information exchange proceeds in women than in men, or that there is greater hemispheric specialization, and less exchange, in men (de Lacoste-Utamsling & Holloway, 1982).

It has been suggested that excess testosterone, or an unusual sensitivity to testosterone during fetal life, could alter brain anatomy so that the right hemisphere becomes dominant for language-related abilities and the person is left-handed. Mathematical ability is generally thought to be a right hemisphere function and it is supposed that under ideal conditions superior right hemisphere talents in art, music, and mathematics emerge; however they may be associated with disorders of the immune system. There may be genetic links between testosterone production, sensitivity to testosterone and the activity of the immune system. Twenty per cent of one group of mathematically talented students were left-handed, which was more than twice the normal incidence of left-handedness, and 60 per cent had some disorder of the immune system, such as allergies and asthma–an incidence five times that in the general population. Less gifted students were also less likely to be left-handed or to have immune disorders. If testosterone is active in the way suggested, then boys should be more likely than girls to be left-handed, to have problems in connection with the immune system, to stutter, to be dyslexic, and to shine at mathematics. Among 50000 American children tested for an aptitude in mathematics 260 boys achieved high scores, but only 20 girls did. A similar search for verbally talented youths yielded an equal proportion of boys and girls (Kolata, 1983). Such differences are not limited to man, for deviations in the metabolic activity of the left and right halves of the neonatal rat brain are demonstrable. Female rats direct their tails preferentially to the right, whereas those of males tend to be moved in the opposite direction (Ross, Glick & Meibach, 1981).

Sexually dimorphic changes on a microscopic scale are evident in the brain outside the hypothalamus, for the sizes of the nuclei in the amygdala of squirrel monkeys differ according to sex, with the nuclei being larger in males than in females (Bubenik & Brown, 1973). By comparison, the nuclear diameters in the suprachiasmatic nuclei in males and females were similar. The basis of the sex difference remains unclear, for it may be attributed to androgenization during fetal life, or reflect the variation in hormones in circulation in males and females. There are also the results of a comparison of the preoptic areas of juvenile macaque monkeys, where neurons in the preoptic areas of males have more bifurcations of the dendrites and a higher incidence of spines than those of females (Ayoub, Greenough & Juraska, 1983). These observations concur with those made in other laboratory animals, but a note of caution has been struck by the failure to discern any sexual difference in the volumes of the mouse equivalent of the sexually dimorphic nucleus of the rat (Young, 1982).

Under organ culture conditions oestradiol and cortisone improved the maintenance of chick embryo cerebellar explants (Vernadakis & Timiras, 1967), while oestradiol and testosterone enhanced the proliferation of neuronal processes in fragments of hypothalamic tissue collected from new-born mice (Toran-Allerand, 1978). Oestrogen has also been shown to facilitate the formation of synapses on dendritic shafts in medial amygdaloid tissue collected from female rats immediately after birth and transferred to the anterior chamber of an eye of an adult ovariectomized host (Nishizuka & Arai, 1982). Other observations in this vein have been summarized elsewhere (Donovan, 1980), and support the idea that gonadal hormones affect the patterns of dendritic organization and synaptic connections made between cells. Such patterns may be gender specific. Oestradiol possibly encourages the selection or preservation of the appropriate target sites of axonal processes, and on this basis the female would seem to possess connections that are lacking in males.

A curious feature of the action of androgen upon the developing brain is the presumption that androgen is converted to oestrogen by the hypothalamus of the fetus in the course of defining the future mode of reproductive activity (Naftolin, Ryan & Petro, 1971a, b; Naftolin *et al.*, 1975). Aromatization of androstenedione is demonstrable in the hypothalamus and limbic system of human fetuses, as well as the conversion of testosterone to oestradiol-17β. However, Dixson (1980) has emphasized that the aromatization hypothesis is not applicable to rhesus monkeys, for dihydrotestosterone propionate, a non-aromatizable androgen, has the same effect as testosterone proprionate upon the fetal brain and the same activational effects upon sexual and aggressive responses in adults. The human might respond likewise.

Thyroid hormones

The thyroid gland of the human fetus is active very early in development and can concentrate iodine and manufacture thyroxine from around the third month of gestation. Further, the ratio of thyroxine to triiodothyronine is similar in thyroid glands collected from fetuses and adults. Because the thyroid gland of the anencephalic fetus lacking a pituitary gland can concentrate iodide and synthesize thyroxine it has been presumed that these functions possess some degree of autonomy from hypophysial control. The concentration of thyroid-stimulating hormone in the serum and pituitary gland of the human fetus is very low until about 8 weeks, when a rise sets in to reach a plateau at around 22 weeks. The marked increase in serum TSH is accompanied by a progressive elevation in blood thyroxine concentration, which is independent of changes in the maternal blood level (Timiras & Cons, 1982).

Brain development is disturbed in cases of fetal and neonatal hypothyroidism, although with early treatment the prognosis is good. Sokoloff & Kennedy (1973) point out that in the mature individual the effects of thyroid dysfunction in most tissues are manifest through alterations in energy exchange, but that the brain does not react in this way. On the other hand, in the young animal the effects of thyroid hormone upon growth, development and maturation predominate and then the brain is most dramatically affected. Consequently, cretinism produces a morphologically and functionally undeveloped brain and mental deficiency. Thyroid hormones promote and are essential for the postnatal maturation of the brain. Proper levels of thyroid hormones and corticosteroids are necessary for normal rates of germinal cell proliferation in the brain, cessation of cell division, the formation of neurons from precursor cells, axonal and dendritic growth, neuronal migration and the formation of the correct number and types of synaptic relationships (Lauder, 1983). Although it is well known that the brain weight of human cretins may be 40 per cent below normal, with narrowed cerebral gyri and a thinning of the cerebral cortex, Adams & Rosman (1978) were not convinced of the occurrence of brain lesions demonstrable microscopically in cases of hypothyroidism, even when cretinism was accompanied by life-long idiocy. However, there is no doubt that normal brain development is disrupted. Brain growth was not altered in monkeys subjected to neonatal hypothyroidism (Holt, Cheek & Kerr, 1973), but protein and RNA synthesis and ganglioside deposition were depressed although DNA synthesis was not altered. Even in cases where the thyroid gland has failed to differentiate, the cretin may appear normal. Alongside somatic changes, such as slowed growth, an inertia and an indifference to the environment develops during early childhood and speech is delayed. Disturbances in motor function may also emerge. Overall, mental development is slowed and ultimately defective (Sokoloff & Kennedy, 1973).

More marked changes are apparent in cases of endemic cretinism arising from a dietary deficiency of iodine. In one study in New Guinea it seemed that the defective development of upper motor neurons in the pyramidal system produced severe weakness and hypotonia in the arms and legs, so that walking was achieved late in childhood. Severely defective children could not stand or walk unsupported and some could not even sit. The face lacked expression and most afflicted children were mute and even deaf (Choufoer, van Rhijn & Querido, 1965). When tests for general intelligence, motor skills, concentration and perceptual capacity especially adapted to the Indonesian situation were applied to villagers subject to endemic goitre, and compared with the findings from a control village, significant differences emerged (Querido, Bleichrodt & Djokomoeljanto, 1978).

Although in untreated cretinism intelligence is impaired, with adequate and early replacement therapy the prognosis can be extremely good. There is a general tendency for the IQ to increase as development proceeds, and in a few spectacular cases the IQ may jump by 30–40 points (Money, 1975b). The variability in response to treatment may result from familial circumstances and educational opportunity, the time of onset of thyroid deficiency, the degree and duration of thyroid hormone lack prior to treatment, and the adequacy of replacement therapy. Nevertheless, it is important that treatment should begin before three or four months of age, and some argue that it is necessary to commence therapy almost immediately after birth (Bass, Pelton & Young, 1977). Point is given to this argument by the relatively high incidence of neonatal hypothyroidism, which lies somewhere in the region of one in 4000 to one in 7000 births (Hetzel & Hay, 1979).

Neonatal hyperthyroidism transiently advances muscular development and if sustained results in a growth spurt and perhaps precocious puberty. Hyperkinesis, irritability and an abbreviated attention span are evident (Sokoloff & Kennedy, 1973; Money, 1975b). Long-lasting changes (hyperactivity, intellectual and perceptual–motor difficulties) have been reported in children with neonatal Graves' disease rendered euthyroid (Hollingsworth & Mabry, 1976), and sometimes children suffering from sporadic cretinism fail to achieve satisfactory intellectual development despite early and seemingly adequate treatment with thyroid hormone. This lack of response has been attributed to the inadvertent induction of hyperthyroidism in the course of therapy (Adams & Rosman, 1978).

Growth hormone

Animal studies, largely with rats, have pointed to a marked action of growth hormone on the growth of the brain, although clinical studies argue to the contrary. Among the responses observed in rats are increases in the number and length of dendrites, increased brain weight, DNA content, cortical cell density, an increase in the ratio of neurons to glia, and an increase in the number of cortical neurons alongside an enhancement of learning ability (Donovan, 1980).

Growth hormone deficiency in childhood does not seem to be associated with changes in cognition and memory, although there may be psychological immaturity. The effects upon intelligence have been the subject of greater debate. Meyer-Bahlburg, Feinman, MacGillivray & Aceto (1978) point out that previous diagnostic endocrine procedures are below current standards, that medical data regarding diagnostic classification, associated endocrine abnormalities and the onset of growth hormone deficiency, as well as the possible factor of brain damage, are usually not presented, and that the socioeconomic status of the patients has rarely been taken into account. With these points in mind, their study of 29 patients with growth hormone deficiency indicated a basically normal IQ distribution and no deficiency in specific mental abilities. In commenting upon the discrepancies between animal and clinical studies they note that most animal investigators have tested the effects of growth hormone given to the pregnant mother, and that studies of growth hormone deficiency are few. Meyer-Bahlburg *et al.* (1978) also note that in man social factors overlay the effects of biological factors on behaviour to a much larger extent than in laboratory animals, and that, since in many growth hormone deficient dwarfs the growth retardation does not become apparent before the second year of life, the exact onset of growth hormone deficiency is not known. Hypopituitary, growth hormone-deficient dwarfs also frequently adopt an immature, dependent attitude, with low esteem and a lack of aggressiveness that may stem from their short stature rather than from disturbances of brain function. Upon treatment with growth hormone, and an increase in stature, aggression may become manifest (Kusalic, Fortin & Gauthier, 1972).

Adrenal hormones

Rather little is known about the effects of adrenal steroids upon brain maturation in the human infant, although Weichsel (1977) was concerned about the potential neurological hazards of glucocorticoid therapy in infancy and childhood. Work on the rat and mouse indicates caution, for overdosage with adrenal corticoids during the first few days of life permanently reduces the total number of cells in the brain, probably by inhibiting cell multiplication (Balázs, 1972). Interest in this area was stimulated by the finding that rats handled or otherwise manipulated during infancy showed a fall in subsequent emotional reactivity. There was also a reduction in the responsiveness of the adrenal glands to later environmental stimulation. The two phenomena appeared to be linked on the basis that the infant rats responded to stimulation by secreting corticosterone, which acted to modify brain organization in such a way as to diminish subsequent emotional and adrenocortical reactivity. However, although the obser-vations remain well-founded, the case for involvement of the pituitary–adrenal system in any behavioural change remains unproven (Ader, 1975).

Although the effects of overdosage of rats with corticosteroids or with thyroid hormone appear to be similar, on the basis of a fall in the number of brain cells, the behavioural consequences differ. With hypercorticoidism there is a retardation in some forms of innate behaviour (such as swimming), the animals are more emotionally labile, and their ability to perform acts involving fine motor co-ordination is impaired. Adaptive behaviour is not disturbed, in contrast to the response to overdosage with thyroid hormone. Balázs (1972) notes that the timing of the consequences of overdosage with adrenal or thyroid hormones differs, in that corticoids inhibit cell multipli-cation mainly during the treatment period, whereas thyroid hormone affected cell formation mainly after a delay of one or two weeks from the start of treatment. Since the differentiation of various cell types within the brain is not synchronous, the outcome of any form of hormone treatment depends to a large degree upon the cell type developing at that time. Lauder (1983) concludes that corticosteroid treatment produces a reversible inhi-bition of cell proliferation, except in those cells already nearing their last divisions, whereas excess thyroid hormone stimulates cell proliferation just after birth in rats, but results in early cessation of cell division later in the postnatal period. Thyroid hormones also seem to influence the rate of cell migration, axonal and dendritic growth, and synaptogenesis.

There is increasing evidence that some of the actions of thyroid hormones in the developing brain are mediated through monoamines, for the normal synthesis and degradation of 5-hydroxytryptamine, noradrenaline and dopamine are disrupted in the brain of the hypothyroid young rat (Lauder, 1983). Equally, normal tryptophan hydroxylase activity (needed for the synthesis of 5-hydroxytryptamine) is related to the blood level of corticosteroid.

8

Hormones and male sexual behaviour

An unexpected difficulty in initiating discussion of the effects of hormones on human sexual behaviour is the absence of satisfactory definitions of some of the elements or components. Such definitions are available for laboratory species, but seldom adopted in clinical studies. Davison, Kwan & Greenleaf (1982) regard libido as the sum of the affective–cognitive processes which result in the tendency to engage in sexual behaviour. The elements of libido involve conscious events which reflect sexual interest and cover the enjoyment, pleasure or satisfaction derived from participating in or thinking about sexual activity, as well as the importance attributed to the manifestation of sexuality. Potency is defined as the capacity to respond to sexual stimuli with physiological genito-pelvic responses, such as erection and ejaculation. It is possible to distinguish between libido and potency under experimental conditions in the laboratory rat, but much more difficult in man. Put another way, most attention in animal studies is devoted to a well-defined response (such as lordosis) to some experimental intervention, whereas human studies attribute considerable weight to subjective feelings and motivation. This is inevitably an over-simplification, for the occurrence of marked individual differences in the ease with which sexual excitement occurs has been described in a wide variety of species. Beach (1942) was prompted to set out a general rule stating that the specificity of a stimulus adequate to elicit mating responses varies inversely with the sexual excitability of the individual.

Sexual behaviour can also be seen as a series of stimulus–response patterns evoked by a range of stimuli acting through a nervous system appropriately primed by hormonal action. Accordingly, it can be disrupted at several steps, but continues if the break is by-passed in one way or another. Not only can the influence of hormones wax and wane, but the intensity of the provocative stimulus required to initiate sexual interaction can vary. This is illustrated by the so-called Coolidge effect, which refers to the fact that a sexually satiated male shows renewed vigour when presented with a fresh female. The American President Coolidge is said to have noted this while observing farmyard activities (Bolles, 1975). A carry-over from sexual activity is also evident when intercourse with a receptive female is followed by a prolonged period of sexual excitability during which mating is attempted with incentive animals previously inadequate to elicit copulation (Beach, 1942).

Gonadal steroids

The effects of castration in the adult serve well as a starting point for discussion, for it is clear that sexual function can be retained after loss of the testes. Married eunuchs were common in biblical times, and Beach (1948) documented the early literature attesting to the retention of sexual function in men castrated many years earlier. He noted that the frequency of accounts describing the survival of normal sexuality following castration need not obscure the fact that in many, if not the majority of, cases the human male exhibits a gradual loss in mating ability as a result of removal of testes. A similar point was made by Kinsey, Pomeroy, Martin & Gebhard (1953), who argued that castration had little or no effect upon the sexual responsiveness of many of the males surveyed, and that the gradual decline in sexuality after castration was due in large part to the ageing process. They were sufficiently persuaded by these observations to remark that the data then available did not justify the opinion that the public could be protected from socially dangerous types of sex offenders by castration. Davidson (1972) observed that potency was speedily lost in some men but retained in others, and more recently concluded (Davidson, Kwan & Greenleaf, 1982) that there is little doubt that sexual behaviour (operationally defined as activities leading to orgasm) is drastically reduced or completely suppressed in a high percentage of men after castration. On the other hand, a substantial proportion of castrates retain a significant degree of sexual function, with estimates varying between 10 and 63 per cent. These authors comment that no systematic attempts have been made to assess factors such as the preoperative level of sexuality, ageing, the psychological effects of loss of the gonads, and the influence of the problems (medical or legal) leading to castration. They further note that it is also not clear what sexuality is really like for those retaining some function, or to what degree sexual desire, enjoyment, satisfaction and orgasm are retained, as opposed to efforts to satisfy their partners or retain some semblance of activity.

Loss of the gonads is not to be equated with a lack of sex hormones, although as much as 98 per cent of the testosterone in circulation is produced by the testes. After castration only about 2 per cent of the testosterone previously available remains, but the production of androstenedione by the adrenal glands is not affected and the peripheral conversion of this steroid to oestrogen means that oestrogen production is about one-half of normal; in some cases the net result is that the preponderance of oestrogen may actually result in feminization (Wilson, 1982).

Sexuality in men can also be suppressed by treatment with an anti-androgenic drug, such as cyproterone acetate (Rubin, Reinisch & Haskett, 1981), and this observation points to an important role of androgen in sexual behaviour, although the fact that these compounds usually have progestogenic properties needs to be borne in mind. In one study of serious sex offenders the effect of cyproterone acetate was compared with that of ethinyl oestradiol and both steroids had depressed sexual interest and the frequency of masturbation at the end of 6 weeks (Bancroft, Tennent, Loucas & Cass, 1974). In another, medroxyprogesterone acetate (Depo-Provera) was given to a series of male sex offenders in combination with counselling therapy (Money, Wiedeking, Walker & Gain, 1976). The steroid elevated the threshold for sexual imagery, and the effect waned when the steroid was discontinued. Oestrogens may be given to men in the course of treatment for cancer of the prostate gland and impotence is a very frequent side-effect (Meyer-Bahlburg, 1978).

Decreases in pubic and facial hair, muscular size, strength, testicular volume and the frequency of sexual activity are all marks of ageing in men, and it is supposed that there is a fall in testosterone secretion with increasing years. However, this supposition has been hard to prove, for the results of studies purporting to document the decline have been criticized on the basis that the subjects were probably ailing in some way. Elderly males in excellent general health have not shown the expected decline in plasma androgen concentration. Vermeulen (1983) stresses the wide scatter in plasma testosterone values at all ages, and points out that some elderly men have androgen concentrations comparable to those of the young. It also seems that significant falls in the blood testosterone level are not seen before the seventh decade, and a clear-cut decrease only after that. A study of 220 men aged between 41 and 93 years led Davidson, Kwan & Greenleaf (1982) to conclude that the correlations between sexual activity and plasma androgen concentration were of a low order, and that performance was less affected than libido. Sexual activity has been seen to wane in exceptionally healthy men (Tsitouras, Martin & Harman, 1982) and these authors concluded that the level of testosterone was but one of several factors that might contribute to a decline in sexual activity with age. There was only a modest association between serum testosterone and sexual vigour.

An additional problem in evaluating the correlation between a fall in plasma testosterone concentration and a diminution in sexual activity arises from the presumption that fluctuations in plasma steroid levels, above a certain value, have physiological meaning. Once a functional threshold has been reached, then elevations above that concentration may have little significance for the expression of sexual behaviour, although gonadotrophin secretion may be affected. There seems to be no correlation between the frequency of sexual thoughts, orgasm and the plasma testosterone concentration in young men (Raboch & Stárka, 1973; Kraemer *et al.*, 1976; Brown, Monti & Corriveau, 1978), or between androgen levels and copulatory behaviour in rats (Damassa, Smith, Tennent & Davidson, 1977) and guinea-pigs (Harding & Feder, 1976). Skakkebaek *et al.* (1981) have shown that sexual behaviour can be stimulated by testosterone undecanoate in hypogonadal men in cases where the plasma level of the androgen had not been restored to normal values. Similarly, the data of Salmimies *et al.* (1982) indicate that there is a wide individual variation in the threshold of plasma testosterone below which function is impaired, with the threshold varying between 2 and 4.5 ng/ml in a population where the normal range is 3–10 ng/ml. All patients with blood levels of testosterone below 2 ng/ml benefited from testosterone treatment, as well as others with testosterone levels in the normal range. The results of a number of earlier studies exploring the correlations between circulating levels of testosterone and sexual activity have been somewhat confusing (Bancroft, 1980), while more subtle correlations between certain components of the sexual response and androgen level may still obtain. When the latency between exposure to erotic videotapes and 75 per cent of maximum penile tumescence was measured in men and correlated with serum testosterone concentrations the higher blood levels of testosterone accorded with a shorter latency to maximal tumescence, and, to a lesser extent, with a shorter latency to detumescence (Lange, Brown, Wincze & Zwick, 1980).

Sexual behaviour can be dissociated from hormonal action in other circumstances. As will be described in connection with aggressive behaviour (Chapter 10), damage to the temporal lobes of the brain appears to favour the verbal and physical expression of sexual interest, perhaps by removing a previously exercised inhibition. These changes, which can be quite striking, are manifest in the absence of any increase in the plasma concentrations of gonadal steroids.

Although testosterone is the major circulating androgen in men, some consideration needs to be given to the question of whether it is solely responsible for the promotion of sexual behaviour. Point is given to this issue by the facts that oestrogen can restore androgen-dependent behaviour in castrated sheep and deer, that androgenic effects can be produced by implanting oestradiol into the brain, and that testosterone can be metabolized to 5α-dihydrotestosterone, and to oestradiol-17β (Bancroft, 1980). Aromatization of testosterone to oestradiol can be achieved by human hypothalamic tissue (Naftolin *et al.*, 1975), and, as described earlier (Chapter 7), the masculinization of the hypothalamus of the mammalian fetal male may involve the conversion of androgen to oestrogen. However, ethyl oestradiol suppresses male sexuality (p. 123).

Despite a number of caveats, androgen replacement therapy can be effective in restoring sexual function in men. This is illustrated by the work of Davidson, Camargo & Smith (1979), who studied the response of 6 hypogonadal men to monthly injections of testosterone enanthate or placebo. The total frequency of erections consistently increased or decreased, according to the treatment, within a week or so of the rise or fall in plasma testosterone level, as did the frequency of coitus and of nocturnal erections. Concordant observations have been reported by others (Skakkebaek *et al.*, 1981). In men with Klinefelter's syndrome, with a sex chromosomal configuration of XXY, the body is eunuchoid, the testes are small and sexual drive is diminished (Raboch, Mellan & Starka, 1979). Treatment with testosterone, alongside developing a masculine phenotype and the male secondary sexual characteristics, can produce increased sexual interest, with heterosexual fantasies, penile erections and overt sexual behaviour (Rubin, Reinisch & Haskett, 1981). One puzzling feature of the response to androgen is that in experimental animals neuronal activity is affected very quickly (within minutes) by the application of gonadal steroids to the brain (Chapter 5) but there is a latent period of days or weeks before the sexual behaviour of animals or of hypogonadal men is affected (Davidson, Camargo & Smith, 1979; Skakkebaek *et al.*, 1981), with the earliest response being an increased frequency of sexual thoughts and excitement.

In reflecting upon the way in which sexual function is influenced by androgen, Bancroft (1980) has given considerable weight to sexual imagery. Since withdrawal and replacement of testosterone therapy in hypogonadal men was associated with a waning and a waxing of sexual thoughts, and since these changes preceded effects on erection and ejaculation, he suggested that the effects on erectile potency are mediated strictly by increased sexual appetite or libido, as well as by a separate effect upon ejaculation. In this he was influenced by the results of a collaborative study indicating that the erectile responses of 2 castrates and 6 hypogonadal men to erotic films were not significantly different from those during androgen treatment, or from those of normal controls. However, the response to a self-selected sexual fantasy that the subject was asked to imagine as vividly as possible and sustain for two minutes was suppressed in the untreated condition but restored upon treatment with testosterone. It is relevant that the treatment of sex offenders with cyproterone acetate and oestrogen decreased their response to fantasy more than that to films (Bancroft *et al.*, 1974).

Confirmation of the production of erection in hypogonadal men by erotic films has been provided by Davidson, Kwan & Greenleaf (1982), who also found that these responses remained unaffected during testosterone therapy. However, the responses to sexual fantasy were robust and unaffected by androgen deficiency or replacement, and these workers were struck by the finding that the rapid detumescence seen in normal volunteers after the stimulus was withdrawn was lacking in the hypogonadal men, even when distractions were applied. There is conflict between these observations and the clinical reports of severe sexual dysfunction in hypogonadal or castrate men, who often relate their deficiencies in sexual capacity to problems with erection – which can be reduced or abolished by testosterone treatment. Davidson, Kwan & Greenleaf (1982) suggest that a neglected factor in this regard is a pleasurable awareness of sexual response in which sensory feedback from the genitalia assumes importance, and where testosterone might act to lower the threshold of genital receptors whose activation stimulates sexual desire as well as erection. The same receptors may also facilitate detumescence.

Sexual activity may itself increase gonadotrophin and gonadal hormone secretion in men, although the case is not as strong as in other species. Raised blood levels of testosterone after coitus were reported by Fox *et al.* (1972) and Kraemer *et al.* (1976), while Pirke, Kockott & Dittmar (1974) noted similar changes in subjects viewing a sexually stimulating film. A rapid, and transient, rise in LH was noted by LaFerla, Anderson & Schalch (1978), who also observed that an interview on sexual topics could be effective.

Changes in plasma testosterone concentration have been seen in other circumstances which do not necessarily have any sexual connotation. Work with non-human primates has shown that social dominance is an important factor, with high-ranking males having more testosterone in circulation than lower-ranking males (Keverne, 1979). Experimental re-arrangement of established rankings, by introducing new males into the society, resulted in a rise in plasma testosterone in the victorious males, and a decline in the losers. One experimental approach to this problem in man has been to compare the plasma testosterone levels in men playing doubles tennis matches for prizes, where there was a trend toward high testosterone levels in the winners, and toward lower levels in the losers. The rises were linked to feelings of elation, and were also noted among the winners of a series of lotteries who reported a similar change in mood (Mazur & Lamb, 1980). Particularly stressful circumstances, as exemplified during the early period of training for officers in an infantry school, can depress androgen secretion, although normal plasma testosterone levels were restored as training continued (Kreuz, Rose & Jennings, 1972).

Animal research leaves little doubt that sex hormones influence behaviour through actions upon the hypothalamus and limbic system, but the nature of the action is less clear. The biochemical basis of such steroid action has been touched upon earlier, but there is little understanding of the way in which the cellular changes become integrated into patterns of behaviour. The investigations of Klüver & Bucy (1937) and Schreiner & Kling (1956) on the effects of damage to the amygdaloid nuclei upon the behaviour of several species drew attention to the relationship between the limbic system and sexual function. Associated with a reduction in aggression, hypersexual behaviour became manifest in monkeys within 30–60 days after placement of the lesions. Male lynxes, cats and agoutis also showed hypersexual behaviour in the form of attempts to copulate with any likely object, not necessarily a member of the same species. In cats, these behavioural changes could be prevented by lesions placed in the hypothalamus (Kling & Hutt, 1958) and this result implies that the amygdala may normally be restraining hypothalamic activity. Concordant observations have been made in man (Klüver, 1952; Chapter 10). It is relevant that diminished or absent libido and impotence, as well as neuroendocrine abnormalities indicative of hypogonadism and hyperprolactinaemia, may be evident in cases of temporal lobe epilepsy (Spark, Wills & Royal, 1984), although changes in sexual interest are not necessarily the main factor. An alternative view is that in cases of amygdaloid damage there is a loss of discrimination on the part of the male, so that a sexually appropriate response can be triggered by a variety of normally inappropriate stimuli.

Peptide hormones

Alongside the prominence given to steroids in the control of sexual behaviour, the peptide hormones themselves may be influential. There is now considerable evidence from animal experimentation that peptides influence sexual behaviour. Gonadotrophin-releasing factor specifically induces mating behaviour in the hypogonadal rat, although it is ineffective in intact individuals. Spayed females treated with oestrogen alone, GnRF alone or oestrogen in combination with either LH, FSH or TRF displayed little or no lordosis behaviour or signs of sexual receptivity, but spayed animals primed with oestrogen in combination with either progesterone or GnRF showed a high incidence of lordosis, although the response to GnRF was not as great as that to progesterone. The sexual receptivity produced by GnRF appeared about 2–3 hours after injection, lasted about 6 hours and seemed to be an all-or-none phenomenon unrelated to dosage. Gonado-trophin-releasing factor accelerated ejaculation in intact male rats and in castrated rats maintained on testosterone. Further, the local injection of GnRF into the medial preoptic area and arcuate–ventromedial nuclear region of the hypothalamus potentiated lordosis in rats, as did injections into the central grey area of the midbrain, where the peptide has been detected. Infusion of an antiserum to GnRF into the third ventricle decreased the lordosis behaviour normally observed in the oestrogen–pro-gesterone-primed ovariectomized rat.

In adult hypogonadal men treated with GnRF, Mortimer *et al.* (1974) found that sexual function improved before any appreciable rise in plasma testosterone concentration was noted, but other work (Benkert, 1975; Davies *et al.*, 1976; McAdoo *et al.*, 1978; Evans & Distiller, 1979; Moss, 1979) has not yielded striking or consistent results. Curiously, such clinical evidence as there is points to an effect of GnRF in men and not in women, in contrast to the observations in rats.

Prolactin has also been implicated in the control of libido, in that men with hyperprolactinaemia produced by pituitary tumours or acromegaly and complaining of impotence have reported an increase in potency after surgery, radiotherapy or treatment with the prolactin-secretion inhibitor bromocriptine. The improvement is matched by a fall in plasma prolactin and a rise in plasma testosterone, so the effects could be due to an interference with testicular function brought about by high levels of prolactin. However, a direct effect of the peptide hormone on the brain cannot be excluded (Franks, Jacobs, Martin & Nabarro, 1978; Carter *et al.*, 1978).

Adrenocorticotrophic hormone injected into the CSF of rabbits generates recurrent episodes of penile erection accompanied by copulatory move-ments, often culminating in ejaculation. The sexual stimulation may be so intense that the animals may ejaculate up to a dozen times during the first two or three hours after hormone administration. Curiously, during the episodes of stimulation the males show no interest in the opposite sex. In sexually experienced rats ACTH 1–24 markedly shortens the latency to ejaculation and decreases the number of mounts and intromissions prior to ejaculation, but does not increase the incidence of copulation in sexually sluggish males. These effects are not exerted by the 4–10 sequence of the ACTH molecule, so indicating that different parts of the ACTH structure are concerned with this response and with learning (Chapter 13). Androgens are essential for this effect in that castration abolishes the sexual response, as does treatment with cyproterone acetate (Serra & Gessa, 1983).

Homosexuality

In view of the insubstantial nature of the evidence involving androgens in the manifestation of male sexual behaviour, it is not surprising that there is even less hard data relating changes in hormone levels to homosexual behaviour in men. These have been reviewed by Meyer-Bahlburg (1982), who states that of a total of twenty-four studies published since 1971, only four found lower testosterone means for homosexual than for heterosexual males, eighteen studies showed no systematic difference, and two showed elevated levels of testosterone. Assessments of the production rates of testosterone, or of free or bound testosterone, gave essentially similar results. The data on oestrogen levels from seven investigations were negative or inconsistent, and the fifteen studies available on gonadotrophin levels presented essentially negative results. The existence of more subtle changes in hypothalamo-pituitary function may be foreshadowed by the observations of Boyar & Aiman (1982), who worked with male-to-female transsexuals considering themselves to be females trapped in the body of a man. In some the 24-hour mean serum concentration of LH and the LH pulse frequency or amplitude was raised, and an increased pituitary response to LHRH was evident, although the sex steroid hormone kinetics appeared to be normal (Aiman & Boyar, 1982).

The possibility that homosexuality in men could stem from an inadequate masculinization of the brain during fetal life has been elaborated upon by Dörner (1979; Chapter 7). On this basis differences in brain function would underlie the condition and overt changes in blood hormone levels need not arise. Further, appropriate prophylactic treatment during fetal life should greatly reduce the incidence of the condition. This view has been vigorously attacked by Sigusch, Schorsch, Dannecker & Schmidt (1982) on behalf of the German Society for Sex Research. They assert that it is rash to draw analogies from the sexual motor patterns of the rat to the sexual life of humans, that prenatal or perinatal hormonal influences may differ markedly between man and other species, and that clinical observations of prenatal hormone disturbances do not support the hypothesis of Dörner. The differences in the positive feedback action of oestrogen in homo- and heterosexual men are considered to be minor, with many exceptions, and have not been replicated elsewhere.

The number of cases reported by Dörner showing lower levels of free plasma testosterone, and higher plasma levels of FSH, in 'effeminate' homosexual men in contrast to heterosexual men is regarded as extremely small and unconvincing, while the distinction between 'effeminate' and 'non-effeminate' homosexuals is said to require explanation. Sigusch *et al.* also regard the use of statistics indicating that a larger proportion of homosexuals were born during the war years than at other times as biologically unsound. The main thrust of these comments centres upon the assumption that homosexuality is an illness, whereas the critics consider that manifest homosexuality is a personality structure, and not a sign of malfunction. When treatment is necessary in cases where an individual has failed to integrate personality and environment, then recourse should be made only to psychotherapy. The information available is clearly being viewed from opposing standpoints and this is valuable in defining points of conflict, but it should be added that whilst the case for an hormonal basis for homosexual behaviour still needs to be established, there is no justification for any discouragement of further exploration of this field. Thus, quite recently, a distinct difference between the responses of female hetero-sexuals, male heterosexuals and male homosexuals to an injection of oestrogen was demonstrable, in that the changes in the plasma concen-trations of LH in the male homosexuals lay between the quite different curves from heterosexual men and women. An enhancement in LH se-cretion observed in females some 60 hours after oestrogen injection was lacking in the heterosexual men (Gladue, Green & Hellman, 1984). None of the life-long homosexual males showed a typically female response pattern, for the reactions in the women were earlier and of greater magnitude than those of the men.

9

Hormones and female sexual behaviour

Patterns of behaviour

Students of sexual behaviour in the female have found it convenient to distinguish between three components in the overall pattern. These are *receptivity*, which relates to the preparedness of the female to accept the male; *proceptivity*, which describes the role of the female in initiating and inviting coitus; and *attractiveness*, covering those non-behavioural features of the female which promote a sexual approach from the male (Beach, 1976). In lower primates hormones have been considered to influence each component, although the information for the woman is less than adequate. Androgen may favour proceptivity in the monkey, oestrogens may be concerned with receptivity, proceptivity and attractiveness, and progesterone may have inhibitory actions (Baum, Everitt, Herbert & Keverne, 1977). However, as Beach (1976) comments, there is no substantial body of evidence that would allow direct comparisons of hormonal effects in women with those known to exist in the females of other species. Feminine sexual characteristics have not been conceptualized in women in terms of attractivity, proceptivity and receptivity and inevitably there is much that is confusing in the human literature.

The menstrual cycle

The distribution of sexual activity through the menstrual cycle has often been studied, perhaps because of conflicting findings. Of 32 studies, sexual activity was found to be increased premenstrually in 17, postmenstrually in 18, highest during menstruation in 4, and greatest around the time of ovulation in 8 (Schreiner-Engel, 1980). Sanders & Bancroft (1982) point to a number of reasons for these discrepancies. One concerns the accurate identification of the phase of the menstrual cycle and underlines the desirability of hormone measurements. Another relates to the methods of recording sexual behaviour, for retrospective accounts are regarded as unreliable and the use of general terms such as 'libido' or 'sexual gratification' can be confusing. Efforts to describe separately the incidence of the various components of sexual behaviour have been lamentably few. Other complicating factors include the avoidance of sexual activity during menstruation, or an increased frequency of coitus on either side of the period of abstinence. With closer analysis other possibilities emerge. If the sexual interest of the woman is examined (as distinct from male–female interaction) then there is some suggestion that autonomous or female-initiated behaviour is at a peak around the time of ovulation, as assessed from the onset of menstruation (Adams, Gold & Burt, 1978).

The human female is not peculiar among primates in being sexually receptive throughout the menstrual cycle. In general, intact non-primate mammals show sexual receptivity for only a brief period during the oestrous cycle, at around the time of spontaneous ovulation. But among the primates, intact females of several species of Old World monkeys and apes copulate throughout the menstrual cycle with little variation in frequency (stumptail macaque, orang-utan) or with a higher frequency in the follicular phase than in the luteal phase of the cycle (other macaques, baboons and chimpanzees). In contrast, copulation is usually restricted to the periovulatory period in prosimians, some New World monkeys, such as the squirrel monkey, and gorillas. As Feder (1984) comments, these data illustrate an enormous variability in hormone–behaviour interactions across primate species and make free extrapolation of information from one species to another hazardous.

In a study involving 55 women in whom detailed hormone measurements established that the menstrual cycles were normal, with one-third of the women complaining of the premenstrual syndrome, one-third reporting premenstrual symptoms but not seeking medical help, and the rest being relatively symptom free, there was no evidence of a mid-cycle or periovulatory peak in sexual activity (Sanders & Bancroft, 1982). There was a general tendency for sexuality to vary with general well-being, and definite evidence of a post-menstrual increase in sexual interest and activity and of a lesser increase in sexual interest premenstrually.

Progesterone is known to exert a variety of effects on sexual behaviour. Prior exposure to progesterone, before the periovulatory surge of oestrogen, is required for oestrus in the sheep, while in the rat progesterone is needed together with oestrogen for the proper manifestation of heat. However, the lack of correlation between the preovulatory peak of oestrogen during the menstrual cycle and sexual activity argues against a major role of this hormone alone in triggering this behavioural pattern (Persky *et al.*, 1978a;

Bancroft *et al.*, 1983), although a facilitatory action must not be disregarded. Postmenopausally, women produce minimal quantities of oestrogen, yet sexual activity continues and may even be enhanced.

Despite poor understanding of the processes involved, other features of the behaviour of women may be affected by the stage of the menstrual cycle. This matter is covered in more detail later, but one extreme is illustrated by the work of MacKinnon & MacKinnon (1956), who studied 47 consecutive deaths in women of reproductive age. There were 23 suicides, and 20 of the women were in the middle or late luteal phases of the cycle. All nine accidental deaths occurred in the luteal phase. On the other hand, a review of the literature on suicide and the menstrual cycle (Wetzel & McClure, 1972) collected many confusing and contradictory results. Perhaps this is to be expected because of the extreme and terminal nature of the event, but the possibility that women are more prone to accidents late in the menstrual cycle appeared to emerge from other work (Dalton, 1960). Here more than half of the accidents in a series of eighty-four took place during menstruation or the four days before menstrual bleeding. However, the study was retrospective, no attempt was made to check the accuracy of the menstrual phase, and no distinction was drawn between being an active or a passive participant in the accident. No consideration was given to the possibility that menstruation may have occurred prematurely as a result of the accident. The sample was not one of a consecutive series of accident admissions, no control group of women who had had an accident but had not required hospitalization was employed, and crucial details concerning the nature of the accident (e.g. was the woman a driver or a passenger) were omitted (Clare, 1983).

The pass-rate in 'O' and 'A' level school examinations was depressed in a minority of candidates sitting during the premenstrual period or during menstruation (Dalton, 1968), but the magnitude of the changes was not reported or any statistical evaluation of the results provided. Other studies have shown an improvement in reaction time and performance tests during the luteal phase of the cycle, with an optimum occurring 2–4 days before menstruation (Clare, 1983). In a series of 44 admissions, more women entered psychiatric hospitals during the premenstrual or menstrual phases of the ovarian cycle than at other times (Janowsky, Gorney, Castelnuevo-Tedesco & Stone, 1969). This represents one of numerous studies leading to the conclusion that recurrent mental conditions of psychotic proportions flare up premenstrually more often than expected on the basis of chance. But reservations remain in that details of the assessment of menstrual phase or of the nature and duration of illness prior to admission are seldom provided (Clare, 1983).

In considering the relationship of hormones to sexual behaviour it is as well to bear in mind the effects of steroids upon the reproductive tract, for changes in the sensitivity of the genitalia, or the degree of vasocongestion, could be influential. A comparison of subjective changes during sexual arousal with fluctuations in vaginal blood flow was made by Schreiner-Engel, Schiavi, Smith & White (1981) and related to the stage of the menstrual cycle. Subjective reports of sexual arousal did not show any differences in blood flow according to the phase of the menstrual cycle, whereas higher mean levels of physiological arousal (as judged by vaginal photoplethysmography) were evident during the follicular and luteal phases than around the time of ovulation.

Hypogonadism

Studies of the changes in sexual behaviour associated with ovariec-tomy or after the menopause would be expected to provide information of great value in the understanding of the role of sex hormones in influencing human behaviour, but they have proved to be disappointing. In 1939, Pratt believed that subjective factors were of such importance that ovariectomized women could marry, exhibit normal libido and participate in satisfactory marital relations, and there is anecdotal evidence to support that view. However, before the advent of reliable contraceptive techniques an impor-tant factor in the resurgence of sexual interest after gonadectomy may have been the removal of the spectre of pregnancy.

The clearest information should stem from follow-up work on patients subjected to a surgical menopause, but, despite the large number of oophorectomies that have been performed, the material is limited. One complication is that removal of the ovaries is very frequently accompanied by hysterectomy, and the psychological consequences of this operation can be marked (Dennerstein & Burrows, 1982). The incidence of subsequent sexual dysfunction was lower in patients who were well-informed about the nature of the operation. From the physiological point of view removal of the uterus should not disturb hormonal balance to any marked degree, but the quality of orgasm could be reduced through loss of the stimulation provided by penile pressure upon the cervix and neighbouring structures (Zussman, Zussman, Sunley & Bjornson, 1981).

In the absence of replacement therapy, menopausal symptoms after ovarian removal are usually more severe than those associated with the natural menopause (Studd, Chakravarti & Oram, 1977). However, after examining the endocrine changes and associated symptomatology in 100 premenopausal women subjected to this operation, Chakravarti *et al.* (1977) concluded that the occurrence of post-operative symptoms in individual patients could not be accounted for on the basis of the known changes in the concentrations of circulating steroids or of gonadotrophins. Sixty-two women complained of depression at interview, one to thirty-one years after surgery, and 48 reported insomnia. Ninety-four of the 100 patients had experienced hot flushes after the operation and these set in within six weeks in 84 of them. Although the occurrence of hot flushes can readily be attributed to the withdrawal of oestrogen, is associated with an acute release of LH and can be reduced by treatments that depress pulsatile LH release, the mechanisms involved in the generation of the episodes remain obscure (Lightman, Jacobs & Maguire, 1982; Duncan, 1982; Linsell & Lightman, 1983). It might also be noted that the menopause is not always associated with a lack of oestrogen. Some 40 per cent of one group of women showed well-oestrogenized vaginal smears through into their seventh decade (McLennan & McLennan, 1971).

By reason of the increasing popularity of hormone replacement therapy in postmenopausal women the case for some beneficial effects of treatment should be strong. In order to eliminate any bias on the part of the investigator or subject, Dennerstein and Burrows (1982) considered only studies utilizing double-blind placebo-controlled methodology. The results were disappointing in that several procedural difficulties limited interpretation. These included the inadequate description and definition of the endocrine status of the women studied, as well as the problem of defining and measuring the behavioural changes of the menopause. Differing drugs were used in varying doses and the possible persistence of steroids in the circulation during the placebo phase of treatment also needed to be taken into account. Nevertheless, oestrogen treatment did appear to be beneficial and Dennerstein & Burrows (1982) were led to carry out their own double-blind crossover study, with each treatment of ethinyl oestradiol, levonorgestrel, or ethinyl oestradiol and levonorgestrel (Nordiol), or placebo, being sustained for three months. The 36 women given all four treatments showed significant agreement in their preferences, with ethinyl oestradiol being top of the list and Nordiol, levonorgestrel and placebo following in that order. After three months ethinyl oestradiol was associated with significantly more vaginal lubrication, sexual enjoyment and desire than placebo. The frequency of orgasm was reported at monthly intervals and the highest number occurred with ethinyl oestradiol treatment, followed by Nordiol, levonorgestrel, and, lastly, placebo. But there was no effect upon the frequency of intercourse. There were highly significant differences between individual patients and in patient–drug interaction. Overall, it seems that a deficiency of oestrogen may not necessarily be the cause of sexual problems at this time of life, but might provide a biological vulnerability that may tilt women with a somewhat tenuous sexual adjustment toward sexual dysfunction. Then more than oestrogen may be needed to restore the situation.

Androgens

Androgens have often been used to increase libido in women, but the physiological case for their application requires reinforcement. There is a rise in plasma testosterone and androstenedione toward mid-cycle (Yen, 1980), but no peak in sexual activity at this time. However, the adrenal glands produce the androgens testosterone, androstenedione, dehydroepiandrosterone and dihydrotestosterone and these may provide between 50 and 90 per cent of the endogenous supply. Sexual behaviour in women is depressed by adrenalectomy, but this is a major surgical intervention and comparison with normal individuals is hazardous. Conversely, some women given testosterone show increased libido and sexual activity, although large and pharmacological doses of steroid have been given (Gray & Gorzalka, 1980; Brown, 1981). These have produced clitoral hypertrophy and an increased clitoral sensitivity that might provide the basis for enhanced sexual desire or awareness. Against this idea can be quoted the observations that paraplegic women lacking sensation below the waist have also experienced increased libido with androgen administration. With more moderate doses of testosterone given to women complaining of sexual unresponsiveness there was, contrary to expectation, no benefit attributable to testosterone (Mathews, Whitehead & Kellett, 1983).

The possible mechanisms of action of androgen in increasing sexual interest in women may require the mediation of monoamines. In the female rhesus monkey the decrease in receptivity seen after adrenalectomy can be reversed by treatment with p-chlorophenylalanine (PCPA), a drug that reduces the concentration of serotonin in the brain, as well as by androgens. Drugs like PCPA that reduce the effects of serotonin may potentiate the response to androgen (Bancroft, 1983), but other explanations are possible.

Because of the long latent period between a rise in sex hormone level and any effect upon behaviour, Bancroft, Sanders, Davidson & Warner (1983) examined the association between average or mid-cycle testosterone levels and average levels of sexuality throughout the cycle. They distinguished between those women who masturbated and those who did not and found that in the former there was a high correlation between testosterone concentration and the frequency of masturbation, but no correlation with the frequency of sexual activity with the partner, or with sexual feelings. For the women who did not masturbate the correlation was negative: the higher the level of testosterone the lower the incidence of sexual feelings or activity.

Here another complicating factor intrudes, for Bancroft *et al.* (1983) noted an association between testosterone and life style, with women living alone or working full-time having higher testosterone levels than those married or co-habiting or working part-time. They postulate that testosterone is associated with personality development and the adoption of life styles that are in conflict with conventional female heterosexuality. It is hard to reconcile these observations with those, for example, of Persky *et al.* (1978b) who, in contrast to their failure to demonstrate any link between plasma oestrogen level and the sexual response of young women, observed that testosterone was influential. High plasma testosterone levels at mid-cycle were associated with an increase in intercourse frequency, and the mean testosterone level across three consecutive menstrual cycles was significantly correlated with the capacity to form interpersonal relationships and sexual gratification. This study was extended to include a group of women who were 30 years older (average ages 24 *versus* 54 years), and the assay of other androgens (Persky *et al.*, 1982). The younger women had markedly higher levels of androgen than their elders, but their levels of sexual desire and degree of sexual arousal were not significantly different. Still, the frequency of sexual intercourse was higher in the young, and the young also felt more sexually gratified than the older women.

Oral contraceptives

Oral contraceptives have now been used by millions of women and the effect of these steroids upon female sexuality should be well understood. However this is not the case (Sanders & Bancroft, 1982). The frequency of coitus may be higher in women on the pill than in other groups of women, but this may simply indicate that most sexually motivated women preferred this method, or that these are the women who find oral contraceptives acceptable. It is also less easy to refuse the importunate male partner.

The distribution of sexual activity in women taking oral contraceptives has been compared with that of a control group given a placebo (Udry, Morris & Waller, 1973). There was no difference in overall sexual activity between the groups, but the women on placebo showed a decline in sexual activity during the luteal phase which was not apparent in the oral contraceptive group. This was attributed to the presence of endogenous progesterone during the natural cycle which affected the male so that his desire for coitus was lessened. With the pill any pheromonal restraint that progesterone exercised would be removed. Others have described an increase in female-initiated sexual behaviour around the time of ovulation in married women using contraceptive devices other than the pill–an increase which was lacking in oral contraceptive users (Adams, Gold & Burt, 1978). A peak of female-initiated sexual activity in pill-taking women occurred over the first four or five days of the pill cycle. The women on oral contraceptives described by Bancroft, Davidson, Warner & Tyrer (1980) expressed most sexual interest toward the end of the pill-free week, when there was a rise in the concentration of endogenous oestradiol and androgen in the blood.

Homosexuality

As in the case of the male, there does not seem to be any hormonal difference between the majority of adult homosexual and heterosexual women, although about one-third of homosexual (including gender-identity disordered or transsexual) women show somewhat elevated testosterone levels that nevertheless remain far below the range for men (Meyer-Bahlburg, 1982). If such an increase in testosterone were to be substantiated it would still need to be ascertained whether the change was causal, or was a consequence of stressful activation of the adrenal glands producing androstenedione which could then be converted peripherally to testosterone.

Neurotransmitter function

The behavioural changes brought about by gonadal steroids may well be mediated by alterations in neurotransmitter function, as noted on several occasions previously. Sexual receptivity is promoted in oestrogen-primed ovariectomized rats by progesterone, and treatment with reserpine or tetrabenazine (monoamine depletors) can be substituted for progesterone. The inhibition of monoamine oxidase activity decreases the response to progesterone. Pharmacological doses of oestrogen given to rats depress monoamine oxidase activity, whereas progesterone has the opposite effect. Oestrogen has also been shown to reduce the release of noradrenaline from electrically stimulated slices of rat brain (Rausch *et al.*, 1982). Heat is enhanced in rats by inhibition of serotonin synthesis, and treatment with drugs causing the depletion of serotonin in the brain can replace the synergistic effect of progesterone given with oestrogen to generate sexual receptivity. The elevation of serotonin levels in the brain inhibits the display of oestrus. There are also suggestions that the inhibition of serotonin synthesis can increase libido in man. In view of the fact that castration and subsequent therapy with gonadal steroid substantially affect the turnover of dopamine, noradrenaline and serotonin in the brain, it is natural to presume that the changes in sexual behaviour wrought by the monoamines and by the sex steroids are directly connected. This is probably a gross oversimplification, for interference with dopamine turnover, for example, influences virtually all forms of goal-directed behaviour, including food intake, water intake and motor behaviour, as well as sexual interaction. Sensory input may be important in that noradrenergic neurons in the brains of rodents seem to influence the behavioural responses to tactile and olfactory cues relating to coitus (Everitt, 1983).

Peptides

Alongside the substantial mass of information covering the actions of oestrogen and progesterone upon the brain in controlling sexual behaviour in animals, a smaller mound concerning the part played by peptide hormones may be beginning to grow. Gonadotrophin-releasing factor is one such peptide (Chapter 8), while a case may be in the course of construction for prolactin. Here the microinfusion of prolactin into the dorsal midbrain of the oestrogen-treated ovariectomized rat increased lordosis behaviour, while the comparable injection of an antiserum to prolactin had the opposite effect. These observations could be artefactual in nature, were it not for the fact that in parallel experiments a prolactin-like material was detected immunochemically in cells in the mediobasal hypothalamus. The cells were located in a band extending laterally from the arcuate nuclei to just ventral to the ventromedial nuclei, and from the rostral tip of these nuclei to a premammillary level. Fibres containing prolactin-like immunoreactivity occurred throughout the midbrain central grey matter, especially ventral and lateral to the cerebral aqueduct, where there was a dense plexus of branching fibres (Harlan, Shivers & Pfaff, 1983). These cells, like those in the hypophysis that secrete prolactin, might be sensitive to oestrogen and increase their production of prolactin under the influence of the steroid. In turn, prolactin or a prolactin-like substance might facilitate the expression of sexual behaviour.

The premenstrual syndrome

At first sight, premenstrual tension would seem to provide a classic example of a hormone-related behavioural disorder, and has been so regarded since attention was first drawn to the condition by Frank (1931). The regular occurrence of psychological symptoms such as depression, tension, anxiety, irritability, nervousness, aggression and lethargy, alongside systemic changes like weight gain, abdominal pain, breast tenderness and hypoglycaemia, in association with a particular phase of the menstrual cycle points toward the involvement of ovarian or hypophysial hormones. However, as Symonds (1981) has pointed out, when the definition is extended to include the time around ovulation, the post-ovulatory phase and up to four days into menstruation (Dalton, 1977), then some twenty days of each month is covered and attention directed away from the few days before menstruation and toward almost any cyclical symptom. By

1968, the list of symptoms felt to vary with the menstrual cycle extended beyond 150 and was drawn from practically every medical speciality. The tremendous diversity of symptoms in the literature, as well as the inconsistency of their reported frequency, reflects the multiplicity of interest in the field and the complete lack of comparability in the methodologies employed, as well as the variety of populations studied (Rubinow & Roy-Byrne, 1984). Others have gone further and expressed considerable scepticism that the syndrome exists at all, particularly as 'the premenstrual syndrome' has been regarded as a mitigating factor in serious crimes (Brahams, 1981).

Among the methodological problems arising in the study of this condition are the use of women attending special clinics and so somewhat self-selected, and the highlighting of symptoms that are common among women, and disregarded by many. The published figures on psychiatric ill-health, psychiatric treatment and psychiatric admissions suggest that women are more prone than men to negative affect symptoms, but such variations as are said to occur within the menstrual cycle in the rates of violence and motor accidents do not lead to a higher rate for women than for men (Lancet, 1981). The baseline from which variations can be gauged is ill-defined, and the data could match suggestions of a mid-cycle syndrome of lowered crime, fewer epileptic seizures, increased self-esteem and elation, increased sexual desire and activity.

A review of the psychiatric aspects of premenstrual complaints left Clare (1983) sceptical of the reported correlations between this phase of the sex cycle and the commission of violent crime, largely because of lack of precision in monitoring the menstrual cycle or defining a particular phase, and overmuch reliance upon recollection on the part of the women concerned. Women who had premenstrual complaints were not more likely to have been more aggressive or violent than the uncomplaining. Many years ago McCance, Luff & Widdowson (1937) found considerable discrepancies between the daily symptom records of 167 women and the results of a questionnaire on menstrual cycle symptoms administered before the records began. According to the literature then available there should have been a great increase in the incidence of depression at or about the time of the menstrual period, but the records showed a fairly even distribution of depression throughout the menstrual cycle. There was a tendency for the incidence to increase just before and during the early stages of the period, but there was by no means the overwhelming incidence that other investigations had led them to expect. Some women may not actually experience changes in relation to specific periods of the menstrual cycle but believe that they experience them, and others led to believe that they were in the premenstrual phase of the cycle reported significantly worse premenstrual symptoms than those led to believe that they were intermenstrual (Ruble, 1977). Little indication of meaningful fluctuations in the enjoyment of daily activities or of mood emerged in another study in which the participating women filled in a series of questionnaires during the course of the investigation. Indeed, the lack of a relationship between moods or enjoyment of activities and the phase of the menstrual cycle came as somewhat of a surprise to many of the subjects (Abplanalp, Donnelly & Rose, 1979).

The existence of the premenstrual syndrome should not be taken for granted, and in future discussions the suggestion that the premenstrual syndrome should be defined as a symptom-complex that reaches its peak in the week preceding menstruation and is generally relieved by the onset of the menstrual flow (Symonds, 1981) has its attractions. Thus there was no overt psychiatric disorder during the luteal phase in 42 women whose behavioural changes were classified according to research diagnostic criteria, but if the duration was reduced from two weeks to two days all met the diagnosis of major depressive disorder premenstrually. They predominantly showed irritability, tension and affective lability (Haskett, Steiner, Osmun & Carroll, 1980). There is a highly statistically significant association between the reporting of premenstrual symptoms and psychiatric ill-health. Psychiatrically ill premenstrual women are more likely to complain of psychological or behavioural symptoms than psychiatrically healthy women, although both groups report premenstrual physical symptoms to a similar degree. This emerged in a study of 521 women attending their family doctor for a variety of reasons, or 171 respondents to an advertisement in a women's magazine seeking volunteers suffering from premenstrual symptoms prepared to take part in a research investigation (Clare, 1983). Cyclical patterns in feelings of well-being were discerned by Sanders, Warner, Backström & Bancroft (1983), and these seemed to be intensified in the women drawn from a gynaecological clinic and complaining of the syndrome. More objective evidence of some change in behaviour during the menstrual cycle may come from study of the changes in electrical skin resistance (galvanic skin response, GSR) accompanying a repetitive auditory stimulus. With repetition of the stimulus the GSR wanes and a point of habituation is reached, defined as the first stimulus point in a series of 21 stimuli where no GSR was obtained for at least three successive stimuli. Normal women showed an abrupt lowering of the threshold of habituation (or a lowering of arousal) around ovulation, and this change was lacking in anovulatory cycles. Habituation may be taken as a measure of responsivity, sensitivity or arousal to familiar stimuli (Friedman & Meares, 1979).

The physical changes reported to occur in the premenstrual syndrome are those expected from involvement of the ovarian hormones. The changes commonly include weight increase, abdominal swelling, peripheral oedema, breast swelling, abdominal pain, backache, headache and vertigo (Symonds, 1981). But when these symptoms are examined in detail there is a distressing lack of consistency. Although gains in weight are frequently observed in cases of premenstrual tension, as in unaffected women, there appears to be no firm evidence of significant changes in sodium and water balance, and a notable lack of correlation with symptoms of bloatedness and breast engorgement. The fact that diuretics can be beneficial awaits explanation.

If the links with hormonal changes occurring during the menstrual cycle are examined in detail, then premenstrual tension has been attributed to a relatively low progesterone concentration, or to the changing level of progesterone as it declines from the maximal plasma concentration during the second half of the cycle. Other possibilities include an overly high blood level of oestrogen, the withdrawal of oestrogen, and the ratio of oestrogen to progesterone (Rausch *et al.*, 1982; Rubinow & Roy-Byrne, 1984). None of the explanations has proved satisfactory, and Backström *et al.* (1983) could find no difference in progesterone, oestradiol, testosterone or androstenedione levels between women showing marked or minimal cyclical changes in mood, although the negative mood changes were closely linked to the luteal phase of the menstrual cycle. Likewise, Clare (1983) found no significant association between lowered progesterone levels during the luteal phase of the cycle and premenstrual complaints. Of ten studies of progesterone levels in relation to menstrually-related mood disturbances, five showed reduced progesterone in the mid–late luteal phase of patients with the premenstrual syndrome compared with controls, one showed a subgroup (30 per cent) of patients with significantly low progesterone, one showed elevated progesterone in the early mid-luteal phase and three showed no abnormality in progesterone secretion. Interpretation of these findings is further complicated by the use of unclear or retrospective entry criteria, presentation of group rather than individual data, failure to fully describe the rating instruments employed, assignment to diagnostic group on the basis of median split rating scores or comparison of ovulatory and menstrual symptom rating scores, and the selection of non-uniform blood sampling times and intervals and the use of unspecified and unequal numbers of samples per patient. Similar problems have plagued assessments of oestrogen concentrations in the premenstrual syndrome, with four studies reporting elevated oestrogen levels and elevated oestrogen–progesterone ratios during the late luteal phase, one study reporting a significant correlation between oestrogen level and symptoms of anxiety and irritability, and four studies showing oestrogen mean values and oestrogen–progesterone ratios in the normal range (Rubinow & Roy-Byrne, 1984).

The changes in sodium and water balance seen in some cases of premenstrual tension have implicated the mineralocorticoids of the adrenal cortex, and in particular aldosterone. There is some evidence that fluctuations in aldosterone levels may parallel the emotional lability during the menstrual cycle, and that aldosterone secretion may be altered in patients. However, there is little evidence that aldosterone activity in women with premenstrual tension is elevated. Since aldosterone secretion is promoted by the peptide angiotensin the role of this factor has come under scrutiny. Angiotensin is known to act upon the brain (Chapter 2) and is produced in increased amounts during the luteal phase of the menstrual cycle (Rausch *et al.*, 1982).

Prolactin can also affect mineral and water balance and has been implicated in the aetiology of premenstrual tension. Plasma prolactin concentrations may be raised in affected women (Halbreich, Assael, Ben-David & Bornstein, 1976) as a secondary response to the stress of the condition, but this view did not commend itself to Carroll & Steiner (1978) in presenting the case for a more direct influence of the pituitary hormone. They emphasized that the timing of the onset and offset of both physical and psychological dysphoric symptoms corresponded with the luteal elevation and menstrual decrease in serum prolactin levels. Still, Clare (1983) could find no association between raised prolactin levels and premenstrual or psychiatric symptomatology, although episodic hormone secretion, and the existence of a diurnal rhythm in prolactin secretion, poses problems. Most workers have collected blood samples for assay during the morning, when prolactin levels are low, whereas differences might emerge more readily between samples collected at night, when most prolactin secretion occurs. But even with these considerations in mind, the later work of Steiner *et al.* (1984) failed to establish any relationship between serum prolactin concentrations and premenstrual tension. Suppression of prolactin secretion in women with high blood levels of prolactin by treatment with bromocriptine has been reported to be beneficial, but this drug could also be acting directly upon dopaminergic systems in the brain, or having a placebo effect. Others (Rubinow & Roy-Byrne, 1984) remain unconvinced of the existence of any effect at all, except an easing of cyclic breast pain.

Indirect evidence for a role of prolactin in the premenstrual syndrome comes from the actions of prolactin in causing the retention of water, sodium and potassium, and consideration of the effects of other treatments which may suppress prolactin secretion or antagonize its peripheral effects. Here the interactions of prolactin with other hormones could be complex, in that high prolactin levels together with low oestrogen may induce depressive symptoms and high prolactin and low progesterone symptoms of anxiety or irritable hostility. On the other hand, high levels of prolactin and oestrogen, a condition which obtains in late pregnancy, may generate euphoria. Sadly, it seems that women who experience euphoria are more likely to succumb to post-partum depression.

An elevation of mood has been reported to occur in women given thyrotrophic hormone-releasing factor, which is known to increase the secretion of prolactin. This conclusion is based upon a heightened sense of well-being, or on a greater incidence of smiling and laughing. Winokur, Amsterdam, Mihailovíc & Caroff (1982) gave TRF or saline on a double-blind basis to normal young women. The peptide produced side-effects, such as a sense of urinary urgency, mild nausea, light-headedness and occasional tingling sensations in the arms, alongside suggestions that anxiety was diminished and a sense of relaxation increased. The expected rises in plasma TSH were produced, but, regrettably, prolactin was not assayed.

10

Hormones and aggression

It is generally known that hormones can generate aggressive behaviour, for the quieting of domestic animals by the removal of the testes (and hence of testicular hormones) is a practice of long antiquity. The rut in stags, like the breeding season in rams, is marked by the development of aggressive, as well as sexual, behaviour and is abolished by castration. This procedure has often been regarded as effective in reducing excessive aggressive behaviour in man, although close analysis of the type of behaviour studied leads to a less optimistic view and limits generalization to sexual offenders, where success has been reported in the treatment of the sexual aggression of the rapist by this means (Meyer-Bahlburg, 1981). Antiandrogenic drugs, such as cyproterone acetate and medroxyprogesterone, have been used to reduce aberrant sexual behaviour and a reduction in plasma testosterone concentration of some 50–75 per cent seems to be necessary, with the effects being specific for disordered sexual thoughts and behaviours; non-sexual violent outbursts are less affected (Rubin, Reinisch & Haskett, 1981).

Among the difficulties inherent in the study of the relationship of hormones to aggression is that concerning definition of the term 'aggression', although most would take this to mean behaviour aimed at inflicting damage to persons or property. The range of behaviours that might be regarded as falling under this heading has been reviewed by Brain (1979), who distinguishes between hazard, role-related, criminal, sexual, sex-role related and clinical categories. Because of such variety it may be unreasonable to search for a common physiological mechanism upon which hormones might act (Conner, 1972), unless this forms the lowest common denominator in a range. Experimental work has not proved very helpful, for much has been concerned with pain- or shock-induced aggression in rats, or isolation-induced fighting in male mice, where the relevance to the human situation is dubious. Nevertheless, brain systems can generate aggressive behaviour, with the limbic complex being particularly prominent. In general, forebrain structures appear to inhibit aggressive responses while parts of the amygdala may be excitatory. A man who killed his wife and mother and later shot 38 people from the tower of the University of Texas was found at autopsy to have a tumour in the amygdaloid area, and many other cases of violent behaviour stem from temporal lobe epilepsy (Johnson, 1972). There is the striking case of a young man of 19 who suffered a series of seizures accompanied by paroxysms of aggressive and violent behaviour, when attacks on his mother, brother or nurses occurred. Since the attacks persisted in spite of all medical therapy, the anterior portions of both temporal lobes were removed surgically, with devastating consequences. There was a loss of memory, a lack of recognition of close friends and relatives and the development of an insatiable appetite. Further, there was a complete loss of all emotional behaviour, with no rage reactions and a marked resistance to stimuli aimed at evoking rage. These changes persisted, although the generalized epileptic attacks reappeared several months after the operation (Terzian & Ore, 1955). In numerous other cases, electrical stimulation of the amygdala or hippocampus was followed by aggressive behaviour directed at the therapist which lasted until the current was switched off, when it ended abruptly. As in the case just described, bilateral lesions in the temporal lobe abolished attacks of rage seemingly generated within the amygdala (Stevens *et al.*, 1969; Moyer, 1981). Nevertheless, the association is by no means conclusive and it is argued that there is no consistent evidence linking temporal spike phenomena to aggression (Kligman & Goldberg, 1975).

A decade ago, the US National Institute of Neurological Diseases and Stroke convened a meeting of leaders in basic science and clinical research to review and evaluate the literature and other unpublished data on brain function and aggressive behaviour (Goldstein, 1974). Some participants could not conceive of a rationale for lesions of the limbic system in any non-epileptogenic clinical condition in man. This was not to say that they discounted the likelihood that the limbic system, and in particular the amygdala, was a high priority candidate for such lesions, but simply reflected the lack of solid information on the reciprocal connections between the neocortex and limbic system structures. In the course of a survey of the relationship of the limbic system to aggression, Eichelman (1983) highlighted the contradictions in the literature, for alongside the cases in which damage to the limbic system has been associated with violent behaviour or rage must be weighed the reports of patients with limbic lobe lesions who were not aggressive, and there are many. Likewise, not all of the attempts to reduce aggressive behaviour by deliberate placement of lesions in the amygdala have been successful.

In monkeys, a marked increase in agonistic behaviour, a reduction in fear towards normally frightening objects such as snakes or man, hyperorality, including coprophagia and uriposia, and inappropriate sexual behaviour have all been reported to follow damage to the amygdaloid nuclei, while a lack of maternal behaviour, a tendency toward reduced social interactions and a decrease in social rank has also been seen. Changes of this nature were first observed in the experiments of Klüver & Bucy (1937) and this behavioural complex has come to be known as the Klüver–Bucy syndrome. Sometimes heightened aggression has been noted, and Kling (1974) thought that this paradoxical effect was restricted to females. However, no striking effects of bilateral amygdaloid lesions upon behaviour or endocrine function in female rhesus monkeys emerged in other work (Spies *et al.*, 1976). There was no suggestion of any increase in overt aggression or of threat directed toward adult males. Attack behaviour can be elicited by electrical stimulation of the brains of rhesus monkeys, but the outcome is influenced by social and sexual factors (Dixson, 1980). The human counterpart of the Klüver–Bucy syndrome in monkeys is well-known, and the case of Terzian & Ore (1955) is but one example. Hypersexuality commonly occurs (Gerstenbrand, Poewe, Aichner & Saltuari, 1983), but this lacks any hormonal basis and rather reflects loss of behavioural inhibition derived from higher centres. The hypersexuality is expressed both verbally and in attempted sexual interaction without signs of shame.

There is reasonably good evidence that androgens impose a masculine pattern of aggression upon the brain when present at the appropriate developmental stage. Most information comes from the rat, although androgens given prenatally to rhesus monkeys increase sexually dimorphic aggressive behaviours such as rough-and-tumble play, pursuit, and threat behaviour pre-pubertally (Goy & Phoenix, 1971). Sex differences in aggressiveness are readily apparent in children well before puberty, with physical assaults upon peers being a very stable behavioural parameter among boys, but not girls, over the first ten years of life. Alongside the imposition of a pattern of sexual behaviour to be manifest in adult life, exposure to steroids early in development could modify other behavioural characteristics, such as aggression (Goldstein, 1974; Reinisch, 1974). Female rhesus monkeys exposed to androgen *in utero* show more rough-and-tumble play and threat behaviour than their normal female peers, but information concerning man must be gleaned from clinical studies.

Androgen-insensitive children may perform poorly in tests of dominance, while studies of cases of congenital adrenal hyperplasia are inconclusive. Meyer-Bahlburg & Ehrhardt (1982) point out that even if androgens were shown to be effective, then several additional extra-neural factors may complicate interpretation. Thus, the condition of the genitalia (incompletely masculinized in males, virilized in females) may influence gender identity and self-image. The level of physical activity may influence the choice of playmates and affect the chance of aggression-producing encounters in the peer group, while the degree of muscular development is likely to affect the outcome of aggressive encounters with peers and lay the foundations of the future expression of aggressive behaviour. All of these factors may be operative in patients, with particularly good evidence for an increase in the level of physical activity in cases of congenital adrenal hyperplasia.

Other children have been exposed to abnormal concentrations of progestogens and oestrogens during fetal life as a result of treatment of the mother for threatened abortion. Some progestational drugs have exerted androgenic effects and caused masculinization of the genitalia. The survey of Meyer-Bahlburg & Ehrhardt (1982) suggested a slight increase in aggressiveness in girls showing some sign of genital masculinization, as well as an increase in aggression-related activities in males and females exposed to various progestogens and in males exposed to combinations of diethylstilboestrol and progesterone. Only inconsistent results were available for males and females treated with progesterone and for males given diethylstilboestrol, and there was some decrease in aggressiveness in boys from diabetic pregnancies exposed to oestrogen–progesterone combinations. But a variety of problems remain. It is not clear whether the pregnancy disorder for which hormones were given may have affected the neural development of the offspring, while the sample sizes and number of control studies are few. [A study of the effect of medroxyprogesterone acetate, regarded as an anti-androgen, showed a trend toward diminished aggression in subjects exposed to the drug, as compared to matched controls, but Meyer-Bahlburg & Ehrhardt (1982) could reach no firm conclusions about the influence of sex hormones in the development of aggressive behaviour.]

As we have seen, clinical studies with virilized children concur with the laboratory findings in monkeys in that more rough-and-tumble play and tomboy behaviour is manifest (Reinisch, 1976; Dixson, 1980). Even so, tomboy behaviour is not to be equated with aggressive behaviour, as Money & Schwartz (1976) concluded from a retrospective review of 15 virilized girls, 11 of whom considered themselves superior to their peers in athletic ability. Tomboyism was self-defined by such traits as a lack of interest in stereotypically girlish doll play or in games such as jump rope, and a preference for competitive sports and athletics. As a group, the girls were not given to striving for leadership or to asserting dominance over others, and there were few instances of fighting or the manifestation of anger. The lack of aggressiveness could be accounted for by pressure on the part of parents to emphasize feminine characteristics during the upbringing of their child, but this did not prevent the expression of tomboyism. It is also possible that the superior physique of the children inhibited challenge by their peers, but it could be argued that in order to be accepted by a group of boys a tomboy girl must not be too assertive or dominant. Aggressiveness might in this way be inhibited by other social needs. However, the work of Money and his colleagues with virilized children has not escaped criticism (Quadagno, Briscoe & Quadagno, 1977) on the basis that the measures of aggressive behaviour were considered to be crude and that the incidence of aggressive behaviour may have been underestimated because of the reluctance of the affected children and their parents to report non-sex-stereotypic behaviour. One point hindering cross-species comparisons is that testosterone is used in most experimental studies to cause masculinization in females, whereas other androgens are involved in pathological conditions in human female fetuses. In turn, a selective or discriminative action on the part of individual androgens is predicated, but not proven.

Adolescence is associated with an increase in aggressive behaviour in males and the change can be related to an increase in androgen production at this time. However, observations in a range of primates indicate that prepubertal castration does not prevent a male from occupying an elevated position in the dominance hierarchy and that androgen treatment does not necessarily enhance aggressiveness or dominance (Dixson, 1980). Castration has much less effect upon the aggressive behaviour of male monkeys than upon sexual responses, with social factors being more important than androgen in controlling aggressive interaction. The trouble from the point of view of scientific investigation is that social and hormonal factors interact. Not only can hormones influence social behaviour, but, in turn, social factors can influence the secretion of hormones (Mazur & Lamb, 1980). Thus the analysis and interpretation of observations can prove to be complicated.

In discussing the effects of testosterone on human behaviour the studies on normal volunteers should be separated from those on aggressive and violent prisoners. Normal individuals show no consistent correlation between the concentrations of testosterone in circulation and various psychological measures of hostility and aggression, whereas measures of plasma testosterone in overtly aggressive, assaultive and violent male prisoners have been more in agreement in demonstrating a relationship between such behaviour and steroid level (Rubin, Reinisch & Haskett, 1981). Plasma testosterone levels often do not differ between fighting and non-fighting prisoners, or correlate well with paper-and-pencil tests of irritability and hostility, but groups of prisoners with long records of crimes against the person have been reported to have higher testosterone levels than control prisoners. Comparisons of testosterone levels between aggressive and non-aggressive prisoners suggest a positive association between a high hormone level and aggressive behaviour, but

> 'some of the authors had to turn all stones before they could come up with any positive findings. Also, all reports appear incomplete with regard to the number of variables tested statistically which obviates the evaluation for spuriousness of correlations. Thirdly, none of these studies confirm each others' positive findings, mostly because of lack of comparability of sample selection criteria and assessment methods.'

(Meyer-Bahlburg, 1981.)

The difficulties in interpretation are well-illustrated by the report of Matthews (1979), who describes a pathologically aggressive prison inmate who was given the anti-androgenic drug cyproterone acetate. When taking this compound the prisoner experienced a reduction in sexual drive and a marked decrease in aggressive impulses, with a reversion to his customary condition when the drug was withdrawn. This result prompted a comparison of plasma testosterone concentrations between 11 men with a history of, and convicted for, violent crime, and 11 detainees pair-matched for age, height, weight and time spent in prison after conviction for non-violent crimes and with no history of aggressive tendencies. There was no difference in the plasma levels of testosterone and the suspicion remains that the attention given to this steroid may be mis-directed, with the influence of other steroids requiring re-examination. Under more normal circumstances, those of boys in a Stockholm suburb, an association between plasma testosterone concentrations and self-reports of physical and verbal aggression has been seen. A relationship between a lack of frustration tolerance, or impatience, and testosterone levels also emerged which was not related to adolescent physical development (Olweus, Mattsson, Schalling & Löw, 1980).

One of the disturbances associated with the chromosomal abnormality of an XYY karyotype in men is a tendency toward persistently violent behaviour, and in this light the plasma androgen levels in such individuals have been measured. The values obtained, while showing a large variability, have almost always been comparable to those of controls and rarely above the normal range. However, the antisocial acts of XYY men show a dearth of violent episodes toward other persons (Rubin, Reinisch & Haskett, 1981). In a double-blind controlled study of 12 XYY and 16 XXY men (Schiavi, Theilgaard, Owen & White, 1984), the XYY men showed significantly higher plasma concentrations of testosterone, FSH and LH than matched control groups while the XXY men had higher levels of FSH, LH

and prolactin, but low concentrations of testosterone. Th_
differences is not clear. There was a higher incidence of crimina_
in the XXY men than among the controls, but this could be attri_
lower intellectual level. There was also no support for the idea tha_
men are particularly violent or aggressive. A correlation emerged betw_
increased blood levels of testosterone and criminal convictions across all _
the men surveyed, but this was not linked to aggressive tendencies.

Fearfulness may be the opposite side of the coin to aggressiveness, although the outward manifestation of behaviour need not reflect internal feelings and the simultaneous expression of some components of fear and aggression is often seen, as in the aggression of the desperately afraid. In rodents the female is less fearful than the male, while in man the reverse appears to be true. There is a preponderance of women among patients suffering from the phobias, and women report more fears than men. In rats, oestrogen appears to reduce fearfulness, as indicated by less fearful behaviour during oestrus and upon treatment with the hormone. Androgen is of little significance in this regard (Gray, 1971).

Underlying much of the preceding discussion is the presumption that men are more aggressive than women – an expectation that may be unjustified (Frodi, Macaulay & Thome, 1977). Human males have been shown to be more aggressive than females in a variety of contexts, and, clinically, boys are approximately four times as likely as girls to show antisocial behaviour, which frequently includes an aggressive element. Sex differences are apparent in aggressive behaviours at the toddler stage of development and are maintained through childhood and adolescence and across cultures (Shaffer, Meyer-Bahlburg & Stokman, 1980). It may be that women shy away from physical aggression more than men, but little difference emerges from careful comparisons. It also seems that this type of behaviour is powerfully shaped by training in childhood and by social forces, which points to caution in the interpretation of hormonal responses. The relentless search for a link between testosterone secretion and aggressiveness also merits review, for there are other hormones that might be just as influential but devoid of androgenic activity.

Increases in irritability and aggression may be attributes of the premenstrual syndrome, but are variable in frequency. One reviewer of the prevalence of premenstrual irritation concluded that 6–13 per cent of women experienced severe premenstrual irritability, while 20–60 per cent regularly show irritation of moderate intensity (Floody, 1983). Much depends upon the survey technique employed and this varies from questionnaires sent to women selected randomly from the records of physicians, and from the review of the histories of women treated for the premenstrual syndrome or severe premenstrual tension, to questionnaires sent to university students, the wives of graduate students, or to nurses. None can be taken to represent the population at large. Studies of overt aggression, primarily by institutionalized women, and of mood fluctuation in more diverse populations, concur in suggesting that women experience increases in aggressiveness near the time of menstruation, decreases in aggressiveness near ovulation, or both types of change. But even if this conclusion were to approach the truth, there is little understanding of the hormonal basis. Androgens can increase the aggressiveness of female monkeys, but behavioural changes in intact female primates in parallel with changes in endogenous oestrogen levels have been difficult to discern. The significance of androgens in influencing aggression in women has been explored by Persky (1974), who followed the changes of plasma testosterone in 29 normal young women and observed peak values around the time of ovulation. However, there was remarkably little variation in the measures of anxiety, hostility or depression, and no peak in aggressiveness at mid-cycle. The therapeutic value of progesterone in reducing irritability and aggressiveness in women is similarly doubtful.

It was pointed out thirty years ago that aggressive animals have higher concentrations of noradrenaline in their adrenal glands than typically non-aggressive animals, and other studies suggested that anger, hostility or aggressive impulses were associated with rises in blood pressure possibly indicative of noradrenaline release (Mason, 1968b). Some have found that individuals who tend to be aggressive and more apt to display hostility and anger tend to excrete more noradrenaline, and that adrenaline excretion is more likely to predominate in individuals who characteristically react in a passive anxious manner, but the thoughtful appraisal of the literature by Mason (1968b) sets out the many problems and pitfalls of work in this area.

11

Hormones and the control of food intake

The control of food intake is no simple matter, with factors such as smell, taste, appearance, the conditioned reflexes attached to a meal, and internal influences, such as hypothalamic activity, the products of digestion, and gastro-intestinal and other hormones all contributing. Yet the precision evident in the mechanisms controlling food intake is seldom appreciated. This accuracy is demonstrable by a few calculations, such as one based upon the observation that an average woman gains about 11 kg between the ages of 25 and 65. During this period she eats roughly 20 tons of food, and yet her weight increase corresponds to an average daily error of only 350 mg of food over the amount needed for energy balance (Hervey, 1969).

The role of the hypothalamus

Numerous elements interact in the control of eating behaviour, which is itself far from simple (Lytle, 1977). Consider the variables introduced by meal size, meal length, intermeal interval, the selection of a balanced diet from the nutrients available, the influence of food palatability, dietary preferences and religious taboos. Even if attention is focussed upon the neurohumoral mechanisms, distinctions should be made between the signals arising from various parts of the digestive tract, such as the mouth, stomach and intestine. It is thus not surprising that a variety of factors act through the hypothalamus to control food intake. This is not the place to discuss the neural mechanisms in detail, although lesions in the ventro-medial nuclei of the hypothalamus of rats have long been known to cause obesity whereas bilateral lesions of the lateral hypothalamus produce aphagia. In turn, it has been suggested that the lateral hypothalamus contains a feeding centre whose influence is counterbalanced by a satiety centre located in the medial hypothalamus. Medial and lateral hypothalamic damage produces extremes of eating and undereating in humans, as well as in rats and other animals (Panksepp, Bishop & Rossi, 1979). However, the old-established view of the hypothalamus as integrating the influences of two opposing centres has lost ground in the light of information indicating that the hypothalamus acts by signalling a set point for body weight, and that it is the set point that is affected by hypothalamic damage. When animals rendered obese by medial hypothalamic lesions are starved to cause a loss of weight and are then allowed free access to food they put on weight to reach the pre-starvation level, and no more. In turn, the set point theory has been attacked on the grounds that rats can be made obese by offering them a high-fat or 'junk-food' diet, that after short-term starvation rats fail to reach the weight or set point expected from normal growth-velocity curves, that there is a rapid weight gain before hibernation in mammals or in fat stores in birds before migration, and that there is an increase in body weight during pregnancy. These observations suggested to Morley & Levine (1983) that the set point is, at the least, extremely labile. Current concepts relating to eating and its disorders are surveyed in Stunkard & Stellar (1984).

The concept of two distinct centres located in the ventral hypothalamus is also regarded as a gross over-simplification (Morley, 1980; Morley & Levine, 1983). The so-called satiety centre in the medial hypothalamus is associated with two major tracts–a serotoninergic pathway originating in the raphe nuclei of the pontine–midbrain area and passing through the ventromedial hypothalamus, and the ventral adrenergic bundle, which passes through the perifornical area in the ventromedial hypothalamus and gives projections to the lateral hypothalamus. Lesions in the globus pallidus of the basal ganglia or of the substantia nigra in the midbrain produce aphagia, as do lesions of the lateral hypothalamus. Destruction of the ventral adrenergic bundle by either electrolytic lesions or the local action of pharmacological poisons also leads to a syndrome, including hyperphagia and obesity, which is similar to, but not identical with, that seen following damage to the ventromedial hypothalamus. The ventrolateral hypothalamus is associated with the dopaminergic nigrostriatal tract, and pharmacological or other damage to this pathway induces hypophagia and weight loss.

As well as feeding, these tracts appear to be associated with the reward or pleasure centres of the brain. Grossman (1979) concluded that the ventromedial satiety mechanism may influence feeding, in part because it exercises important inhibitory functions with respect to the individual's hedonic response to sensory input, and in part because it exercises control over endocrine and metabolic processes that regulate energy use and storage. Catechol- and possibly also indoleaminergic projections from the lower brain stem, as well as inputs from the amygdala and periamygdaloid cortex, seem to influence food intake but the nature of their action is as yet poorly understood. There is also the important point that rats with lesions in the lateral hypothalamus show a number of permanent disturbances, in addition to hyperphagia, which can modify behaviour in general. Thus there is no feeding in response to a reduction in blood sugar level, a depressed drinking response upon dehydration, the salivary reflexes are depressed, the feeding response to sodium deficiency is reduced, and learning in taste aversion tests is impaired. There is also depressed arousal, motor impairment, depressed affect, and a depressed tolerance for stress (Shepherd, 1983). The consequences of damage to the lateral hypothalamus are thus hardly restricted to an interference with food intake. These considerations can be set out in a slightly different way, for in the eyes of Norgren & Grill (1982) the hegemony of the hypothalamus in the control of feeding behaviour was broken by two seemingly disparate developments. First came the discovery of long ascending catecholaminergic systems passing through the hypothalamus to innervate the limbic system, basal ganglia and neocortex, with the realization that destruction of the dopaminergic system arising from the substantia nigra and ventral tegmental areas reproduced the behavioural deficits arising from lateral hypothalamic destruction in the absence of any damage to the hypothalamus. And then came appreciation of the fact that the hypothalamic lesions that abolished eating also induced profound neglect of sensory stimuli over a range of modalities. In turn, pharmacological lesions of the dopaminergic system in the midbrain were also seen to result in sensory neglect. A descending influence of the hypothalamus also needs to be taken into account, for after section of the vagus nerve in the neck stimulation of lateral hypothalamic sites that previously elicited feeding behaviour ceases to have that effect. In this light it is not necessary for hormones to act upon the hypothalamus to influence behaviour: they could act at some distance.

The autonomic activities of the hypothalamus figure in suggestions that obesity is caused by an imbalance between sympathetic and parasympathetic activity, and disturbance of pancreatic function (Powley & Laughton, 1981; Bray, Inoue & Nishizawa, 1981). Section of the vagus nerve depresses food intake and reduces the hyperinsulinaemia in animals with lesions in the ventromedial nuclei, and removal of the pancreatic islets from any direct neural influence (by transplantation of fetal pancreatic tissue to the kidney capsule after destruction of the endogenous pancreatic islets) prevents the development of hyperphagia, or the increase in serum insulin seen after damage to the ventromedial nuclei. These observations imply that the hyperinsulinaemia of hypothalamic obesity is primarily under neural control, although the relative contributions of the sympathetic and parasympathetic systems remain uncertain. Because long-term vagotomized animals can still be rendered hyperphagic by hypothalamic lesions, and over-eating occurs in lesioned diabetic animals given exogenous insulin, it is unwise to attribute hyperphagia solely to overactivity of the pancreatic islets (Panksepp, Bishop & Rossi, 1979). Visual and olfactory stimuli provoke insulin secretion in humans (Parra-Covarrubias, Rivera-Rodriguez & Almarez-Ugalde, 1971) and there are suggestions that this response is more readily evoked in the obese than in normal individuals.

Metabolic signals

Over the years many have tried to identify the metabolic signal used by the hypothalamus to control food intake. Glucose has long been a prime candidate, with hunger resulting when the blood sugar level fell below a certain threshold, and satiety when the glucose concentration returned to normal. This concept provided the basis of the glucostatic theory, with variations emphasizing the rate of glucose utilization, and the operation of insulin-sensitive cells. There are glucose receptors in the hypothalamus: the local application of glucose or insulin affects the firing rate of neurons. Other candidates for the role of metabolic signal include fatty acids and amino acids, and they may well all act in concert (Castonguay, Applegate, Upton & Stern, 1983; Morley & Levine, 1983).

A possible direct action of insulin upon the hypothalamus in controlling food intake has attracted particular attention. Insulin receptors have been detected in the rat brain, with the highest concentrations being found in the olfactory bulb, cerebral cortex and hypothalamus. Insulin itself was present in some areas in concentrations ten times that of plasma, and was indistinguishable from purified insulin in a variety of assays and test procedures. The induction of peripheral insulin excess, or lack, does not affect the brain concentration of the hormone and there is evidence for the synthesis of insulin by neural tissue (Havrankova, Brownstein & Roth, 1981). Others (van Houten & Posner, 1981) have speculated that insulin may act directly to influence the activity of nerve terminals in the arcuate nucleus and median eminence region of the hypothalamus: that this area may 'sense' the blood level of insulin. In this way, insulin could serve as a signal in the mechanisms controlling food intake and hunger. Insulin can enter the brain through the circumventricular organs, which provide gaps in the blood–brain barrier, but movement is slow and limited. The experimental introduction of insulin into the hypothalamus is known to alter the electrical activity of neurons, to activate central glucostatic reflexes, to suppress feeding and to modify the turnover of noradrenaline.

There is a strong physiological connection between the degree of adiposity and the plasma concentration of insulin, and support for the idea that insulin levels may provide the signal controlling food intake and the maintenance of a steady body weight (Porte & Woods, 1981). Overeating or weight gain would be accompanied by an increase in plasma insulin concentration that would operate to curb appetite and limit any further gain in weight. The fact that insulin secretion varies from hour to hour, or even from minute to minute, depending upon feeding, exercise, arousal, stress and emotional state, need not detract from this view, for studies of the CSF concentration of insulin in experimental animals indicate that, so far as the brain is concerned, the rapid fluctuations in plasma insulin are greatly damped. Therefore, CSF insulin concentrations could provide an integrated signal representative of the overall plasma insulin concentration.

In general, it seems that hormones acting to enhance anabolic processes tend to increase feeding, while many catabolic hormones have the opposite effect (Panksepp, Bishop & Rossi, 1979). Insulin is a good example of an anabolic hormone, while glucocorticoids serve to illustrate the catabolic category. High doses of glucocorticoids cause loss of appetite and body weight in animals, as do adrenaline, thyroxine and glucagon. The anabolic effects of the androgens, as body-builders, are well-known; oestrogens do not act in this way. Some observers have been impressed by the similarity between the effects of oestrogen administration and anorexia nervosa and have attempted to account for the syndrome on the basis of changes in oestrogen metabolism. Oestrogen reduces food intake and weight gain and it has been suggested that the neural structures concerned with feeding become hypersensitive to, and functionally depressed by, the steroid. In view of the low oestrogen concentrations in the blood of anorexic women, the increase in sensitivity of the control circuits would have to be marked; this remains to be proved.

Peptides
Because of the involvement of neuropeptides in other behavioural activities, including drinking (Chapter 2), it is not surprising that these substances influence food intake and meal size. Among the peptides reported to reduce meal size may be listed cholecystokinin, bombesin, somatostatin and caerulin. Most effort however has been devoted to the study of cholecystokinin, particularly as early work indicated that extracts of intestinal mucosa reduced meal size, and cholecystokinin is known to be released from the duodenal mucosa upon exposure to fatty acids in order to cause contraction of the gall bladder and discharge of bile into the intestine and an increased release of an alkaline pancreatic secretion (Woods *et al.*, 1981). Purified or

synthetic cholecystokinin reduces meal size in many species, including man, in a dose-dependent manner and there is evidence that the ingestion of foods that promote the secretion of cholecystokinin (such as egg yolk) reduces food intake. On this basis, cholecystokinin might act, in the absence of other factors like high palatability, to end a meal. The locus of action of cholecystokinin is not known and may be outside the brain. Somatostatin also limits food intake when given intraperitoneally, but not after intra-ventricular injection, so that a peripheral effect is indicated.

Several factors illustrate the behavioural specificity of cholecystokinin (Smith, 1983). Doses of up to 8 μg/kg inhibit food intake in food-deprived rats, but do not inhibit water intake in thirsty rats. When cholecystokinin inhibits food intake it does not produce any significant toxic effects in animals or man (Billington, Levine & Morley, 1983), and when the peptide inhibits sham-feeding in animals it elicits the behavioural patterns of satiety. Further, all of the known biological actions and receptor binding of cholecystokinin depend upon the presence of a sulphate group on the tyrosine moiety at the seventh position from the carboxyl end. Adjustment of the position of the sulphate group depresses biological activity.

At least part of the satiety action of cholecystokinin is exerted at the periphery, for the mechanism appears to involve the dispatch of signals down the vagus to generate some response in the gut that, in turn, elicits a further signal. This is illustrated by the observations of Moran & McHugh (1982) that doses of cholecystokinin too small to restrict food intake in rhesus monkeys nevertheless inhibited gastric emptying, and that if these small doses were combined with a small gastric load of physiological saline then a substantial inhibition of food intake resulted. As saline is not considered to cause the release of cholecystokinin, the operation of some other factor in the region of the stomach and acting synergistically with the peptide is implied. The abdominal vagus of the rat has three branches, and gastric vagotomy abolishes the satiating effect of cholecystokinin, whereas section of the coeliac or hepatic branches do not. It is thus likely that gastric vagal afferent fibres are involved in the limitation of food intake, through a contractile effect upon smooth muscle in the stomach, through a reduction in the rate of gastric emptying, or through a direct action on the vagal afferents.

Another point in favour of cholecystokinin as a physiological satiety factor arises from the use of a specific competitive antagonist, proglumide. This substance blocks the satiety effect of exogenous cholecystokinin, as well as the action of the peptide on pancreatic secretion and on gall bladder and intestinal motility. It has also increased the food intake of rats given a food pre-load (to release endogenous cholecystokinin) followed by a test meal 20 minutes later (Shillabeer & Davison, 1984).

Despite the attractions of cholecystokinin as a satiety hormone, a big question concerning the physiological nature of the observations remains. Harvey (1983) has argued that a satiety effect of cholecystokinin should be seen with doses that produce (say) half the maximum gall bladder contraction. This would correspond with the degree of gall bladder contraction seen after a fatty meal (variable, but usually between 30 and 70 per cent). The doses of the peptide producing a satiety effect in man have been 12 to 30 times the dose necessary to cause the customary degree of gall bladder contraction occurring post-prandially, and in one study where only a six-fold greater dose was used food intake seemed to be increased rather than decreased.

Endogenous opiates appear to be involved in the generation of a drive to feeding, as shown by the response to naloxone (the opiate antagonist), which reduces food intake in the obese, in patients with the Prader–Willi syndrome or traumatic hypothalamic hyperphagia, and in normal individuals in whom feeding was induced by 2-deoxyglucose. Conversely, exogenous and endogenous opiates can stimulate food intake. The functions of opiates may spread to the integration of several systems, for the deprivation of food in the rat produces significant analgesia, and in the hungry rat there is an increase in endogenous opiate activity (Morley, 1980; Morley & Levine, 1983). Caution must be exercised in transferring the results of animal studies to the human situation, for the role of endogenous opioids in modulating feeding behaviour may be species dependent (Lowy & Yim, 1983). There is now an extensive literature dealing with the possible role of opiates in the control of appetite (Morley, Levine, Yim & Lowy, 1983), but much is concerned with the rat, whose pattern of food intake differs considerably from that of man. Rats consume most of their food during the dark phase of the lighting cycle, whereas the hamster, another laboratory rodent, consumes small intermittent meals at approximately 2-hourly intervals. It may be significant that many observations made on the rat are not transferable to the hamster. A further complication is that some foodstuffs contain biologically active peptides, akin to the peptides found in the brain and gut. Some are opiate-like peptides, and, by analogy with the endorphins, have been called 'exorphins', but they seem to have less effect upon food intake. Rather do they slow the passage of food along the intestinal tract and promote greater absorption (Harvey, 1983).

Numerous other peptides influence feeding, although it can be difficult to distinguish between physiological and pharmacological effects. Calcitonin is a peptide hormone secreted by the C cells of the thyroid gland and serves to reduce the concentrations of calcium and phosphorus in the plasma by promoting bone resorption and calcium release and, more rapidly, by decreasing the reabsorption of calcium, phosphorus and other electrolytes in the kidney (Freed, Bing, Andersen & Wyatt, 1984). Numerous physiological stimuli serve to increase calcitonin secretion, including feeding, calcium and the gut hormones cholecystokinin and gastrin, as well as glucagon, triglycerides and amines. Many of these stimuli arise from feeding, but the fact that eating promotes calcitonin secretion in man remains controversial. The point is important because of the experimental evidence that post-prandial increases in the blood level of calcitonin may exert an anorexic action and so limit food intake. Injections of calcitonin reduce food intake in rats and monkeys, but the information for man is controversial and increased concentrations of calcitonin in the blood of patients with anorexia have not been reported. Any lack of change in anorexic patients is not necessarily significant, as anorexia may stem from a variety of causes. Calcitonin probably acts on the brain by inhibiting the uptake of calcium by hypothalamic neurons.

Corticotrophin-releasing factor is another peptide whose activities extend to an influence over feeding, possibly as part of an overall response to stress. Accordingly, there is the suggestion that the anorexia associated with stress may arise from an increase in CRF activity within the hypothalamus (Morley, 1980; Morley & Levine, 1983).

Monoamines

The monoamines are inevitably closely involved in the control of food intake (Lytle, 1977; Panksepp, Bishop & Rossi, 1979). The satiety mechanism is thought to be under positive serotoninergic control, and food intake restrained, in that serotonin agonists produce anorexia. Conversely, pharmacological depletion of serotonin in the brain causes hyperphagia. However, since waking, sexual behaviour and aggressiveness are also inhibited by this means there is uncertainty over the specificity of the response. Likewise, much experimental work on the role of the monoamines, and upon the appetite-suppressing effects of amphetamine (a monoaminergic agonist), has been undertaken in the belief that dual hunger and satiety mechanisms were operative in the hypothalamus and in ignorance of the actions of peptides.

The application of noradrenaline to the medial hypothalamus of experimental animals induces feeding, and depletion reduces food intake. Dopamine acts as an appetite stimulant and may be involved in stress-induced eating in the rat. Fittingly, dopamine antagonists suppress deprivation-induced feeding. A further possible participant is γ-aminobutyric acid, which inhibits the serotoninergic satiety system and frees the noradrenergic feeding component from restraint. Monoamines could influence food intake, at least in part, by altering the secretion of hormones from the pituitary gland. Thus, an increase in ACTH output would secondarily raise the blood level of glucocorticoids and in turn perhaps affect the appetite. Growth hormone is another factor that might operate in this way. The rate of secretion of this hormone varies as a function of changes in plasma levels of glucose and amino acids, and the subsequent increase in lipolysis and the production of fatty acids could serve as a satiety signal. On the other hand, many people tend to increase their food intake when they are emotionally upset or under stress (Lytle, 1977), and these are circumstances when growth hormone secretion would be expected to be high (Chapter 12).

Anorexia nervosa

It is natural to proceed from a review of the brain mechanisms controlling food intake to a discussion of anorexia nervosa, although it should be emphasized that the connection remains fragile, and could be erroneous. Still, hormonal changes are prominent in the condition and cannot be neglected.

The factors responsible for the appearance of anorexia nervosa have attracted much thought in recent years, particularly as the incidence of this disease has been said to be rising. Although regarded as a disease of modern society, the condition was carefully described more than 300 years ago, and it is suggested that there may be 10000 severely affected patients in Britain at any one time (Crisp, 1983). The weight loss produced by vigorous dieting can generate amenorrhoea in women, and in some cases many progress to a disturbed perception of body image, as well as disturbance of the feelings of hunger and satiety. In a discussion of the aetiology of anorexia, Hsu (1983) outlined six main theories. There is the socio-cultural theory, which highlights the pressures for physical attractiveness exerted by society; the family pathology theory, which emphasizes family pressures; and the individual psychoanalytical theory, concerned with the struggle for a self-respecting identity. Then there is the developmental psychobiology theory, reflecting the need of the individual to avoid adolescent and related family turmoil, even if the price paid in terms of the illness is high; the primary hypothalamic dysfunction idea, which takes account of the role of the hypothalamus in the control of food intake; and, lastly, the view that anorexia is simply an atypical affective disorder. None of the theories need represent the sole answer to the clinical problem, and none is based upon neuroendocrine principles. The very diversity of view illustrates the dilemma of the physician.

Originally it was thought that the reproductive changes seen in anorexic women were simply a consequence of loss of body weight, or of starvation, but closer study, or changes in the patient population, makes it seem that anywhere between 20 and 65 per cent of women developing anorexia cease to menstruate prior to dieting or weight loss (Katz & Weiner, 1980). However, the difficulty of determining the timing of symptoms retrospectively needs to be borne in mind. Most patients resume menstruation when the body weight has returned to about 90 per cent of the normal value, but in some amenorrhoea persists.

The malnutrition arising from famine conditions sharply increases the incidence of amenorrhoea, and delays sexual maturation; the converse also applies, with improvements in the diet and plane of nutrition advancing the onset of puberty and improving fertility. Vigorous exercise alters body composition, reduces the amount of fat, and may lead to amenorrhoea. About one-third of competitive long-distance runners aged between 12 and 45 may suffer menstrual dysfunction, with the incidence of amenorrhoea being linked with the number of miles run weekly, a shift in the percentage of body fat, and the amount of stress experienced by the athlete in the course of training (Dale, Gerlach & Wilhite, 1979; Baker, 1981). Menarche is delayed in young ballet dancers by about three years, or, in swimmers and runners, by about 0.4 year for each year of pre-menarchial training (Warren, 1980; Frisch *et al.*, 1981). The delay has been attributed to a shift in body composition, with an alteration in the ratio of fat to other tissues. Alternative explanations include hormonal changes, an increased production of catecholamines and opioid peptides, an increased metabolic clearance of sex hormones, and adjustments in the metabolism of thyroid hormones (Rebar & Cumming, 1981), although Malina (1983) argues that the difference arises almost accidentally, because girls with delayed menarche select athletic pursuits. The later maturing girl has, on the average, longer legs for her stature, relatively narrow hips and a generally linear physique, alongside less weight for height and less fatness than her earlier maturing peers. Later maturation is associated with better performance on most motor tasks such as dashes, jumps and throws. Malina (1983) also suggests that early maturing girls are led away from participation in sports by social pressures, whereas the converse applies to late maturers.

About 20 per cent of women athletes cease menstruating before starting running, and a close parallel between anorexia nervosa and compulsive physical activity has been drawn by Yates, Leehey & Shisslak (1983), who speculate that both patterns of behaviour represent attempts to establish a personal identity. They point out that obligatory runners resemble anorexic women in terms of family background, socioeconomic class, and such personality characteristics as inhibition of anger, extraordinarily high self-expectations, tolerance of physical discomfort, denial of potentially serious disability, and a tendency towards depression. Anorexic women, and members of their families, are often compulsively athletic, and obligatory runners may demonstrate a bizarre preoccupation with food and an unusual emphasis on lean body mass. Of course, not all serious runners fall into this category, but there are athletes who demonstrate a single-minded commitment to physical effectiveness, such that depression and anxiety set in when running is not possible.

There is a fall in gonadotrophin secretion in anorexia nervosa (Brown *et al.*, 1983), with the blood level of LH being directly correlated with body weight and rising with recovery. In patients losing 25–40 per cent of body weight, the patterns of gonadotrophin secretion studied over the course of 24 hours show similarities with those of prepubertal girls. There can be a low level of LH throughout the 24-hour period, or only very small rises in LH output during sleep. With recovery, a reversion to the adult pattern is commonly, but not invariably, seen. In some way, the sensitivity of the pituitary gland to GnRF is depressed in anorexic patients, with the women showing the greatest weight loss producing the smallest increases in LH after an injection of GnRF. The return of responsiveness on the part of FSH to GnRF correlates linearly with the increase in body weight, while that for LH best fits a log–linear correlation (Brown *et al.*, 1983). Additionally, the secretion of FSH in response to GnRF returns to normal before that of LH. Repetitive treatment with GnRF is effective in restoring the sensitivity to releasing factor of the hypophysis to normal, even when the disease persists, and normal ovarian function can be restored. This observation supports the idea that the secretion of endogenous GnRF is disturbed in some way in the disease. Quite small alterations in the frequency of the episodic pulses generated by the hypothalamus could be responsible. Males are much less susceptible to anorexia nervosa than females, and account for less than 10 per cent of patients. Gonadotrophin secretion is similarly disturbed.

Basal growth hormone levels are elevated in some patients, but fall to normal upon an increase in calorie intake. The fall occurs before any gain in weight. A rise in plasma growth hormone is also seen during fasting, and is reversed during feeding, so that the changes in growth hormone secretion in anorexia nervosa are regarded as being secondary to the decrease in food intake (Brown *et al.*, 1983). The blood level of triiodothyronine can also be reduced, and is correlated with the fall in body weight.

Approximately half of the sufferers with anorexia nervosa exhibit elevated 24-hour mean levels of plasma cortisol, and this proportion is similar to that seen in cases of major depressive illness (Walsh, 1982). The abnormality subsides with recovery, but interpretation of these observations is not simple, for in the anorexic patient the metabolism of cortisol is slowed, while in depressed people cortisol metabolism is normal. Further, the slowed metabolism of cortisol may be due to reduced thyroid activity as a consequence of the lowered calorie intake. Adrenal steroids also reduce the sensitivity of the pituitary gland to TRF. On the other hand, although emaciated patients with anorexia nervosa secrete about the same quantity of cortisol daily as normal controls, when the cortisol secretion rate is related to body size then the production of cortisol by anorexic patients is seen to be significantly increased, and falls with recovery. Such observations have prompted the drawing of parallels between anorexia and depressive illness, particularly as some cases have responded to antidepressant therapy, but they could well reflect non-specific changes brought about by malnutrition.

Bulimia nervosa

Stressful conditions can cause eating (Morley, Levine & Rowland, 1983). This is evident from ethological studies, where animals approaching danger may indulge in a bout of grooming or eating before, or while, deciding to fight or flee. Mild tail pinching in rats can induce a variety of oral behaviours, including eating and gnawing, in the absence of attempts to escape or attack the source of irritation. Such behaviour may be reflected in man by nail biting under stress. Bulimia nervosa, or bulimarexia, may represent an extreme example of stress-induced eating. This syndrome is characterized by episodic binge eating, followed by vomiting in most cases, and may occur in association with anorexia nervosa. Pyle, Mitchell & Eckert (1981) have stressed that the onset of bulimic behaviour tends to be precipitated by a traumatic event occurring during a period of voluntary dieting. In their studies, 30 of 34 patients recalled some traumatic event associated with the onset of bulimic behaviour; the most common being loss or separation from a significant person in their life. Twenty-four people reported that a major trigger of individual binges was unhappiness, although others referred to anxiety, frustration or anger. Although stress may precipitate an episode, the sensation of stress does not appear to be alleviated by eating. There is no evidence that hormones are directly concerned in the genesis of bulimia nervosa, although animal studies indicate that the opioid peptides and corticotrophin-releasing factor might be involved (Morley, Levine & Rowland, 1983).

The link between anorexia nervosa and bulimia is steadily being strengthened, for it seems that 40–50 per cent of patients with primary anorexia exhibit bulimic behaviour. Anorexic patients behave as endogenously depressed individuals in showing resistance to the lowering of plasma cortisol by dexamethasone, and bulimic patients respond likewise. There may also be a delayed response in the secretion of TSH after giving TRF, and an abnormal secretion of growth hormone (Gwirtsman, Roy-Byrne, Yager & Gerner, 1983).

12

Hormones and emotion

Theoretical considerations of emotional behaviour have blossomed since Charles Darwin published his book on *The Expression of the Emotions in Man and Animals* in 1872. Numerous attempts at conceptual modelling have been made but not one has proved adequate. A recent effort, for example, assumes that there are eight basic emotions playing major adaptive roles in animals and man (Plutchik, 1980). These encompass fear and terror, anger and rage, joy and ecstasy, sadness and grief, acceptance and trust, disgust and loathing, anticipation, and surprise. Although progress is being made in relating particular patterns of hormonal activity to these facets of emotional life, there is relatively little understanding of the meaning of such patterns. Indeed, it may be that hormonal patterns are not classifiable into these categories, as is shown by the complexity of the hormonal changes seen under conditions of emotional stress – a situation which in any case does not easily fit into the classification noted above. Other theories emphasize evolutionary, ethological or sociobiological aspects, or direct attention toward changes in consciousness or cognition (Plutchik & Kellerman, 1980), and it is clear that a full appreciation of the role of hormones in emotional processes awaits advances in our grasp of the mechanisms generating emotional states. In this context, it may be surprising that innumerable studies of the physiology of mood and emotion are in print. This is largely because of preoccupations with the role of the catecholamines, and the possible actions of antidepressant drugs, for nearly all aspects of catecholamine metabolism touch upon behaviour and involve one or other aspect of their part in neurotransmission (McGeer & McGeer, 1980). In turn, catecholamine activity can be modulated by hormones, so that there is a ready means by which the endocrine system can influence emotion. Similarly, the neuropeptides described earlier are distributed in the brain in a fashion that makes them further candidates for influencing mood and emotion, and numerous behavioural effects have been described.

There is also the possible operation of neuropeptides as neuromodulators to be taken into account. Thus the neurohumoral bases of emotional reactions engage the attention of many clinicians and researchers and impinge upon many aspects of neurobiological function.

Emotional responses show several of the features of motivated behaviour. They can be purposive, adaptive, intense, persistent and periodic and, again like motivated behaviours, involve hypothalamic activity. The influence of hormones is exemplified by the extremes of thyroid hormone activity, for the hypothyroid individual, lacking adequate amounts of the hormone, is depressed, withdrawn and unhappy, while the hyperthyroid patient, burdened with an excessive hormone secretion, is irritable and emotionally extremely labile. Thus, thyroid hormones seem to provide an optimal setting for emotional reactions, with too much hormone leading to frenetic neurotransmitter activity and too little resulting in slowed neuronal interaction. Cortisol provides a good example of the way in which emotional responses can be influenced by a hormone in a seemingly unpredictable fashion. Raised blood levels of this steroid are known to produce euphoria in some individuals and depression in others (Chapter 3). Perhaps the outcome depends upon the level of monoamine turnover, or the degree of neurotransmitter tone. Another possibility needing to be explored is that neuropeptide function might be altered.

By assaying the plasma concentration of each of a range of hormones during a variety of emotional states, researchers have aimed to associate particular patterns of hormone secretion with particular moods. However, the endeavour has not been successful and has rather served to show that the assay findings provide an index of neurotransmitter function within the brain that is secondarily affecting hormone secretion. In fact, hormone assays are now serving to provide insight into the types of neuronal system active in the brain at the time of blood sampling, and are being used in the dissection of individual reactions to stress, as well as of the impact of different modes of stress. In this connection it is as well to recall that because of the involvement of brain aminergic systems in both the generation of emotional behaviour and the control of endocrine function (Chapter 3), the pharmacological manipulation of aminergic activity in an effort to alleviate emotional disturbances will have repercussions for the neuroendocrine system and that changes in the secretion of pituitary hormones can be expected.

It has never been easy to distinguish between the physiological responses to fear and anger. More than thirty years ago Ax (1953) followed the changes in heart rate, ballistocardiograph, respiratory rate, face and finger skin temperature, skin conductance and muscle tension in subjects led to generate fear or anger in a contrived situation. The broad spectrum of responses differed in that the number of rises in diastolic blood pressure, falls in heart rate, rises in skin conductance and increases in muscle potential were greater in anger than fear, and it was concluded that the reactions to anger were similar to those produced by adrenaline and noradrenaline together, and those to fear by noradrenaline alone. However, no index alone served to distinguish uniformly between the two states, and it appears that the level of sympathetic activity simply sets the pitch of the emotional response, with the outcome being dependent upon the circumstances in which the individual finds himself. This is illustrated by the varying responses to stress, described a little later on.

Anxiety may be regarded as a normal inborn response to threat, whether it be of bodily injury, attitudes or self esteem, or to the absence of people or objects that signify and assure safety. Subjective manifestations of anxiety range from a heightened sense of awareness to a deep fear of impending disaster, while the objective signs consist of an increased responsiveness to stimuli, restlessness and autonomic activation, with changes in heart rate and blood pressure (Kandel, 1983). Emotional reactions can be conditioned, as in rats given electric shocks to the feet in association with a flash of light or sound. Some look upon an emotional reaction simply as one end-result of a general arousal, in that there are suggestions that general emotional arousal facilitates aggressive behaviour, with the aggression being triggered, or restrained, by appropriate environmental cues. On this basis, there should be a common physiological response to emotional arousal, but the response elicited by a hormone can vary according to the cognitive state of the individual. In many people anxiety itself may form the primary or only manifestation of disease, and have no apparent cause. There is a range of anxiety disorders, and they can be divided into four categories: the phobic disorders, characterized by fear and avoidance of certain objects or situations and consequent restriction of normal activities; anxiety states, where there is fear, apprehension or anxiety without identifiable cause; and post-traumatic stress disorders, which represent pathological reactions to accidents and natural disasters and manifest themselves by nightmares, intrusive recollections and a compulsive reliving of past events. The fourth group, the atypical anxiety disorders, covers patients who appear to have primary anxiety but do not fall into the preceding categories (Brown, Mulrow & Stoudemire, 1984). Such a classification has the merit of simplicity, but will not satisfy all psychiatrists.

Rage and fear represent the most commonly reported behavioural disturbances with hypothalamic damage in adults and children over 2 years of age (Plum & Van Uitert, 1978). Characteristically, fully co-ordinated episodic outbursts of rage and fear occur, with normal behaviour being maintained between the storms. The emotions usually burst forth in response to a threatening stimulus, such as restraint or a delay in feeding, and generally include an intense autonomic component. Lesions having these effects involve the basal hypothalamus and the critical sites concern either the pathways descending from the cerebral cortex to the hypothalamus, or the ventromedial nuclear region where these inputs converge. In both situations the inhibitory influence of the telencephalic input to the hypothalamus is lost.

Direct evidence for involvement of the hypothalamus in emotional responses has come from studies of the consequences of electrical stimulation of this organ in conscious animals. In the cat, Hess & Akert (1955) reported that the animal assumes a typical defence posture, extends the claws and lashes the tail. There is hissing, spitting and growling, retraction of the ears and erection of the hairs on the back. At this stage of excitement, a slight movement on the part of the experimenter will serve to make him the object of a brisk and well-directed assault. When the stimulation is stopped there is a rapid breakdown of the syndrome, and a resumption of the customarily friendly attitude. Because the precise nature of the response depends upon the external stimuli provided by the experimenter, and not upon the parameters of the electrical input, such a complete pattern of behaviour is unlikely to arise simply from activation of a motor mechanism. Subsequent studies indicated the existence of two distinct patterns of behaviour: one 'affective–defensive', which included many of the features noted earlier, and another characterized by a relative absence of affective display, but in which stalking predominated. The affective reaction could be produced from much of the medial hypothalamus, whereas the latter response resulted from more lateral stimulation (Chi & Flynn, 1971).

Since the hypothalamus is part of the limbic system, it is no longer surprising that interference with the amygdaloid nuclei and other forebrain structures leads to marked changes in emotional behaviour. The limbic system receives a wide variety of visceral afferent stimuli and is a prime locus of the feedback action of hormones. Attacks of rage and aggression have been seen clinically in patients with lesions in the medial temporal lobes and orbital frontal cortex (Poeck & Pilleri, 1965) and an increase in aggressive behaviour is a common accompaniment of temporal lobe epilepsy (Devinsky & Bear, 1984). As part of the limbic system, the septum would be expected to be involved in the generation of emotional behaviour, and abnormal affective behaviour was evident in a series of patients with a tumour of this region (Zeman & King, 1958). Experimentally, damage to the amygdala produces emotional placidity. Wild, aggressive and fearful lynxes, agoutis and monkeys can be handled immediately after recovery of consciousness (Schreiner & Kling, 1956). Placidity has similarly been induced in the cat, dog, phalanger and man. Electrical stimulation of the amygdala in man elicits rage, violent and aggressive behaviour, and, with repetition of the stimulus, a feeling of intense fear and a desire to flee (Heath, Monroe & Mickle, 1955; Stevens *et al.*, 1969). Bilateral temporal lobe ablation has resulted in placidity (Terzian & Ore, 1955) and when lesions were made in the posterior hypothalamus of patients with pathologically aggressive behaviour they became markedly calm, passive and tractable, with an initial decrease in spontaneity. Intelligence was not impaired (Sano *et al.*, 1970).

In recent years it has become clear that the locus ceruleus, a noradrenergic centre located at the base of the fourth ventricle (Chapter 3), plays a major role in the control of anxiety. Electrical stimulation of this region in man produces feelings of fear and imminent death, while in monkeys stimulation of the locus causes alerting. As the intensity of stimulation increases the animals chew, grind their teeth, grasp the chair, pull their hair, wring their hands and struggle to escape. Such behaviours are also seen when monkeys are threatened by man or are given drugs activating the locus ceruleus. Bilateral lesions in the locus reduce the expression of anxiety in monkeys, as do drugs depressing neural activity in the area and known to decrease human anxiety (Redmond & Huang, 1979). One such drug is clonidine, while others that increase the activity of the locus ceruleus, like piperoxane and yohimbine, produce anxiety. There still remain doubts about the role of the locus ceruleus, in that selective destruction of the noradrenergic system of the rat by means of treatment with 6-hydroxydopamine does not produce the same changes as lesions made by electrolysis. It is also noteworthy that in rats, depletion of brain noradrenaline alone may not be sufficient to induce certain behavioural changes and that adrenalectomy is required in addition. Loss of the adrenal steroid corticosterone appears to be the factor concerned and it may be relevant that corticosterone binds strongly to the hippocampus, which also receives a substantial noradrenergic input (Mason & Fibiger, 1979). As Redmond & Huang (1979) suggest, the locus could serve as part of an alarm system with increasing levels of activation generating, in turn, attention, carefulness, interest, surprise, alerting, astonishment, alarm, anxiety, fear, panic and terror.

Changes in the excretion of noradrenaline and adrenaline were early used as an index of sympathetic involvement in the physiological response to emotional situations, and Elmadjian (1959) concluded that 'fight' sympathetic responses or active aggressive emotional displays were primarily associated with noradrenaline discharge and the 'flight' response or tense, anxious, but passive, emotional displays with adrenaline. Other work with astronauts in training support the general conclusion that noradrenaline excretion is associated with active aggressive action, and adrenaline excretion with apprehension and anxiety (Goodall, 1962). Of course, these peripheral changes in catecholamine activity do not necessarily parallel the changes occurring within the brain.

Stress

Studies of the endocrine response to fear, anxiety and stress were very important in early work on brain–endocrine interactions. At that time, in the 1950s, most attention was directed to the way in which a variety of apparently noxious influences enhanced ACTH secretion and adrenal steroid output; now, more subtle influences are being explored, for adverse physical stimuli need not necessarily activate the hypothalamo-pituitary system. Of possibly greater significance is the strangeness, unfamiliarity, or novelty of the stimulus (Mason, 1968a; Rose, 1980), for it is clear that individuals differ in their response to undesirable life events. There is also a problem in defining the term 'stress'. For some, any stimulus that provokes ACTH and adrenocortical hormone secretion is regarded as a stress, but then a particular stimulus may be stressful only for some individuals. Other investigators prefer to regard a particular stimulus as uniformly stressful, even though some individuals may not react in the anticipated manner. Surgery powerfully activates the hypothalamo-pituitary–adrenocortical system and cortisol secretion, but the prospect of surgery can be just as effective, as can admission to hospital, the prospect of a college or university examination, or the prospect of exhausting physical exercise. With repeated exposure to stress adaptation may occur. This has been shown in monkeys given the task of avoiding an electric shock by pressing a lever; considerable increases in cortisol secretion occurred over the first test period, but steadily lessened over subsequent occasions until little reaction was evident. Naive parachutists show a very large increase in cortisol, growth hormone and prolactin secretion at the time of their first jump, and this also wanes with experience, although accomplished parachutists may still show a brief anticipatory spurt of cortisol release before a jump takes place. The converse situation of a fall in adrenal steroid secretion under some circumstances has been much less studied, although a fall in adrenocortical activity at weekends has been documented for man and monkey (Mason, 1968a).

The individual differences in the response to stress appear to be related to defence or coping behaviour. In a classical study, Wolff and his colleagues (Wolff, Friedman, Hofer & Mason, 1964; Wolff, Hofer & Mason, 1964) looked at the output of adrenal steroids in the urine of parents watching their child die of leukaemia. Some parents were extremely demonstrative and even hysterical when discussing their child's illness, but excreted relatively normal amounts of corticosteroids. Other parents were much quieter, yet were deeply disturbed and showed an increased output of adrenal hormones. It also emerged that certain individuals coped with the emotional problem by denying the illness, and only when the denial was challenged did adrenal activation occur. Similar findings were obtained in a study of adrenal cortical function in young men during their first month of basic training in the US Army, where the level of steroid secretion was related to the degree to which they were able to isolate or protect themselves by any means possible from the demands of basic training and the likelihood of being severely humiliated or threatened by it. The less isolation or protection achieved, the greater the rate of adrenal hormone release. Concordant observations have been made under the hazardous conditions of the war in Vietnam (Rose, 1980).

Growth hormone is another factor that must be included in the constellation of hormones released in greater amount in association with stressful stimuli. Again, surgery, physical exercise, stressful interviews, watching particular films, examinations, venipuncture, and psychological testing are all effective, but growth hormone secretion is not generally as readily enhanced as that of ACTH, or, in turn, cortisol (Rose, 1980). In part, the dissociation may be related to stimulus intensity, for subjects showing growth hormone responses also show significant increases in cortisol secretion. Cortisol secretion was not always accompanied by growth hormone release, perhaps indicating that a greater provocative stimulus is needed to cause growth hormone release alongside that of cortisol. There is also the observation that subjects judged to be anxious but engaged during an episode of cardiac catheterization showed a rise only in cortisol secretion, whereas those who were anxious but not engaged with others secreted growth hormone as well as cortisol. The plasma growth hormone level was increased in about half of a group of middle-aged to elderly individuals interviewed about events surrounding the potential loss of a spouse hospitalized two months earlier. Those showing a raised blood level of growth hormone had higher anxiety scores, and the greater the defensiveness of the subject, the lower was the threshold at which anxiety evoked a response (Kosten *et al.*, 1984). Paradoxically, in children social stresses may serve to inhibit growth hormone secretion, so producing the condition known as psychosocial dwarfism.

Physical stresses, such as surgery or exploratory procedures, increase the secretion of prolactin, but less is known about the response to psychological or emotional stimuli (Rose, 1980).

There is thus little doubt that psychological variables such as novelty, unfamiliarity and challenge are highly effective in modulating the activity of the pituitary gland. But there is much less agreement about the influence of long-continued environmental pressures. This point is underlined by the results of a study of growth hormone and cortisol secretion in a group of 416 American air traffic controllers based in the New York and New England areas (Rose *et al.*, 1982b). Serial blood samples were collected over a 5-hour period through indwelling venous catheters supplying a pump attached to the waist on as many as five occasions over three years. Samples were taken while the controllers were separating aircraft, and during break periods. Neither cortisol nor growth hormone concentrations were very consistent over time within individuals, and the secretions of cortisol and growth hormone did not seem to be related. There was a significant fall in cortisol secretion as the day progressed, whereas average growth hormone secretion appeared to be higher during the afternoon than during the morning. Apparently the controllers secreted more cortisol and less growth hormone than other groups of males. There was very little relationship between a host of biological, psychological or work-related variables and average cortisol and growth hormone concentrations (Rose *et al.*, 1982a), perhaps because of the low level of consistency of hormone levels on the different days the men were studied. However, when the men were compared with themselves under a variety of conditions it was seen that on the days with higher cortisol levels the men did more work, and showed more aroused behaviour. They also reported more subjective difficulty; more unusual events were noted and they came to work reporting slightly more depression and fatigue. Yet the differences were small, and when a high work load day was chosen as the criterion variable cortisol was raised, but only modestly. The men with the greatest increases in work load did not necessarily show the greatest increases in plasma cortisol levels.

These findings allow the conclusion that adaptation of the adrenocortical system to initially disturbing or provocative events may occur rather quickly (Rose, 1980), and that there is a seeming lack of adrenal activation in individuals accustomed to stress. Helicopter medical orderlies in Vietnam failed to increase 17-hydroxycorticosteroid excretion (an indicator of adrenal hormone secretion) on flying days, by comparison with non-flying days, and there was no increase in plasma cortisol in experienced truck drivers during periods when truck driving was particularly difficult. Urinary 17-hydroxycorticosteroids were not significantly elevated among air traffic controllers at O'Hare airport in Chicago, when compared to controls, although Rose *et al.* (1982a) found some men who showed an increase in plasma cortisol as the work load increased. These individuals did not seem to be subjected to more stress, for they were judged by their peers to be more competent than average, were more satisfied with their jobs and considered that their superiors allowed them more freedom in performing their duties than others.

On a humbler plane, in discussing the response to chronic stress Rose (1980) quotes work to the effect that a shift from employment on a salaried basis to piece-work increases adrenal activity. When employees in a confectionery factory were switched from piece-work payment to a guaranteed salary, urinary steroid and catecholamine excretion fell, while sheet metal workers showed an increase in these parameters when they were shifted from a regular salary to piece-work.

Adrenal medulla

The adrenal medulla was early implicated in the endocrine response to emotional or physical stress, as is evident from the prominence given to the fight-or-flight concept of Cannon (1929). However, the blood levels of the catecholamines, noradrenaline and adrenaline, do not necessarily provide a good index of adrenal medullary activity, for the sympathetic system contributes largely to the production of noradrenaline, and much of this amine in the blood represents an overflow from the sympathetic nerve endings. Further, the sympathetic system is commonly activated alongside the adrenal medulla, so that the relative contributions of the peripheral sympathetic system and adrenal medullary secretion can be difficult to discern. There is the additional complication that catecholamines occur in the cells of the adrenal medulla alongside a variety of opioid peptides. Indeed, the peptides and the catecholamines seem to be stored together in intracellular vesicles and be secreted jointly in response to stimulation (Iversen, 1984). Thus, assessment of adrenal medullary function by assay of catecholamines may only reveal part of the response. Even so, it seems that public speaking doubles the plasma adrenaline concentration and increases that of noradrenaline by 50 per cent, whereas the reverse occurs with mental arithmetic. During harassment, type A individuals (coronary prone) have a greater elevation of plasma adrenaline than type B subjects (non-coronary prone). Depressed people show increased basal levels of plasma noradrenaline and adrenaline, and these have been related to the degree of anxiety (Axelrod & Reisine, 1984).

Tumours of the adrenal medulla, or of other chromaffin tissue, known as phaeochromocytomas produce excessive quantities of noradrenaline and, to a lesser extent, adrenaline, and patients often manifest psychoses and acute anxiety states that proceed to panic. These signs develop in addition to the expected hypertension arising from the actions of the catecholamines on the heart and blood vessels. Metenkephalin may also be produced in high concentration by phaeochromocytomas, thus complicating diagnosis.

Many activities increase urinary catecholamine excretion. Examinations, watching distressing films, mental arithmetic, physical exercise and gravitational stress have all been utilized in experimental studies. There are suggestions that conditions characterized by novelty, anticipation and unpredictability are associated with rises in adrenaline output. As control is gained over the situation, adrenaline production falls. Noradrenaline secretion may be more related to attention-demanding or vigilance situations (Rose, 1980). Unlike cortisol secretion, the catecholamine response to effective stimuli does not seem to wane with repeated exposure. Parachutists continue to show an increased catecholamine secretion when jumping at a time when other endocrine responses have been reduced. The stimuli increasing catecholamine production are not necessarily aversive, as is evident from the continued response of enthusiastic parachutists. Pleasurable game playing or sexual excitement are effective in this regard, but may also produce increased arousal or vigilance.

The secretion of noradrenaline and adrenaline can be affected by erotic stimuli. Levi (1969) showed erotic films to a mixed cinema audience and collected urine from the 50 men and 53 women before and after the screening. The excretion of catecholamines was measured and compared with the results of self-ratings of sexual arousal. Both sexes showed similar increases in urinary noradrenaline excretion, but the increase of adrenaline in men was greater than that observed in women. Sexual arousal in the male subjects was greater than in females, and whereas the self-ratings for sexual arousal correlated with catecholamine excretion in the females they did not do so in the men. Bland films of natural scenery did not induce any emotional or adrenal activation, and indeed, decreased catecholamine excretion in healthy women.

The concurrent response of both divisions of the adrenal gland to appropriate provocation has been studied less often, although comparison of the alterations in catecholamine production and cortisol output can be most informative. In one such investigation (Ward *et al.*, 1983) the responses to a range of stimuli were examined in subjects from whom a series of blood samples were collected through an indwelling catheter placed in an arm vein. A cognitive stressor (mental arithmetic), physical stressors (hand grip, knee bends), and passive painful stressors (venipuncture or cold) were used. Plasma adrenaline concentrations increased most in response to the cognitive stressor and noradrenaline concentrations were most elevated in response to the passive painful stressors. Secretion of the two catecholamines, then, does not necessarily proceed in harmony, but interpretation may be complicated by the slower clearance of noradrenaline from the blood than adrenaline. Other responses to psychological arousal have been followed by Frankenhaeuser and her colleagues (Franken-haeuser, 1982), who addressed themselves to two components, effort and distress, where effort represented positive aspects of the stress experience, and distress the opposite. In their eyes, effort without distress is a joyous, happy state, accompanied by catecholamine secretion together with a suppression of cortisol secretion. Effort with distress is accompanied by an increase in both catecholamine and cortisol secretion. Mental work carried out under conditions of either stimulus underload or stimulus overload is considered typically to evoke feelings of effort as well as distress, and a rise in catecholamine and cortisol secretion. Distress without effort is related to feelings of helplessness and depression and may be accompanied by cortisol secretion. Women appear to be less prone than men to increase catecholamine secretion in response to demands for achievement, so that during rest and relaxation, sex differences in catecholamine excretion are generally slight, but in challenging performance situations (intelligence tests, a colour–word conflict task, an arithmetic task) the increase in plasma adrenaline and noradrenaline seen in males was much less evident in females, although the women performed just as well, or better, than men. The sex difference is not unalterable, for women students selected from a male-dominated school of engineering in Sweden increased their adrenaline excretion almost as much as did their male fellow students when performing a cognitive-conflict task. Does this observation indicate that the increase in catecholamine excretion is achievement-oriented?

Efforts have been made to separate the emotional states associated with the secretion of adrenaline and noradrenaline from the metabolic actions of the amines in order to determine whether the anxiety apparent under stressful conditions is a necessary factor in provoking release of the hormones, or whether the change in affective state results from the peripheral effects of these factors. This is an old question, for long ago James and Lange suggested that emotion was the perception of the peripheral concomitants, while others maintained that the affect was purely central in origin (Schachter, 1975). One way of distinguishing between the two alternatives is to inject volunteers with adrenaline or noradrenaline and to ask them to describe their feelings. This was done over sixty years ago, and only a minority of subjects reported an emotional experience. Most felt as if they were afraid, or as if they were happy, but they did not actually feel fear or happiness. However, this work suffered from the criticism that the subjects knew that they were being given something and that it might affect their sensations. In an oft-quoted study this reservation was addressed by injecting adrenaline or placebo into subjects led to believe that they were being given vitamins and exposed to conditions calculated to engender euphoria or anger (Schachter & Singer, 1962; Schachter, 1967). When placed with a stooge acting in a euphoric–manic fashion, the subjects given adrenaline quickly caught the mood of the occasion, joined in the whirl of activity and invented near-manic activities of their own. In marked contrast, the subjects given adrenaline and provided with a plausible explanation of the possible effects tended simply to sit and stare at the stooge in mild disbelief. Similar results were obtained when anger was manifest by the stooge: uninformed adrenaline subjects grew openly annoyed and irritated, while those informed about the possible side-effects of adrenaline or given a placebo maintained their equanimity. Thus it seems that given a state of physiological arousal for which no simple explanation was available, states of euphoria or anger could be generated readily, depending upon the emotional setting. Once an explanation was available for the physiological feelings, it was much less easy to influence mood, whether as amusement, anger, euphoria or fear.

The peripheral autonomic nervous system, though not essential for affect, colours emotional feelings, as is illustrated by a study of paraplegics and quadraplegics carried out by a paraplegic (Hohmann, 1966). The patients were grouped according to the level of the spinal lesion, on the basis that the higher the lesion the greater might be the depression of sympathetic activity, and the higher the lesion the less the emotion that the subjects might feel. The postulated correlation was evident in that emotional reactions without feeling were repeatedly described by patients with cervical lesions. When the changes in emotionality were related to the height of the spinal cord lesion, it was seen that as less autonomic control was retained, so there was a greater loss in emotionality, or the greater the retention of visceral sensation the greater the intensity of emotional experiences. Quite often the subjects described themselves as thinking mad, rather than feeling mad.

13

Hormones and learning and memory

Learning and memory are closely integrated and difficult to separate from the experimental or clinical point of view. Thus, one definition states that learning is an adaptive change in behaviour caused by experience, with memory being specified as the storage and recall of previous experiences (Shepherd, 1983). Over the years, concepts of the physiological basis of learning and memory have changed considerably, although current studies are still handicapped by a lack of understanding of the processes involved. The hippocampus has featured in much work, particularly since surgical removal of the hippocampus was found to cause loss of recent memory. However, loss of memory can also arise from damage to other brain structures without interference with the hippocampus and removal of the hippocampus in monkeys and rats does not produce the relatively complete loss of memory seen in man. From the hormonal point of view, discussion is simplified by general acceptance of the principle that plastic changes at synapses are responsible for the retention of a memory trace. There is less certainty concerning the nature of the plastic changes, but many of the alterations in learning and memory produced by drugs, electric shock, or hormones are explicable on this basis. The evidence as a whole argues for some form of regional biochemical, or even behavioural specificity, but the magnitude and general nature of the biochemical reactions render it unlikely that any of the metabolic changes observed represent the stored information. Rather, they may just indicate the general cellular activation necessary for learning to occur (Dunn, 1980).

Numerous studies have shown that learning and memory are affected by treatments that influence catecholamine metabolism (McGaugh, 1983). Learning and retention are enhanced by amphetamine, and impaired by drugs such as diethyldithiocarbamate and reserpine that decrease levels of catecholamines. Studies of the effects upon learning and memory of lesions of the locus ceruleus or lesions of the dorsal noradrenergic bundle with neurotoxins that severely deplete forebrain noradrenaline, like 6-hydroxy-dopamine, have yielded mixed results, although the consequent impairment is potentiated by removal of the adrenal glands. Retention of a memory trace is also impaired by the central administration of drugs that interfere with the synthesis of catecholamines: catecholamine agonists facilitate retention and catecholamine antagonists act in the opposite sense.

Despite the natural emphasis on the central effects of drugs influencing catecholamine turnover and memory, it is as well to bear in mind that peripherally released catecholamines may be of significance. Experimental work, largely with rats, indicates that drugs which affect peripheral, but not central, levels of the amines, like syrosingopine and guanethidine, attenuate retention. These observations raise intriguing questions, for catecholamines do not readily cross the blood–brain barrier and thus a central action of peripherally released amine appears unlikely.

As with other functions, the hypothalamus is of importance in memory. Loss of memory in man was first correlated with neoplastic damage to the mammillary bodies, but other regions of the hypothalamus, and in particular the ventromedial nuclei, were involved (Plum & van Uitert, 1978), and there are cases of amnesia where the mammillary bodies remain intact. Most patients suffering loss of memory with hypothalamic disease manifest a classic Korsakoff syndrome, with loss of a short-term memory but a relative preservation of immediate and long-term recall.

The hippocampus is essential for short-term memory, as is shown by the effects of bilateral removal of the hippocampus and hippocampal gyri (Penfield & Milner, 1958), but a major hippocampal projection to the hypothalamus, the fornix, can be cut without producing amnesia. Plum & van Uitert (1978) postulate that the hypothalamus compensates for the loss of the fornix by using hippocampal projections that travel to critical hypothalamic sites through amygdalofugal paths crossing the lateral hypothalamus to end in the ventromedial nuclear region. According to this view, memory loss would occur only when disease destroyed this critical, terminal, ventromedial zone for memory or both the amygdalofugal and the fornix projections for it. What is not at issue is the significance of the hypothalamus.

ACTH-like peptides

Pointers toward the direct participation of pituitary hormones in behavioural processes emerged from studies of conditioned avoidance behaviour, where hypophysectomy led to severe impairment which could in turn be corrected with ACTH, α-MSH and vasopressin. Fragments of these hormones, devoid in themselves of endocrine effects, were as active as the parent molecules in improving the behavioural reactions of hypophysec-tomized animals, and it was recognized that the effects of ACTH-related peptides were short-lived, whereas those produced by vasopressin were longer-lasting. The term 'ACTH-related' should be read only in a structural sense, for short peptide chains such as ACTH 4–7 or ACTH 4–10 need not be generated solely via a larger parent molecule. They may be synthesized elsewhere and may not necessarily retain any adrenal cortex-stimulating activity.

Modification of the ACTH molecule can readily enhance the behavioural activity, and allow oral administration. Substitution of the methionine in ACTH 4–10 by methionine sulphoxide, of the arginine by D-lysine and tryptophan by phenylethylamine produced a derivative that was 1000 times more active than ACTH 4–10, while other larger peptides with potency ratios of 100 000, 300 000 or even 1 000 000 are known. These may bind more strongly at receptor sites, or be broken down less readily (De Wied, 1969; De Wied & de Kloet, 1980).

ACTH and related peptides delay the extinction of shuttle box or pole-jumping avoidance behaviour in rats. The shuttle box requires that the inhabitant moves from one chamber to another on receipt of a sensory signal (usually a light or sound) in order to avoid an electric shock. Similarly, the pole-jumping situation is such that the rat can only escape a shock by climbing a pole mounted in the centre of the cage. The extinction period refers to the period of time that the conditioned avoidance response is maintained when the conditioned stimulus (the light or sound) is presented without the electric shock. The effect of treatment with ACTH-like peptides lasts a few hours and is thought to arise from a temporary increase in motivation. Memory processes may also be affected by ACTH fragments in that the amnesia produced by carbon dioxide inhalation or electroconvulsive shock is alleviated. Avoidance behaviour can be regarded as a form of escape behaviour, is learned rapidly and is persistent. However, as Mason (1983) concludes, extinction behaviour is not a simple activity under the control of a single brain system, but rather is affected by many diverse psychological processes ranging from response inhibition to selective attention, and from secondary reinforcement to frustrative non-reward. The neurochemical basis of extinction has been examined and the process or processes shown to be affected by cholinergic, dopaminergic, noradrenergic, serotoninergic and peptidergic systems in diverse ways. Thus the interpretation of the results of studies involving extinction is no simple matter.

Selective visual attention in man, and motivation, may be facilitated by ACTH 4–10, but the evidence is not yet convincing. Perhaps this is because most studies have employed healthy adults, where these functions may be incapable of much improvement. On the whole, human studies have not consistently supported an effect of ACTH 4–10 upon memory consolidation or retrieval (D'Elia & Frederiksen, 1983), but other analogues may prove to be more active.

Progress is being made in understanding the mode of action of ACTH-like peptides on the brain (Wiegant & De Wied, 1981). A multiplicity of structures is involved in the behavioural effects, in that an intact limbic system–midbrain circuit is essential for the promotion of avoidance behaviour, while the dorsal septal nucleus may be involved in avoidance learning. The dopaminergic nigrostriatal tract participates in the induction by ACTH of excessive grooming in the rat, as does the hippocampus. Further, ACTH-like immunoreactive material is distributed widely through the brain, with cell bodies being located in the arcuate nucleus and terminals being distributed throughout limbic–midbrain areas.

If ACTH were to act as a neurotransmitter or neuromodulator, then changes in the metabolism of cyclic AMP in brain tissue would be expected in the presence of the peptide, and these have been observed. The evidence is not entirely consistent, but analysis of the structure–activity relationships of a series of analogues produced results which correlated broadly with the structural requirements for the induction of excessive grooming. Wiegant & De Wied (1981) considered that the information encoded in ACTH-like peptides is transferred to brain cells by means of the activation and inhibition of adenylate cyclase, by the phosphorylation of a variety of substrate proteins in the synaptic membrane, and by the alteration of calcium mobility. There are other possibilities: ACTH can enhance protein synthesis, so that a general effect of ACTH on the synthesis of proteins in the brain might underlie the benefits on learning. In this way, the effects of stress could be regarded as a by-product of a widespread response, and not necessarily reflect any behavioural specificity on the part of ACTH (Dunn *et al.*, 1982). The fragment of the complete ACTH molecule, ACTH 4–10, that is behaviourally but not hormonally active, promotes protein synthesis in the brain but not in the liver.

Vasopressin and oxytocin

As we have seen, the distribution of the classical neurohypophysial hormones extends outside the hypothalamus, and nerve fibres containing these peptides ramify widely in the brain. Because the results of numerous studies point to vasopressin and oxytocin as being influential in memory processes, great significance is being attached to the peptidergic networks containing these hormones, although proof of many assumptions is slow to emerge.

Vasopressin may affect the acquisition of avoidance behaviour in intact rats, but more powerfully increases the resistance to extinction of shuttle box and pole-jumping avoidance behaviour, particularly after intra-ventricular injection (De Wied & Versteeg, 1979; De Wied & de Kloet, 1980). Like ACTH, vasopressin protects rats and mice against experimentally induced amnesia and may affect the consolidation and retrieval of newly acquired experience. Male rats, trained in a T-maze to run for a receptive female, chose the correct arm of the maze more frequently when given desglycinamide-lysine vasopressin (DG-LVP) than after saline administration—provided success was rewarded with copulation. This vasopressin analogue is practically devoid of endocrine activity. Rats with hereditary diabetes insipidus (Brattleboro strain), and lacking the ability to synthesize vasopressin, are inferior in acquiring and maintaining active and passive avoidance behaviour. They respond normally when tested immediately or very soon after the learning trial, so implying that memory is defective rather than the learning process. Treatment of rats of the Brattleboro strain with vasopressin or DG-LVP restores their avoidance behaviour to normal, while the injection of an antiserum to vasopressin into the third ventricle of intact rats disrupts the response. Vasopressin is evidently involved in the development of avoidance behaviour, and the effect cannot be equated with the endocrine activities of the peptide. Oxytocin, when given intra-ventricularly, has opposing behavioural effects to those of vasopressin and facilitates the extinction of pole-jumping avoidance behaviour. Vasopressin and oxytocin exert antagonistic effects in other situations, as in studies of self-stimulation, hypothalamic neuronal activity, hippocampal θ activity and heroin self-administration.

Structure–activity studies using fragments of the arginine–vasopressin molecule have shown that the peripheral and central activities of arginine–vasopressin can be dissociated and that various short sequences of the parent molecule affect different aspects of memory. Indeed, the fragments can be more potent than the intact molecule, and Burbach *et al.* (1983b) found that the peptide pGlu—Asn—Cys(Cys)—Pro—Arg—Gly—NH2, which arises upon proteolysis of arginine–vasopressin, is highly selective in promoting memory consolidation. In the same vein, it seems that oxytocin may serve similarly as a precursor of peptides of much greater behavioural activity (Burbach *et al.*, 1983a).

Efforts have been made to identify the site of action of vasopressin in the brain, but vasopressin exerts its effect on memory consolidation after injection into a multitude of brain sites, including the hippocampal dentate gyrus, the dorsal septal nucleus, and the dorsal raphe nucleus. Thus, the local injection of vasopressin into these locations immediately after a learning trial facilitated the later retention of a passive avoidance response.

Lesions of the septal complex, dorsal hippocampus and the amygdaloid complex abolish the effect of vasopressin on the maintenance of a conditioned avoidance response and suggest that a functionally intact limbic system is essential for the response to vasopressin (Meisenberg & Simmons, 1983a). Similar treatment with oxytocin attenuated passive avoidance behaviour; but injections into the subiculum, central nucleus of the amygdala and locus ceruleus were ineffective. The experimental work of De Wied and his colleagues (van Wimersma-Griedanus *et al.*, 1983) on the rat indicated that the effect of vasopressin upon retrieval processes seems to be located in the central nuclei of the amygdala, whereas the dorsal septal and dorsal raphe areas are involved in the influence of vasopressin on storage processes. The dentate gyrus of the hippocampus seems to be involved in both storage and retrieval processes. Further complications are introduced by the fact that a range of neurotransmitters may be involved in the behavioural effects of peptides, as well as in the metabolic conversion of the neurohypophysial hormones to behaviourally active fragments. At the receptor level, sites in the septum may recognize vasopressin- and oxytocin-like molecules equally well, while receptors in the dentate gyrus of the hippocampus may discriminate between the two peptide forms.

Brain catecholamines are involved in the responses to neurohypophysial peptides and their analogues (De Wied & Versteeg, 1979; De Wied & de Kloet, 1980). Manipulation of catecholamine metabolism, subsequent treatment with vasopressin, and the examination of distinct areas isolated by microdissection have shown that the turnover of noradrenaline and dopamine is enhanced in those areas affected by vasopressin. Additionally, catecholamine turnover is slower in the brains of rats with hereditary diabetes insipidus than in controls. The amnesia for a passive avoidance response produced by treatment with an analeptic drug was reversed by treatment with arginine vasopressin, given systemically or intra-ventricularly. Bohus, Conti, Kovacs & Versteeg (1982) postulate that some interaction with a catecholaminergic system underlies these responses to vasopressin. The effective sites from which vasopressin affects consolidation and retrieval processes coincide with the brain regions where the fibres of the dorsal noradrenergic bundle system arising from the noradrenergic cell bodies in the locus ceruleus terminate. Vasopressin may act presynaptically, or at the postsynaptic receptors of this system. Chemical destruction (by 6-hydroxydopamine) of the noradrenergic nerve terminals arising from the locus ceruleus prevented the beneficial effect of vasopressin on consolidation processes, but similar lesions in the nucleus accumbens or dorsal raphe nucleus were ineffective. Serotoninergic involvement may be of special significance in the facilitation of retrieval processes by vasopressin, but the mode of action is not understood. Korsakoff's syndrome, the organic brain disease of alcoholics characterized by anterograde and retrograde amnesia, is thought to be caused by lesions along the dorsal noradrenergic bundle in the diencephalon and brain stem, and it is particularly interesting that such patients do not benefit from treatment with the vasopressin analogue desglycinamide–arginine–vasopressin (Laczi *et al.*, 1983). Vasopressin may well act upon the very pathways damaged in this disease.

The suggestions concerning the involvement of vasopressin in memory consolidation and retrieval have not been universally welcomed. One major line of uncertainty concerns the ability of rats with genetic diabetes insipidus (Brattleboro strain) to perform normally in passive avoidance tests. De Wied and his colleagues (De Wied, 1980) have reported that such animals show severe memory impairment that can be improved by treatment with vasopressin, whereas others (Bailey & Weiss, 1979; Hostetter, Jubb & Kozlowski, 1980; Carey & Miller, 1982) could find no evidence of any learning or memory deficit. Bailey & Weiss (1979) also point out that Brattleboro rats manifest other physiological, or physiopathological, changes besides that of diabetes insipidus. There can also be an increase in oxytocin secretion, and disturbances of adrenal steroid synthesis, electrolyte metabolism, growth, and peripheral sympathetic activity.

One novel possibility concerning the action of vasopressin is that it has direct visceral (autonomic) effects that may directly influence other behaviours, such as arousal (Gash & Thomas, 1983). The effects of systemically administered vasopressin can be blocked by the systemic administration of a peptide antagonist of vasopressin that does not cross the blood–brain barrier, so that some peripheral action is indicated (Le Moal *et al.*, 1981). The behavioural effects were produced by doses of vasopressin of the order of those eliciting pressor responses, so that central mechanisms may be triggered through activation of visceral afferents. Oxytocin and vasopressin neurons in the paraventricular nucleus seem to project directly to pre-ganglionic cell groups of both the parasympathetic and sympathetic divisions of the autonomic nervous system, and to the principal sensory nucleus of the vagus and glossopharyngeal nerves (Swanson & Sawchenko, 1983), so that a route for an indirect action of the neurohypophysial peptides can be traced. However, De Wied, Gaffori, van Ree & de Jong (1984) point out that the central administration of vasopressin can produce behavioural effects in the absence of pressor action, and that the central administration of a vasopressor antagonist blocked the behavioural but not the pressor effect of systemically given vasopressin.

Neurohypophysial peptides have been shown to modulate the tolerance of rats to morphine, and this effect may become significant from the psychiatric point of view, particularly as the development of tolerance to narcotic analgesics has been regarded as a process analogous to that of learning and memory. However, the structure–activity relationships between neurohypophysial peptides and their derivatives and tolerance differ from those derived from studies of memory. Further, the memory effects appear to be mediated by noradrenergic systems, whereas the effects upon opiate tolerance utilize a dopaminergic action (Meisenberg & Simmons, 1983a). The development of morphine tolerance is delayed in homozygous diabetic Brattleboro rats and returned to normal upon treatment with vasopressin or DG-LVP. In this regard oxytocin is approximately five times more active than DG-LVP. In another situation daily treatment with DG-LVP reduced the self-administration of heroin in rats in a dose-dependent manner, whereas oxytocin administration slightly increased the amount of heroin taken.

Clinical studies indicate that vasopressin may be helpful in patients suffering from amnesia after car accidents, and in tests of attention and memory in elderly people. Improvement in concentration and motor rapidity have been reported, and learning and memory bettered in specific tests in normal individuals. Since post-traumatic amnesia has also been reported to be resistant to vasopressin or its analogues Meisenberg & Simmons (1983a) argue that the case for the therapeutic value of this neurohypophysial principle remains to be proven. But this view presupposes that the processes causing amnesia are similar. These issues are discussed by Jolles (1983), who points out that many studies in which vasopressin has proved ineffective used patients with a complex pattern of neuropsychological deficits, or other symptoms of brain degeneration, and in whom degeneration of the brain structures upon which vasopressin might be expected to act might already have occurred. Memory difficulties may accompany a variety of diseases and may have differing causes; it is unreasonable to expect any neuropeptide to be effective in all. Patients with diabetes insipidus have not differed from controls in tests of attention or concentration, although their short- and long-term memory was much poorer. Medication was discontinued for ten days before testing. A single injection of lysine vasopressin was beneficial, as was treatment with 1-deamino-8-D-arginine-vasopressin (DDAVP). Long-term memory was also improved in healthy individuals (Laczi *et al.*, 1982). These effects were not associated with changes in water balance.

Other studies have yielded more striking differences (Legros & Lancranjan, 1983). Lysine vasopressin decreased the α, and increased the δ, activity in the EEG of normal volunteers, but large, and sedative, doses of the hormone were used. In other experiments, men over the age of 50 given

LVP performed better in tests of attention, concentration and immediate and delayed recall. For Legros & Lancranjan (1983), the clinical data suggest that vasopressin can stimulate attention, concentration and memory in young and elderly normal volunteers, and can improve retrograde and anterograde amnesia in some patients with post-traumatic memory loss and in some patients with Korsakoff's psychosis. They allow that most of the findings are not consistent, possibly because of heterogeneity among the patients studied and a lack of objective criteria in selecting the responsive individuals. Interestingly, in their own studies with schizophrenic patients given vasopressin a normalization of the circadian rhythms of growth hormone and prolactin was observed. A careful double-blind crossover study of healthy young and elderly men given several discriminatory psychological tests concluded that DDAVP did not simply enhance the general level of arousal but improved both short-term and long-term memory. The subjects did not know when DDAVP or placebo was given and could not distinguish between them, thus subjective influences were avoided (Nebes, Reynolds & Horn, 1984).

Since the powerful pressor and hormonal effects of vasopressin can be avoided by modification of the molecular structure, analogues of neuro-hypophysial peptides that affect retrieval processes may be of great value in the treatment of mental disorders of cognitive origin. Memory loss induced experimentally by carbon dioxide or by the central administration of puromycin can be prevented by pretreatment with vasopressin. The biological half-lives of vasopressin and oxytocin extend only over a few minutes, yet the anti-amnesic effect of vasopressin is evident when the peptide is given one hour or twenty-four hours before an experiment. This suggests that the benefits observed are not due to the presence of vasopressin or a metabolite, but are rather long-term consequences of its evanescent action.

Endogenous opiates

Like ACTH and vasopressin, the opioid peptides are released in response to stressful circumstances, and, again like vasopressin, the opioid peptides might be involved in learning and memory (McGaugh, 1983). Animal studies indicate that retention is enhanced by the opiate antagonist naloxone, and attenuated by opiate agonists. The enkephalins appear to impair avoidance learning, and there are suggestions that such effects are mediated through an adrenergic system, with naloxone releasing an opioid inhibition. The treatment of young men with naloxone improves the selectivity of auditory attention in the presence of competing sources of stimuli (Arnsten *et al.*, 1983), and suggests that opiates are involved in some way. Naloxone may affect the ability of an individual to pay attention to particular stimuli without altering total processing capacity or global arousal levels.

Low doses of exogenous opiates cause retrograde amnesia, whereas very high doses seem to have the opposite effect. It appears to be the rule that agents affecting memory consolidation have an inverted 'U' dose–response curve, usually within a rather narrow dose range, and this inevitably complicates interpretation (Izquierdo *et al.*, 1982). High doses of any drug may influence behaviour through a variety of non-physiological actions and it may be wondered whether an amnesic effect of a neuropeptide is itself physiological: whether it is necessary or desirable to erase memory traces. Izquierdo *et al.* (1982) think that this might be done in order to prevent the simultaneous operation of a huge and ever-increasing number of storage systems, most of which may never be used, and quote Jorge Luis Borges to the effect that perfect memory, in addition to being 'intolerable', is incompatible with the normal process of thinking, for which it is necessary to forget differences in order to make abstractions and to generalize. It should be noted also that opiates can, under certain circumstances and particularly with multi-trial learning, improve performance, so that distinguishing between the many actions of opiates can pose problems. To some extent the dilemma will be resolved as more knowledge is gained concerning the various opiate systems within the brain, alongside understanding of the different opiate receptors involved.

14

What next?

The study of brain–body interactions or 'psychosomatic' medicine, like that of neuroendocrinology, is not of recent creation: an American journal devoted to the subject was founded in 1939 and has thrived since then. This is to be expected, for an understanding of the involvement of hormones in the control of behaviour is an important aspect of psychosomatic medicine, yet progress has been infuriatingly slow. In a Presidential Address to the American Psychosomatic Society a decade and a half ago, John Mason (1970) was moved to remark that 'realistically, we must face the fact that the psychosomatic approach has not as yet had the sweeping, revolutionary impact on medicine of which it appears capable.' At that time he felt that the advances in endocrinology pointed the way to significant progress, for hormone measurement seemed to provide a sensitive, roughly quantitative, and objective index of emotional arousal or distress which was not masked by verbal or overt behaviour.

> 'In the study of a particular patient, hormonal levels can provide clues to the specific life problems or idiosyncratic conflict areas which are associated with unusual disruption of physiologic homeostasis. Hormone levels can help the skillful clinician dissect out the crucial issues perhaps more rapidly and more conclusively than he otherwise normally might.'

And that was before hormone assays were transformed in sensitivity and accuracy by the application of radioimmunoassay, and before the existence of episodic and rhythmic hormone secretion was appreciated. We are now in a far better position to undertake the analyses Mason hoped for, and the opportunities are being grasped, as the material presented earlier has shown.

The application of endocrine methods to psychiatric disease, while providing insight into the pathophysiological changes occurring in patients, has underscored the problem of precisely defining the psychological or psychiatric conditions to which a pattern of hormone secretion can be related. It is not enough to refer to 'depression', or 'schizophrenia'. The endocrine evidence points to different categories or groups of depressed or schizophrenic patients and we wait to see whether clarity and resolution will stem more from the efforts of the psychoendocrinologist than the psychiatrist. Some may also argue that the abnormal behavioural patterns stemming from endocrine disturbances are not psychiatric diseases at all. This thought inevitably leads to considerations of the definition of psychiatric disease, which lies outside our present remit. As yet, investigators are faced with the dilemma of either organizing their research in terms of particular psychological or psychiatric states, or using hormonal changes as indices of particular internal conditions regardless of any behavioural manifestations. The approach adopted seems to depend more upon the prior training of the experimenter than on the demands of the problem.

Evidently the time has come for a reassessment in depth of the relationship between endocrine disease and psychiatric disturbance. Quite often undue attention is given to the rare case which seems to teach a lesson, even though that condition is but one case in a thousand or ten thousand and the conclusions drawn from the less exciting mass are just as important. Some years ago Tattersall (1981) pointed out that at least 1 per cent of the general population has undiagnosed diabetes, so that it is inevitable that 1 per cent of accident victims will have glycosuria when tested in hospital. It is equally evident that a proportion of psychiatric patients will similarly be shown to be diabetic, without the two conditions necessarily being related. Then there are the uncomfortable observations that, for example, hypercalcaemia or parathyroid disease may often be evident in patients showing no behavioural changes, so pointing to the operation of effective adaptive mechanisms. Hormonal disturbances seem to be less common in psychiatric patients than the incautious reader of Chapter 1 might be led to expect, while John Crammer has pointed out to me that a diabetic who becomes manic may not be able to manage his diet sufficiently well to control his disease or be able to treat himself properly with insulin. Interpretation of the relationship of behavioural changes to the disease then becomes further complicated. There is also the diabetic who discovers that he can wield power over his family by means of the syringe.

Ample evidence has been presented in earlier chapters to show that changes in the patterns of hormone secretion occur under a variety of circumstances, whether they be associated with sleep, depression, excitement or emotional stress. This mass of information contrasts with the paucity of material concerning the mechanisms involved in, or the reasons for, the changes. We know incredibly little about the neural or brain mechanisms generating the fluctuations in hormone secretion. How do changes in neuronal activity occurring at the cellular level, with a duration measured in milliseconds, come to be converted into much longer-lasting swings in hypothalamic or pituitary function? How does the hypothalamus manage to control so many functions simultaneously and independently, despite considerable overlap in the structures involved? Is this where peptide specificity assumes importance? Answers to these questions can only come from animal experimentation.

Little thought has thus far been given to the significance of the hormonal changes wrought by psychic stimuli. What physiological benefits are derived? Why is it helpful to increase the plasma concentration of growth hormone under stressful conditions – if beneficial it is? This question has been addressed by Munck, Guyre & Holbrook (1984) in connection with the reactions of the adrenal cortex to stress (Chapter 3), for almost any kind of threat to homeostasis causes an increase in plasma glucocorticoid levels. It has been traditional to assume that the glucocorticoids act to increase the resistance of the individual to stress, but closer scrutiny indicates that glucocorticoids modulate, and largely inhibit, the actions of numerous intercellular mediators (hormones, prostaglandins, enzymes, lymphokines and peptides) that participate in the endocrine, neural, renal and immune mechanisms serving as a first line of defence to such challenges as haemorrhage, metabolic disturbance, infection or anxiety. Thus it may be that stress-induced increases in glucocorticoid levels do not protect against the stress itself but limit the normal reactions of the body to stress, so preventing the excessive endogenous responses that would threaten the individual. Similar reconsideration of other endocrine reactions is likely to be extremely rewarding.

To the non-clinically oriented reader, progress in the study of hormone–behaviour interactions must appear painfully slow. It would seem to be a simple matter to test the influence of a particular agent on suitable subjects and to quickly obtain definitive results. Unfortunately, this is seldom the case, for ethical considerations are paramount, whether they concern the withholding of possibly effective treatment for control purposes or the likelihood of eliciting unwanted side-effects. The effects of other drugs administered concomitantly with the test material can never be neglected and it can be very difficult to pursue an investigation with drug-free patients. This is particularly evident in the psychiatric context, where some of the confusion over the variable responses of depressed individuals given the dexamethasone suppression test or supplied with thyrotrophin-releasing factor (Chapter 3) may be due to the use of patients under anti-depressant therapy, or given an insufficiently long drug holiday. Whereas the laboratory worker strives to achieve uniformity in the experimental conditions and in the animals used, the clinical researcher has to use the patients, or ward staff, who come to hand. And both groups (test subjects and controls) tend to be highly selected, and probably not fully representative of the population at large.

There is no doubt that the list of behaviourally significant peptides present in the brain will be extended greatly in the coming years. It is also only a matter of time before effective agonists and antagonists of many of the peptides discussed earlier are synthesized. Indeed, with the utilization of an antagonist to the peptide cholecystokinin (proglumide, Chapter 11), an acceleration in our understanding of the activities and physiological signi-ficance of this agent is already apparent. The availability of such compounds will bring much new knowledge and clinical benefit, but also pose problems of sociological concern. It is likely that among the new drugs will be some displaying addictive and 'mind-bending' properties far greater than those of the hallucinogens. The couplet 'mind-bending' is used only because we have no inkling of the effects of such drugs upon perception or conscious-ness. Effects on food intake, drinking, affective and sexual behaviour can be predicted, but there will be others.

Ethical problems will assume an even greater profile, for the reaction against the therapeutic use of brain stimulation or lesioning techniques in the treatment of behavioural problems will appear to have been trivial when compared to the outcry against the use of the newer drugs. For not only are the behavioural reactions likely to be more predictable, and subject to control, but the availability of the newer materials will be vastly greater. Only a few centres possess the facilities necessary to undertaken careful work involving brain stimulation or lesioning: but almost every clinic will be tempted to observe the effects of the novel peptides for themselves.

Most productive work in the field of hormones and behaviour has emerged from collaborative efforts between experts in differing disciplines, with an endocrinologist interesting himself in behaviour, a behaviouralist applying the rudiments of endocrinology, or a clinician joining hands with basic scientists. The trouble is that communication between psychologists, psychiatrists, physiologists and endocrinologists is limited. Not surpris-ingly, each discipline tends to confine discussion to its own peer group and joint meetings between the practitioners of different subjects are poorly attended. Happily, with the formation of new interdisciplinary societies and the vigorous growth of journals of neuroendocrine interest information exchange can only get better. This little book may also prove helpful in promoting understanding.

It may be as well to conclude this peep into the future with a cautionary word. Because an effort has been made to provide an up-to-date review of an exciting field, most of the material cited is of recent appearance. This feature should not be taken to indicate that only current work on the relationship between hormones and human behaviour is of any value. That conclusion would be erroneous, for there is much to be learned from the past: after all, truth is eternal, and there are very few new ideas. We simply express them better, and test them a little more elegantly.

REFERENCES

Abbott, D. H., Holman, S. D., Berman, M., Neff, D. A. & Goy, R. W. (1984). Effects of opiate antagonists on hormones and behavior of male and female rhesus monkeys. *Archives of Sexual Behavior*, **13**, 1–25.

Abplanalp, J. M., Donnelly, A. F. & Rose, R. M. (1979). Psychoendocrinology of the menstrual cycle. 1. Enjoyment of daily activities and moods. *Psychosomatic Medicine*, **41**, 587–604.

Adams, D. B., Gold, A. R. & Burt, A. D. (1978). Rise in female-initiated sexual activity at ovulation and its suppression by oral contraceptives. *New England Journal of Medicine*, **299**, 1145–50.

Adams, R. D. & Rosman, N. P. (1978). Hypothyroidism: Neuromuscular system. In *The Thyroid*, 4th edn, ed. S. C. Werner & S. H. Ingbar, pp. 901–10. New York: Harper & Row.

Ader, R. (1975). Early experience and hormones: emotional behavior and adrenocortical function. In *Hormonal Correlates of Behavior*, vol. 1: *A Lifespan View*, ed. B. E. Eleftheriou & R. L. Sprott, pp. 7–33. New York: Plenum Press.

Aiman, J. & Boyar, R. M. (1982). Testicular function in transsexual men. *Archives of Sexual Behavior*, **11**, 171–9.

Akil, H., Watson, S. J., Young, E., Lewis, M. E., Khachaturian, H. & Walker, J. M. (1984). Endogenous opioids: biology and function. *Annual Review of Neuroscience*, **7**, 223–55.

Andersson, B. (1953). The effect of injections of hypertonic NaCl-solutions into different parts of the hypothalamus of goats. *Acta Physiologica Scandinavica*, **28**, 188–201.

Arnsten, A. F. T., Segal, D. S., Neville, H. J., Hillyard, S.A., Janowsky, D. S., Judd, L. L. & Bloom, F. E. (1983). Naloxone augments electrophysiological signs of selective attention in man. *Nature*, **304**, 725–7.

Aschoff, J. (1980). The circadian system in man. In *Neuroendocrinology*, ed. D. T. Krieger & J. C. Hughes, pp. 77–83. Sunderland, Mass.: Sinauer Associates.

Ax, A. F. (1953). The physiological differentiation between fear and anger in humans. *Psychosomatic Medicine*, **15**, 433–42.

Axelrod, J. & Reisine, T. D. (1984). Stress hormones: their interaction and regulation. *Science*, **224**, 452–9.

Ayoub, D. M., Greenough, W. T. & Juraska, J. M. (1983). Sex differences in dendritic structure in the preoptic area of the juvenile macaque monkey brain. *Science*, **219**, 197–8.

Backström, T., Sanders, D., Leask, R., Davidson, D., Warner, P. & Bancroft, J. (1983). Mood, sexuality, hormones, and the menstrual cycle. II. Hormone levels and their relationship to the premenstrual syndrome. *Psychosomatic Medicine*, **45**, 503–7.

Bailey, W. H. & Weiss, J. M. (1979). Evaluation of a 'memory deficit' in vasopressin-deficient rats. *Brain Research*, **162**, 174–8.

Baker, E. R. (1981). Menstrual dysfunction and hormonal status in athletic women: a review. *Fertility and Sterility*, **36**, 691–6.

Baker, S. W. (1980). Psychosexual differentiation in the human. *Biology of Reproduction*, 22, 61–72.

Balázs, R. (1972). Hormonal aspects of brain development. In *The Brain in Unclassified Mental Retardation*, ed. J. B. Cavanaugh, pp. 61–72. London: Churchill Livingstone.

Bancroft, J. (1980). Endocrinology of sexual function. *Clinics in Obstetrics and Gynaecology*, 7, 253–81.

Bancroft, J. (1983). *Human sexuality and its problems*. Edinburgh: Churchill Livingstone.

Bancroft, J., Davidson, D. W., Warner, P. & Tyrer, G. (1980). Androgens and sexual behaviour in women using oral contraceptives. *Clinical Endocrinology*, 12, 327–340.

Bancroft, J., Sanders, D., Davidson, D. & Warner, P. (1983). Mood, sexuality, hormones, and the menstrual cycle. III. Sexuality and the role of androgens. *Psychosomatic Medicine*, 45, 509–16.

Bancroft, J., Tennent, G., Loucas, K. & Cass, J. (1974). The control of deviant sexual behaviour by drugs: behavioural changes of oestrogens and anti-androgens. *British Journal of Psychiatry*, 125, 310–15.

Barrington, E. J. W. (1982). Evolutionary and comparative aspects of gut and brain peptides. *British Medical Bulletin*, 38, 227–32.

Bass, N. H., Pelton, E. W. & Young, E. (1977). Defective maturation of cerebral cortex: an inevitable consequence of dysthyroid states during early postnatal life. In *Thyroid Hormones and Brain Development*. ed. G. D. Grave, pp. 199–210. New York: Raven Press.

Baum, M. J., Everitt, B. J., Herbert, J. & Keverne, E. B. (1977). Hormonal basis of proceptivity and receptivity in female primates. *Archives of Sexual Behavior*, 6, 173–92.

Beach, F. A. (1942). Analysis of factors involved in the arousal, maintenance and manifestation of sexual excitement in male animals. *Psychosomatic Medicine*, 4, 173–98.

Beach, F. A. (1948). *Hormones and Behavior*. New York: Hoeber.

Beach, F. A. (1976). Sexual attractivity, proceptivity and receptivity in female mammals. *Hormones and Behavior*, 7, 105–38.

Beach, F. A. (1981). Historical origins of modern research on hormones and behavior. *Hormones and Behavior*, 15, 325–76.

Benkert, O. (1975). Study on pituitary hormones and releasing hormones in depression and sexual impotence. *Progress in Brain Research*, 42, 25–36.

Benzo, C. A. (1983). The hypothalamus and blood glucose regulation. *Life Sciences*, 32, 2509–15.

Bergland, R. M. & Page, R. B. (1978). Can the pituitary secrete directly to the brain? (Affirmative anatomical evidence.) *Endocrinology*, 102, 1325–38.

Billington, C. J., Levine, A. S. & Morley, J.E. (1983). Are peptides truly satiety agents? A method of testing for neurohumoral satiety effects. *American Journal of Physiology*, 245, R920–6.

Bleuler, M. (1951). The psychopathology of acromegaly. *Journal of Nervous and Mental Disease*, 113, 497–511.

Bleuler, M. (1954). *Endokrinologische Psychiatrie*. Stuttgart: Georg Thieme.

Bleuler, M. (1982). In *Psychiatrists on Psychiatry*, ed. M. Shepherd, pp. 1–13. Cambridge University Press.

Bligh, J. (1973). *Temperature regulation in mammals and other vertebrates*. Amsterdam: North-Holland Publishing Company.

Block, G. D. & Page, T. L. (1978). Circadian pacemakers in the nervous system. *Annual Review of Neuroscience*, 1, 19–34.

Bloom, F. E. (1983). The endorphins: a growing family of pharmacologically pertinent peptides. *Annual Review of Pharmacology and Toxicology*, 23, 151–70.

Bohnet, H. G. & McNeilly, A. S. (1979). Prolactin: assessment of its role in the human female. *Hormone and Metabolic Research*, 11, 533–46.

Bohus, B., Conti, L., Kovács, G. L. & Versteeg, D. H.G. (1982). Modulation of memory processes by neuropeptides: interaction with neurotransmitter systems. In *Neuronal*

Plasticity and Memory Function, ed. C. Ajmone Marsan & H. Matthies, pp. 75–87. New York: Raven Press.

Bolles, R. C. (1975). *Theory of Motivation*, 2nd edn. New York: Harper & Row.

Bolles, R. C. & Fanselow, M. S. (1982). Endorphins and behavior. *Annual Review of Psychology*, **33**, 87–101.

Boston Collaborative Drug Surveillance Program (1972). Acute adverse reactions to prednisone in relation to dosage. *Clinical Pharmacology and Therapeutics*, **13**, 694–8.

Boyar, R. M. & Aiman, J. (1982). The 24-hour secretory pattern of LH and the response to LHRH in transsexual men. *Archives of Sexual Behavior*, **11**, 157–69.

Boyd, A. E., Spare, S., Bower, B. & Reichlin, S. (1978). Neurogenic galactorrhea–amenorrhea. *Journal of Clinical Endocrinology and Metabolism*, **47**, 1374–7.

Brahams, D. (1981). Premenstrual syndrome: a disease of the mind. *Lancet*, **ii**, 1238–40.

Brain, P. F. (1979). *Hormones and Aggression*, vol. 2. Montreal: Eden Press.

Brambilla, F. & Penati, G. (1978). Schizophrenia: endocrinological review. In *Perspectives in Endocrine Psychobiology*, ed. F. Brambilla, P. K. Bridges, E. Endröczi & G. Heuser, pp. 309–421. London: John Wiley.

Bray, G. A., Inoue, S., & Nishizawa, Y. (1981). Hypothalamic obesity: the autonomic hypothesis and the lateral hypothalamus. *Diabetologia*, **20**, 366–76.

Breedlove, S. M. & Arnold, A. P. (1980). Hormone accumulation in a sexually dimorphic motor nucleus of the rat spinal cord. *Science*, **210**, 564–6.

Brown, D. R. & Miller, R. J. (1982). Neurotensin. *British Medical Bulletin*, **38**, 239–45.

Brown, G. M. (1976). Endocrine aspects of psychosocial dwarfism. In *Hormones, Behavior and Psychopathology*. ed. E. Sachar, pp. 253–261. New York: Raven Press.

Brown, G. M., Garfinkel, P. E., Grof, E., Grof, P., Cleghorn, J. M. & Brown, P. (1983). A critical appraisal of neuroendocrine approaches to psychiatric disorders. In *Neuroendocrine Perspectives*, vol. 2, ed. E. E. Müller & R. M. MacLeod, pp. 329–64. Amsterdam: Elsevier Science Publishers.

Brown, G. M., Seggie, J. A., Chambers, J. W. & Ettigi, P. G. (1978). Psychoendocrinology and growth hormone: a review. *Psychoneuroendocrinology*, **3**, 131–53.

Brown, J. J., Curtis, J. R., Lever, A. F., Robertson, J. I. S., de Wardener, H. E. & Wing, A. J. (1969). Plasma renin concentration and the control of blood pressure in patients on maintenance haemodialysis. *Nephron*, **6**, 329–49.

Brown, J. T., Mulrow, C. D. & Stoudemire, G. A. (1984). The anxiety disorders. *Annals of Internal Medicine*, **100**, 558–64.

Brown, W. A. (1981). Testosterone and human behaviour. *International Journal of Mental Health*, **9**, 45–66.

Brown, W. A., Monti, P. M. & Corriveau, D. P. (1978). Serum testosterone and sexual activity and interest in men. *Archives of Sexual Behavior*, **7**, 97–103.

Bubenik, G. A. & Brown, G. M. (1973). Morphologic sex differences in primate brain areas involved in regulation of reproductive activity. *Experientia*, **29**, 619–21.

Buchanan, K. D. (1982). Gut hormones and the brain. In *Clinical Neuroendocrinology*, vol. 2, ed. G. M. Besser & L. Martini, pp. 331–58. New York: Academic Press.

Buijs, R. M., De Vries, G. J., Van Leeuwen, F. W. & Swaab, D. F. (1983). Vasopressin and oxytocin: distribution and putative functions in the brain. *Progress in Brain Research*, **60**, 115–22.

Burbach, J. P. H., Bohus, B., Kovács, G. L., Van Nispen, J. W., Greven, H. M. & De Wied, D. (1983a). Oxytocin as a precursor of potent behaviourally active neuropeptides. *European Journal of Pharmacology*, **94**, 125–31.

Burbach, J. P. H., Kovács, G. L., De Wied, D., Van Nispen, J. W. & Greven, H. M. (1983b). A major metabolite of arginine vasopressin in the brain is a highly potent neuropeptide. *Science*, **221**, 1310–12.

Cannon, W. B. (1929). *Bodily Changes in Pain, Hunger, Fear and Rage: An Account of Recent Researches into the Function of Emotional Excitement*, 2nd edn. Boston: Charles T. Branford.

Cappon, D., Ezrin, C. & Lynes, P. (1959). Psychosexual identification (psychogender) in the intersexed. *Canadian Psychiatric Association Journal*, 4, 90–106.

Cardinali, D. P. (1983). Molecular mechanisms of neuroendocrine integration in the central nervous system: an approach through the study of the pineal gland and its innervating sympathetic pathway. *Psychoneuroendocrinology*, 8, 3–30.

Carey, R. J. & Miller, M. (1982). Absence of learning and memory deficits in the vasopressin-deficient rat (Brattleboro strain). *Behavioral Brain Research*, 6, 1–13.

Carman, J. S., Wyatt, E. S., Smith, W., Post, R. M. & Ballenger, J. C. (1984). Calcium and calcitonin in bipolar affective disorder. In *Neurobiology of Mood Disorders*, ed. R. M. Post & J. C. Ballenger, pp. 340–55. Baltimore: Williams & Wilkins.

Caroff, S., Winokur, A., Snyder, P. J. & Amsterdam, J. (1984). Diurnal variation of growth hormone secretion following thyrotropin-releasing hormone infusion in normal men. *Psychosomatic Medicine*, 46, 59–66.

Carroll, B. J. (1976). Psychoendocrine relationships in affective disorders. In *Modern Trends in Psychosomatic Medicine*, vol. 3, ed. O. Hill, pp. 121–53. London: Butterworths.

Carroll, B. J., Curtis, G. C. & Mendels, J. (1976a). Neuroendocrine regulation in depression. I. Limbic system–adrenal cortical dysfunction. *Archives of General Psychiatry*, 33, 1039–44.

Carroll, B. J., Curtis, G. C. & Mendels, J. (1976b). Neuroendocrine regulation in depression. II. Discrimination of depressed from non-depressed patients. *Archives of General Psychiatry*, 33, 1051–8.

Carroll, B. J. & Steiner, M. (1978). The psychobiology of premenstrual dysphoria: the role of prolactin. *Psychoneuroendocrinology*, 3, 171–80.

Carter, J. N., Tyson, J. E., Tolis, G., Van Vliet, S., Faiman, C., & Friesen, H. G. (1978). Prolactin-secreting tumours and hypogonadism in 22 men. *New England Journal of Medicine*, 299, 847–52.

Castonguay, T. W., Applegate, E. A., Upton, D. E. & Stern, J. S. (1983). Hunger and appetite: old concepts/new distinctions. *Nutrition Reviews*, 41, 101–10.

Catt, K. J. & Dufau, M. L. (1983). The clinical significance of peptide hormone receptors. *Clinics in Endocrinology and Metabolism*, 12, xi–xlv.

Chakravarti, S., Collins, W. P., Newton, J. R., Oram, D. H. & Studd, J. W. (1977). Endocrine changes and symptomatology after oophorectomy in premenopausal women. *British Journal of Obstetrics and Gynaecology*, 84, 769–77.

Charles, G., Wilmotte, J., Quenon, M. & Mendlewicz, J. (1982). Reproducibility of the dexamethasone suppression test in depression. *Biological Psychiatry*, 17, 845–8.

Checkley, S. A. (1978). Thyrotoxicosis and the course of manic–depressive illness. *British Journal of Psychiatry*, 133, 219–23.

Checkley, S. A., Slade, A. P. & Shur, E. (1981). Growth hormone and other responses to clonidine in patients with endogenous depression. *British Journal of Psychiatry*, 138, 51–5.

Chi, C. C. & Flynn, J. P. (1971). Neuroanatomic projections relating to biting attack elicited from hypothalamus in cats. *Brain Research*, 35, 49–66.

Chiodo, L. A. & Bunney, B. S. (1983). Typical and atypical neuroleptics: differential effects of chronic administration on the activity of A9 and A10 midbrain dopaminergic neurons. *Journal of Neuroscience*, 3, 1607–19.

Choufoer, J. C., van Rhijn, M. & Querido, A. (1965). Endemic goiter in Western New Guinea. II. Clinical picture, incidence and pathogenesis of endemic cretinism. *Journal of Clinical Endocrinology and Metabolism*, 25, 385–402.

Christensen, L. W. & Gorski, R. A. (1978). Independent masculinization of neuroendocrine systems by intracerebral implants of testosterone or estradiol in the neonatal female rat. *Brain Research*, 146, 325–40.

Clare, A. W. (1983). Psychiatric and social aspects of premenstrual complaint. *Psychological Medicine*, Monograph Supplement 4, 1–58.

Cogen, P. H. & Zimmerman, E. A. (1979). Ovarian steroid hormones and cerebral function.

In *Cerebral Hypoxia and Its Consequences*, ed. S. Fahn, J. N. Davis & L. P. Rowland. *Advances in Neurology*, **26**, 123–33.

Cohen, M. R., Cohen, R. M., Pickar, D., Weingartner, H., Murphy, D. L. (1983). High-dose naloxone infusions in normals. *Archives of General Psychiatry*, **40**, 613–19.

Cohen, S. I. (1980). Cushing's syndrome: a psychiatric study of 29 patients. *British Journal of Psychiatry*, **136**, 120–4.

Conn, J. W., Cohen, E. L., Lucas, C. P., McDonald, W. J., Mayor, G. H., Blough, W. M., Eveland, W. C., Bookstein, J. J. & Lapides, J. (1972). Primary reninism. *Archives of Internal Medicine*, **130**, 682–6.

Conner, R. L. (1972). Hormones, biogenic amines, and aggression. In *Hormones and Behavior*, ed. S. Levine, pp. 209–33. New York: Academic Press.

Cooper, J. D., Lazarowitz, V. C. & Arieff, A. I. (1978). Neurodiagnostic abnormalities in patients with acute renal failure. *Journal of Clinical Investigation*, **61**, 1448–55.

Corn, T. H. & Checkley, S. A. (1983). A case of recurrent mania with recurrent hyperthyroidism. *British Journal of Psychiatry*, **143**, 74–6.

Cowley, J. J., Johnson, A. L. & Brooksbank, B. W. L. (1977). The effect of two odorous compounds on performance in an assessment-of-people test. *Psychoneuroendocrinology*, **2**, 159–72.

Cramer, E. B. & Ford, D. H. (1982). Morphological response of the nervous system to hormones. In *Hormones in Development and Aging*, ed. A. Vernadakis & P. S. Timiras, pp. 181–206. Lancaster: MTP Press.

Crisp, A. H. (1983). Anorexia nervosa. *British Medical Journal*, **287**, 855–8.

Curry, D. L. (1983). Direct tonic inhibition of insulin secretion by central nervous system. *American Journal of Physiology*, **244**, E425–9.

Cushing, H. (1973). Psychic disturbances associated with disorders of the ductless glands. *American Journal of Insanity*, **69**, 965–90.

Dale, E., Gerlach, D. H. & Wilhite, A. L. (1979). Menstrual dysfunction in distance runners. *Obstetrics and Gynecology*, **54**, 47–53.

Dalton, K. (1960). Menstruation and accidents. *British Medical Journal*, **ii**, 1425–6.

Dalton, K. (1968). Menstruation and examinations. *Lancet*, **ii**, 1386–8.

Dalton, K. (1977). *The Premenstrual Syndrome and Progesterone Therapy*. London: William Heinemann Medical Books.

Dalton, K. (1979). Intelligence and prenatal progesterone: a reappraisal. *Journal of the Royal Society of Medicine*, **72**, 397–9.

Damassa, D. A., Smith, E. R., Tennent, B. & Davidson, J. M. (1977). The relationship between circulating testosterone levels and male sexual behavior in rats. *Hormones and Behavior*, **8**, 275–86.

Davidson, J. M. (1972). Hormones and reproductive behavior. In *Hormones and Behavior*, ed. S. Levine, pp. 63–103. London: Academic Press.

Davidson, J. M., Camargo, C. A. & Smith, E. R. (1979). Effects of androgen on sexual behavior in hypogonadal men. *Journal of Clinical Endocrinology and Metabolism*, **48**, 955–8.

Davidson, J. M., Kwan, M., & Greenleaf, W. J. (1982). Hormonal replacement and sexuality in men. *Clinics in Endocrinology and Metabolism*, **11**, 599–623.

Davies, A. O. & Lefkowitz, R. J. (1984). Regulation of β-adrenergic receptors by steroid hormones. *Annual Review of Physiology*, **46**, 119–30.

Davies, T. F., Mountjoy, C. Q., Gomez-Pan, A., Watson, M. J., Hanker, J. P., Besser, G. M. & Hall, R. (1976). A double blind cross over trial of gonadotrophin releasing hormone (LHRH) in sexually impotent men. *Clinical Endocrinology*, **5**, 601–7.

Deakin, J. F. W., Ferrier, I. N., Crow, T. J., Johnstone, E. C. & Lawler, P. (1983). Effects of ECT on pituitary hormone release: relationship to seizure, clinical variables and outcome. *British Journal of Psychiatry*, **143**, 618–24.

D'Elia, G. & Frederiksen, S.-O. (1983). ACTH 4–10 and memory in psychiatric patients. In *Psychoneuroendocrine Dysfunction*, ed. N. S. Shah & A. G. Donald, pp. 243–54. New York: Plenum Medical Book Company.

Denko, J. D. & Kaelbling, R. (1962). The psychiatric aspects of hypoparathyroidism. *Acta Psychiatrica Scandinavica*, **38**, Supplementum 164.

Dennerstein, L. & Burrows, G. D. (1982). Hormone replacement therapy and sexuality in women. *Clinics in Endocrinology and Metabolism*, **11**, 661–79.

Devinsky, O. & Bear, D. (1984). Varieties of aggressive behavior in temporal lobe epilepsy. *American Journal of Psychiatry*, **141**, 651–6.

De Wied, D. (1969). Effects of peptide hormones on behavior. In *Frontiers in Neuroendocrinology, 1969*, ed. W. F. Ganong & L. Martini, pp. 97–140. New York: Oxford University Press.

De Wied, D. (1980). Behavioural actions of neurohypophysial peptides. *Proceedings of the Royal Society, Series B*, **210**, 183–95.

De Wied, D., Gaffori, O., van Ree, J. M. & de Jong, W. (1984). Central target for the behavioural effects of vasopressin neuropeptides. *Nature*, **308**, 276–8.

De Wied, D. & de Kloet, R. (1980). The brain as target tissue for hormones of pituitary origin: behavioral and biochemical studies. In *Frontiers in Neuroendocrinology*, vol. 6, ed. L. Martini & W. F. Ganong, pp. 157–201. New York: Raven Press.

De Wied, D. & Versteeg, D. H. G. (1979). Neurohypophyseal principles and memory. *Federation Proceedings*, **38**, 2348–54.

Diamond, M. (1965). A critical evaluation of the ontogeny of human sexual behavior. *Quarterly Review of Biology*, **40**, 147–75.

Diamond, M. (1982). Sexual identity, monozygotic twins reared in discordant sex roles and a BBC follow-up. *Archives of Sexual Behavior*, **11**, 181–6.

Dixson, A. F. (1980). Androgens and aggressive behaviour in primates: a review. *Aggressive Behavior*, **6**, 37–67.

Donovan, B. T. (1970). *Mammalian Neuroendocrinology*. London: McGraw-Hill.

Donovan, B. T. (1978a). The portal vessels, the hypothalamus and the control of reproductive function. *Neuroendocrinology*, **25**, 1–21.

Donovan, B. T. (1978b). The behavioural actions of the hypothalamic peptides: a review. *Psychological Medicine*, **8**, 305–16.

Donovan, B. T. (1980). The role of hormones in perinatal brain differentiation. In *The Endocrine Functions of the Brain*, ed. M. Motta, pp. 117–41. New York: Raven Press.

Donovan, B. T. & van der Werff ten Bosch, J. J. (1965). *Physiology of Puberty*. London: Arnold.

Doris, P. A. (1984). Vasopressin and central integrative processes. *Neuroendocrinology*, **38**, 75–85.

Dörner, G. (1979). Hormones and sexual differentiation of the brain. In *Sex, Hormones and Behavior*, ed. R. Porter & J. Whelan, pp. 81–112. Ciba Foundation Symposium 62. Amsterdam: Excerpta Medica.

Dörner, G. (1983). Letter to the editor. *Archives of Sexual Behavior*, **12**, 577–82.

Doty, R. L., Green, P. A., Ram, C. & Yankell, S. L. (1982). Communication of gender from human breath odors: relationship to perceived intensity and pleasantness. *Hormones and Behavior*, **16**, 13–22.

Duncan, S. L. B. (1982). Menopausal flushing: where now? *British Journal of Obstetrics and Gynaecology*, **89**, 975–6.

Dunlop, D. & Chalmers, A. (1984). Diagnostic imaging and venous sampling of the endocrine system. In *Clinical Endocrinology*, ed. W. M. Keynes & P. B. S. Fowler, pp. 36–70. London: Heinemann.

Dunn, A. J. (1980). Neurochemistry of learning and memory: an evaluation of recent data. *Annual Review of Psychology*, **31**, 343–90.

Dunn, A. J., Rees, H. D., Iuvone, P. M., Delanoy, R. L. & Kramarcy, N. R. (1982). Neurochemical effects of behaviorally active peptides: ACTH and vasopressin. In *Neuronal Plasticity and Memory Formation*, ed. C. Ajmone Marsan & H. Matthies, pp. 113–22. New York: Raven Press.

Edwards, C. R. W. (1977). Vasopressin. In *Clinical Neuroendocrinology*, ed. L. Martini & G. M. Besser, pp. 527–67. London: Academic Press.

Ehrhardt, A. A. & Meyer-Bahlburg, H. F. L. (1981). Effects of prenatal sex hormones on gender-related behavior. *Science*, **211**, 1312–18.

Eichelman, B. (1983). The limbic system and aggression in humans. *Neuroscience and Biobehavioral Reviews*, **7**, 391–4.

Ellis, A. (1945). The sexual psychology of human hermaphrodites. *Psychosomatic Medicine*, **7**, 108–25.

Elmadjian, F. (1959). Excretion and metabolism of epinephrine. *Pharmacological Reviews*, **11**, 409–15.

Emson, P. C., Corder, R., Ratter, S. J., Tomlin, S., Lowry, P. J., Ress, L. H., Arregui, A. & Rosser, M. N. (1984). Regional distribution of pro-opiomelanocortin-derived peptides in the human brain. *Neuroendocrinology*, **38**, 45–50.

Epstein, A. N. (1982). The physiology of thirst. In *The Physiological Mechanisms of Motivation*, ed. D. W. Pfaff, pp. 165–214. New York: Springer-Verlag.

Evans, I. M. & Distiller, L. A. (1979). Effects of luteinizing hormone-releasing hormone on sexual arousal in normal men. *Archives of Sexual Behavior*, **8**, 385–95.

Everitt, B. J. (1983). Monoamines and the control of sexual behaviour. *Psychological Medicine*, **13**, 715–20.

Everitt, B. J. & Hansen, S. (1983). Catecholamines and hypothalamic mechanisms. In *Psychopharmacology and Sexual Disorders*, ed. D. Wheatley, pp. 3–14. Oxford University Press.

Fagg, G. E. & Foster, A. C. (1983). Amino acid neurotransmitters and their pathways in the mammalian central nervous system. *Neuroscience*, **9**, 701–19.

Faris, P. L., Komisaruk, B. R., Watkins, L. R. & Mayer, D. J. (1983). Evidence for the neuropeptide cholecystokinin as an antagonist of opiate analgesia. *Science*, **219**, 310–12.

Feder, H. H. (1984). Hormones and sexual behavior. *Annual Review of Psychology*, **35**, 165–200.

Fenoglio, C. M. & King, D. W. (1983). Somatostatin: an update. *Human Pathology*, **14**, 475–9.

Ferin, M. (1983). Neuroendocrine control of ovarian function in the primate. *Journal of Reproduction and Fertility*, **69**, 369–81.

Ferrier, I. N., Johnstone, E. C., Crow, T. J. & Rincon-Rodriguez, I. (1983). Anterior pituitary hormone secretion in chronic schizophrenics. *Archives of General Psychiatry*, **40**, 755–61.

Flerkó, B. (1974). Hypothalamic mediation of neuroendocrine regulation of hypophysial gonadotrophic functions. In *Reproductive Physiology*, ed. R. O. Greep, pp. 1–32. London: Butterworths.

Floody, O. R. (1983). Hormones and aggression in female mammals. In *Hormones and Aggressive Behavior*, ed. B. B. Svare, pp. 39–89. New York: Plenum Press.

Foote, S. L., Bloom, F. E. & Aston-Jones, G. (1983). Nucleus locus ceruleus: new evidence of anatomical and physiological specificity. *Physiological Reviews*, **63**, 844–914.

Fowler, P. B. S. (1984). Hypermetabolic states. In *Clinical Endocrinology*, ed. W. M. Keynes & P. B. S. Fowler, pp. 203–22. London: Heinemann.

Fox, C. A., Ismail, A. A. A., Love, D. N., Kirkham, K. E. & Loraine, J. A. (1972). Studies on the relationship between plasma testosterone levels and human sexual activity. *Journal of Endocrinology*, **52**, 51–8.

Frank, R. T. (1931). The hormonal causes of premenstrual tension. *Archives of Neurology and Psychiatry*, **26**, 1053–7.

Frankenhaeuser, M. (1982). Challenge–control interaction as reflected in sympathetic–adrenal and pituitary–adrenal activity: comparison between the sexes. *Scandinavian Journal of Psychology*, Suppl. **1**, 158–64.

Franks, S., Jacobs, H. S., Martin, N. & Nabarro, J. D. N. (1978). Hyperprolactinaemia and impotence. *Clinical Endocrinology*, **8**, 277–87.

Fras, I., Litin, E. M. & Pearson, J. S. (1967). Comparison of psychiatric symptoms in carcinoma of the pancreas with those in some other intra-abdominal neoplasms. *American Journal of Psychiatry*, **123**, 1553–62.

Frederickson, R. C. A. & Geary, L. E. (1982). Endogenous opioid peptides: review of physiological, pharmacological and clinical aspects. *Progress in Neurobiology*, **19**, 19–69.

Freed, W. J., Bing, L. A., Andersen, A. E. & Wyatt, R. J. (1984). Calcitonin as an anorectic agent. In *Psychoneuroendocrine Dysfunction*, ed. N. S. Shah & A. G. Donald, pp. 83–109. New York: Plenum Medical Book Company.

Freedman, R. & Carter, D. B. (1982). Neuroendocrine strategies in psychiatric research. In *Hormones in Development and Aging*, ed. A. Vernadakis & P. S. Timiras, pp. 619–36. Lancaster: MTP Press.

Friedhoff, A. J. & Miller, J. C. (1983). Clinical implications of receptor sensitivity modification. *Annual Review of Neuroscience*, **6**, 121–48.

Friedman, J. & Meares, R. A. (1979). The menstrual cycle and habituation. *Psychosomatic Medicine*, **41**, 369–81.

Frisch, R. E., Gotz-Welbergen, A. V., McArthur, J. W., Albright, T., Witschi, J., Bullen, B., Birnholz, J., Reed, R. B. & Hermann, H. (1981). Delayed menarche and amenorrhea of college athletes in relation to age of onset of training. *Journal of the American Medical Association*, **246**, 1559–63.

Frodi, A., Macaulay, J. & Thome, P. R. (1977). Are women always less aggressive than men? A review of the experimental literature. *Psychological Bulletin*, **84**, 634–60.

Furlong, F. W., Brown, G. M. & Beeching, M. F. (1976). Thyrotropin-releasing hormone: differential antidepressant and endocrinological effects. *American Journal of Psychiatry*, **133**, 1187–90.

Gandelman, R. (1983). Gonadal hormones and sensory function. *Neuroscience and Biobehavioral Reviews*, **7**, 1–17.

Ganong, W. F. (1984). The brain renin–angiotensin system. *Annual Review of Physiology*, **46**, 17–31.

Garnett, E. S., Firnau, G. & Nahmias, C. (1983). Dopamine visualized in the basal ganglia of living man. *Nature*, **305**, 137–40.

Garver, D. L., Pandey, G. N., Dekirmenjian, H. & Deleon-Jones, F. (1975). Growth hormone and catecholamines in affective disease. *American Journal of Psychiatry*, **132**, 1149–54.

Gash, D. M. & Thomas, G. J. (1983). What is the importance of vasopressin in memory processes? *Trends in Neurosciences*, **6**, 197–8.

Gerner, R. H., Post, R. M., Gillin, C. & Bunney, W. E. (1979). Biological and behavioral effects of one night's sleep deprivation in depressed patients and normals. *Journal of Psychiatric Research*, **15**, 21–40.

Gerstenbrand, F., Poewe, W., Aichner, F. & Saltuari, L. (1983). Klüver–Bucy syndrome in man: experiences with posttraumatic cases. *Neuroscience and Biobehavioral Reviews*, **7**, 413–17.

Gibbons, J. L. (1964). Cortisol secretion rate in depressive illness. *Archives of General Psychiatry*, **10**, 572–5.

Gibbons, J. L. (1983). Endocrine disorders. In *Handbook of Psychiatry*, vol. 2, *Mental Disorders and Somatic Illness*, ed. M. H. Lader, pp. 37–45. Cambridge University Press.

Gillin, J. C., Sitaram, N., Wehr, T., Duncan, W., Post, R., Murphy, D.L., Mendelson, W. B., Wyatt, R. J. & Bunney, W. E. (1984). Sleep and affective illness. In *Neurobiology of Mood Disorders*, ed. R. M. Post & J. C. Ballenger, pp. 157–89. Baltimore: Williams & Wilkins.

Gispen, W. H. (1982). Neuropeptides and behavior: ACTH. *Scandinavian Journal of Psychology*, Suppl. **1**, 16–25.

Gladue, B. A., Green, R. & Hellman, R. E. (1984). Neuroendocrine response to estrogen and sexual orientation. *Science*, **225**, 1496–99.

Glick, B. B., Baughman, W. L., Jensen, J. N. & Phoenix, C. H. (1982). Endogenous opiate systems and primate reproduction: inability of naloxone to induce sexual activity in rhesus males. *Archives of Sexual Behavior*, **11**, 267–75.

Goddard, G. V. (1964). Functions of the amygdala. *Psychological Bulletin*, **62**, 89–109.

Gold, P. W., Chrousos, G., Kellner, C., Post, R., Roy, A., Augerinos, P., Schulte, H., Oldfield, E. & Loriaux, D. L. (1984). Psychiatric implications of basic and clinical studies with corticotropin-releasing factor. *American Journal of Psychiatry*, **141**, 619–27.

Goldfoot, D. A., Kravetz, M. A., Goy, R. W. & Freeman, S. K. (1976). Lack of effect of vaginal lavages and aliphatic acids on ejaculatory responses in rhesus monkeys: behavioral and chemical analyses. *Hormones and Behavior*, **7**, 1–27.

Goldstein, M. (1974). Brain research and violent behavior. *Archives of Neurology*, **30**, 1–35.

Golstein, J., van Cauter, E., Désir, D., Noël, P., Spire, J.-P., Refetoff, S. & Copinschi, G. (1983). Effects of 'jet lag' on hormonal patterns. IV. Time shifts increase growth hormone release. *Journal of Clinical Endocrinology and Metabolism*, **56**, 433–40.

Goodall, McC. (1962). Sympathoadrenal response to gravitational stress. *Journal of Clinical Investigation*, **41**, 197–202.

Goodwin, F. K., Prange, A. J., Post, R. M., Muscettola, G. & Lipton, M. A. (1982). Potentiation of antidepressant effects by L-triiodothyronine in tricyclic nonresponders. *American Journal of Psychiatry*, **139**, 34–8.

Gorski, R. A. (1983). Steroid-induced sexual characteristics in the brain. In *Neuroendocrine Perspectives*, ed. E. E. Müller & R. M. MacLeod, vol. 2, pp. 1–35. Amsterdam: Elsevier Science Publishers.

Goy, R. W. & Goldfoot, D. A. (1975). Neuroendocrinology: animal models and problems of human sexuality. *Archives of Sexual Behavior*, **4**, 405–20.

Goy, R. W. & Phoenix, C. H. (1971). The effects of testosterone propionate administered before birth on the development of behavior in genetic female rhesus monkeys. In *Steroid Hormones and Brain Function*, ed. C. H. Sawyer & R. Gorski, pp. 193–200. Berkeley: University of California Press.

Graham, C. A. & McGrew, W. C. (1980). Menstrual synchrony in female undergraduates living on a coeducational campus. *Psychoneuroendocrinology*, **5**, 245–52.

Gray, D. S. & Gorzalka, B. B. (1980). Adrenal steroid interactions in female sexual behavior: a review. *Psychoneuroendocrinology*, **5**, 157–75.

Gray, J. A. (1971). Sex differences in emotional behaviour in mammals including man: endocrine bases. *Acta Psychologica*, **35**, 29–46.

Greden, J. F., Albala, A., Haskett, R. F., James, N. McI., Goodman, L., Steiner, M. & Carroll, B. J. (1980). Normalization of dexamethasone suppression test: a laboratory index of recovery from endogenous depression. *Biological Psychiatry*, **15**, 449–58.

Green, J. D. & Harris, G. W. (1947). The neurovascular link between the neurohypophysis and adenohypophysis. *Journal of Endocrinology*, **5**, 136–46.

Green, R. (1982). Prenatal androgens, postnatal socialization, and psychosexual development. *Annals of Internal Medicine*, **96**, 496–501.

Groos, G., Mason, R. & Meijer, J. (1983). Electrical and pharmacological properties of the suprachiasmatic nuclei. *Federation Proceedings*, **42**, 2790–5.

Grossman, A., Moult, P. J. A., McIntyre, H., Evans, J., Silverstone, T., Rees, L. H. & Besser, G. M. (1982). Opiate mediation of amenorrhoea in hyperprolactinaemia and in weight-loss related amenorrhoea. *Clinical Endocrinology*, **17**, 379–88.

Grossman, S. P. (1979). The biology of motivation. *Annual Review of Psychology*, **30**, 209–42.

Guillemin, R. (1983). A summary of current studies with somatocrinin, growth hormone releasing factor. *Clinical Research*, **31**, 338–41.

Guillemin, R., Brazeau, P., Böhlen, P., Esch, F., Ling, N. & Wehrenberg, W. B. (1982). Growth hormone-releasing factor from a human pancreatic tumor that caused acromegaly. *Science*, **218**, 585–7.

Gwirtsman, H. E., Roy-Byrne, P., Yager, J. & Gerner, R. H. (1983). Neuroendocrine abnormalities in bulimia. *American Journal of Psychiatry*, **140**, 559–63.

Halbreich, U., Assael, M., Ben-David, M. & Bornstein, R. (1976). Serum prolactin in women with premenstrual syndrome. *Lancet*, **ii**, 654–6.

Hall, E. D. (1982). Glucocorticoid effects on central nervous excitability and synaptic transmission. *International Review of Neurobiology*, **23**, 165–95.

Harding, C. F. & Feder, H. H. (1976). Relation between individual differences in sexual behavior and plasma testosterone levels in the guinea-pig. *Endocrinology*, **98**, 1198–1205.

Harlan, R. E., Shivers, B. D. & Pfaff, D. W. (1983). Midbrain microinfusions of prolactin increase the estrogen-dependent behavior, lordosis. *Science*, **219**, 1451–3.

Harvey, R. F. (1983). Gut peptides and the control of food intake. *British Medical Journal*, **287**, 1572–4.

Haskett, R. F., Steiner, M., Osmun, J. N. & Carroll, B. J. (1980). Severe premenstrual tension: delineation of the syndrome. *Biological Psychiatry*, **15**, 121–39.

Havrankova, J., Brownstein, M. & Roth, J. (1981). Insulin and insulin receptors in rodent brain. *Diabetologia*, **20**, 268–73.

Heath, R. G., Monroe, R. R. & Mickle, W. A. (1955). Stimulation of the amygdaloid nucleus in a schizophrenic patient. *American Journal of Psychiatry*, **111**, 862–3.

Heinsimer, J. A. & Lefkowitz, R. J. (1982). Adrenergic receptors: biochemistry, regulation, molecular mechanism, and clinical implications. *Journal of Laboratory and Clinical Medicine*, **100**, 641–58.

Henkin, R. I. (1980). Sensory manifestations of altered endocrine function. In *Perspectives in Clinical Endocrinology*, ed. W. B. Essman, pp. 195–225. Lancaster: MTP Press.

Hervey, G. R. (1969). Regulation of energy balance. *Nature*, **222**, 629–31.

Hess, W. R. & Akert, K. (1955). Experimental data on role of hypothalamus in mechanism of emotional behavior. *Archives of Neurology and Psychiatry*, **73**, 127–9.

Hetzel, B. S. & Hay, I. D. (1979). Thyroid function, iodine nutrition and fetal brain development. *Clinical Endocrinology*, **11**, 445–60.

Hines, M. (1982). Prenatal gonadal hormones and sex differences in human behavior. *Psychological Bulletin*, **92**, 56–80.

Hohmann, G. W. (1966). Some effects of spinal cord lesions on experienced emotional feelings. *Psychophysiology*, **3**, 143–56.

Hollingsworth, D. R. & Mabry, C. C. (1976). Congenital Graves disease. Four familial cases with long-term follow-up and perspective. *American Journal of Diseases of Childhood*, **130**, 148–55.

Hollister, L. E. (1975). Drugs and sexual behavior in man. *Life Sciences*, **17**, 661–8.

Hollister, L. E., Davis, K. L. & Davis, B. M. (1980). Hormones in the treatment of psychiatric disorders. In *Neuroendocrinology*, ed. D. T. Krieger & J. C. Hughes, pp. 167–75. Sunderland, Mass.: Sinauer Associates.

Holsboer, F. (1983). Hormones. In *Psychopharmacology, Part 2. Clinical Psychopharmacology*, ed. H. Hippius & G. Winokur, pp. 144–61. Amsterdam: Excerpta Medica.

Holt, A. B., Cheek, D. B. & Kerr, G. R. (1973). Prenatal hypothyroidism and brain composition in a primate. *Nature*, **243**, 413–15.

Hostetter, G., Jubb, S. L. & Kozlowski, G. P. (1980). An inability of subcutaneous vasopressin to affect passive avoidance behavior. *Neuroendocrinology*, **30**, 174–7.

van Houten, M. & Posner, B. I. (1981). Cellular basis of direct insulin action in the central nervous system. *Diabetologia*, **20**, 255–67.

Hsu, L. K. G. (1983). The aetiology of anorexia nervosa. *Psychological Medicine*, **13**, 231–8.

Hughes, J., Smith, T. W., Kosterlitz, H. W., Fothergill, L. A., Morgan, B. A. & Morris, H. R. (1975). Identification of two related pentapeptides from the brain with potent opiate agonist activity. *Nature*, **258**, 577–9.

Imperato-McGinley, J., Guerrero, L., Gautier, T. & Peterson, R. E. (1974). Steroid

5α-reductase deficiency in man: an inherited form of male pseudohermaphroditism. *Science*, **186**, 1213–15.

Imperato-McGinley, J., Peterson, R. E., Gautier, T. & Sturla, E. (1979). Androgens and the evolution of male-gender identity among male pseudohermaphrodites with 5α-reductase deficiency. *New England Journal of Medicine*, **300**, 1233–7.

Imura, H., Nakai, Y., Nakao, K., Oki, S. & Tanaka, I. (1982). Control of biosynthesis and secretion of ACTH, endorphins and related peptides. In *Neuroendocrine Perspectives*, vol. 1, ed. E. E. Müller & R. M. MacLeod, pp. 137–67. Amsterdam: Elsevier Medical Press.

Iversen, L. L. (1983). Nonopioid neuropeptides in mammalian CNS. *Annual Review of Pharmacology and Toxicology*, **23**, 1–27.

Iversen, L. L. (1984). Amino acids and peptides: fast and slow chemical signals in the nervous system? *Proceedings of the Royal Society Series B*, **221**, 245–60.

Iversen, S. D. & Iversen, L. L. (1981). *Behavioral Pharmacology*, 2nd edn. New York: Oxford University Press.

Izquierdo, I., Dias, R. D., Perry, M. L., Souza, D. O., Elisabetsky, E. & Carrasco, M. A. (1982). A physiological amnesic mechanism mediated by endogenous opioid peptides, and its possible role in learning. In *Neuronal Plasticity and Memory Formation*, ed. C. Ajmone Marsan & H. Matthies, pp. 89–111. New York: Raven Press.

Jackson, I. M. D. (1981). Evolutionary significance of the phylogenetic distribution of the mammalian hypothalamic releasing hormones. *Federation Proceedings*, **40**, 2545–52.

Jackson, I. M. D. (1982). Thyrotropin-releasing hormone. *New England Journal of Medicine*, **306**, 145–55.

Jain, V. K. (1972). A psychiatric study of hypothyroidism. *Psychiatric Clinics*, **5**, 121–30.

James, V. H. T., Tunbridge, D., Wilson, G. A., Hutton, J. D., Jacobs, H. S., Goodall, A. B., Murray, M. A. F. & Rippon, A. E. (1978). Central control of steroid hormone secretion. *Journal of Steroid Biochemistry*, **9**, 429–36.

Janal, M. N., Colt, E. W. D., Clark, W. C. & Glusman, M. (1984). Pain sensitivity, mood and plasma endocrine levels in man following long-distance running: effects of naloxone. *Pain*, **19**, 13–25.

Janowsky, D. S., Gorney, R., Castelnuovo-Tedesco, P. & Stone, C. B. (1969). Premenstrual–menstrual increases in psychiatric hospital admission rates. *American Journal of Obstetrics and Gynecology*, **103**, 189–91.

Jefferson, J. W. & Marshall, J. R. (1981). *Neuropsychiatric Features of Medical Disorders*. New York: Plenum Medical Book Company.

Johnson, R. N. (1972). *Aggression in Man and Animals*. Philadelphia: Saunders.

Jolles, J. (1983). Vasopressin-like peptides and the treatment of memory disorders in man. *Progress in Brain Research*, **60**, 169–82.

Jürgens, U. (1974). The hypothalamus and behavioral patterns. *Progress in Brain Research*, **41**, 445–62.

Kalogerakis, M. G. (1963). The role of olfaction in sexual development. *Psychosomatic Medicine*, **25**, 420–32.

Kandel, E. (1983). From metapsychology to molecular biology: explorations into the nature of anxiety. *American Journal of Psychiatry*, **140**, 1277–93.

Kastin, A. J., Banks, W. A., Zadina, J. E. & Graf, M. (1983). Brain peptides: the dangers of constricted nomenclatures. *Life Sciences*, **32**, 295–301.

Katz, J. L. & Weiner, H. (1980). The aberrant reproductive endocrinology of anorexia nervosa. In *Brain, Behavior and Bodily Disease*, ed. H. Weiner, M. A. Hofer & A. J. Stunkard, pp. 165–80. New York: Raven Press.

Kelly, J. S. (1982). Electrophysiology of peptides in the central nervous system. *British Medical Bulletin*, **38**, 283–90.

Kelly, W. F., Checkley, S. A., Bender, D. A. & Mashiter, K. (1983). Cushing's syndrome and depression – a prospective study of 26 patients. *British Journal of Psychiatry*, **142**, 16–19.

Keverne, E. B. (1979). Sexual and aggressive behaviour in social groups of talapoin monkeys. In *Sex, Hormones and Behaviour*, ed. R. Porter & J. Whelan, pp. 271–97. Ciba Foundation Symposium 62. Amsterdam: Excerpta Medica.

Kinsey, A. C., Pomeroy, W. B., Martin, C. E. & Gebhard, P. H. (1953). *Sexual Behavior in the Human Female*. Philadelphia: Saunders.

Kirkegaard, C. (1981). The thyrotropin response to thyrotropin-releasing hormone in endogenous depression. *Psychoneuroendocrinology*, **6**, 189–212.

Kleinschmidt, H. J., Waxenberg, S. E. & Cuker, R. (1956). Psychophysiology and psychiatric management of thyrotoxicosis: a two-year follow-up study. *Journal of the Mount Sinai Hospital, New York*, **23**, 131–53.

Kligman, D. & Goldberg, D. A. (1975). Temporal lobe epilepsy and aggression. *Journal of Nervous and Mental Disease*, **160**, 324–41.

Kling, A. (1974). Differential effects of amygdalectomy in male and female nonhuman primates. *Archives of Sexual Behavior*, **3**, 129–34.

Kling, A. & Hutt, P. J. (1958). Effect of hypothalamic lesions on the amygdala syndrome in the cat. *Archives of Neurology and Psychiatry*, **79**, 511–17.

Klüver, H. (1952). Brain mechanisms and behavior with special reference to the rhinencephalon. *Journal-Lancet*, **72**, 567–77.

Klüver, H. & Bucy, P. C. (1937). 'Psychic blindness' and other symptoms following bilateral temporal lobectomy in Rhesus monkeys. *American Journal of Physiology*, **119**, 352–3.

Kolata, G. (1983). Math genius may have hormonal basis. *Science*, **222**, 1312.

Kosten, T. R., Jacobs, S., Mason, J., Wahby, V. & Atkins, S. (1984). Psychological correlates of growth hormone response to stress. *Psychosomatic Medicine*, **46**, 49–58.

Kraemer, H. C., Becker, H. B., Brodie, H. K. H., Doering, C. H., Moos, R. H. & Hamburg, D. A. (1976). Orgasmic frequency and plasma testosterone levels in normal human males. *Archives of Sexual Behavior*, **5**, 125–32.

Kreuz, L. E., Rose, R. M. & Jennings, J. R. (1972). Suppression of plasma testosterone levels and psychological stress. *Archives of General Psychiatry*, **26**, 479–82.

Krieger, D. T. (1983a). The multiple faces of pro-opiomelanocortin, a prototype precursor molecule. *Clinical Research*, **31**, 342–53.

Krieger, D. T. (1983b). Brain peptides: what, where, and why? *Science*, **222**, 975–85.

Kripke, D. F., Risch, S.C. & Janowsky, D. (1983). Bright white light alleviates depression. *Psychiatry Research*, **10**, 105–12.

Kusalic, M., Fortin, C. & Gauthier, Y. (1972). Psychodynamic aspects of dwarfism. Response to growth hormone treatment. *Canadian Psychiatric Association Journal*, **17**, 29–34.

de Lacoste-Utamsling, C. & Holloway, R. L. (1982). Sexual dimorphism in the human corpus callosum. *Science*, **216**, 1431–2.

Laczi, F., Valkusz, Z., László, F. A., Wagner, Á., Járdánházy, T., Szász, A., Szilárd, J. & Telegdy, G. (1982). Effects of lysine-vasopressin and L-deamino-8-D-arginine vasopressin on memory in healthy individuals and diabetes insipidus patients. *Psychoneuroendocrinology*, **7**, 185–93.

Laczi, F., Van Ree, J. M., Balogh, L., Szász, A., Járdánhazy, T., Wágner, A., Gáspár, L., Valkusz, Z., Dobranovics, I., Szilárd, J., László, F. A. & De Wied, D. (1983). Lack of effect of desglycinamide-arginine-vasopressin (DGAVP) on memory in patients with Korsakoff's syndrome. *Acta Endocrinologica, Copenhagen*, **104**, 177–82.

LaFerla, J. J., Anderson, D. L. & Schalch, D. S. (1978). Psychoendocrine response to sexual arousal in human males. *Psychosomatic Medicine*, **40**, 166–72.

Lancet (1981). Editorial: Premenstrual syndrome. *Lancet*, **ii**, 1393–4.

Lange, J. D., Brown, W. A., Wincze, J. P. & Zwick, W. (1980). Serum testosterone concentration and penile tumescence changes in men. *Hormones and Behavior*, **14**, 267–70.

Lauder, J. M. (1983). Hormonal and humoral influences upon brain development. *Psychoneuroendocrinology*, **8**, 121–55.

Legros, J. J. & Lancranjan, I. (1983). Vasopressin in neuropsychiatric disorders. In *Psychoneuroendocrine Dysfunction*, ed. N. S. Shah & A. G. Donald, pp. 255–78. New York: Plenum Medical Book Company.

Le Moal, M., Koob, G. F., Koda, L. Y., Bloom, F. E., Manning, M., Sawyer, W. H. & Rivier, J. (1981). Vasopressin receptor antagonist prevents behavioural effects of vasopressin. *Nature*, **291**, 491–3.

Levey, G. S. & Robinson, A. G. (1982). Introduction to the general principles of hormone–receptor interactions. *Metabolism*, **31**, 639–45.

Levi, L. (1969). Sympatho-adreno-medullary activity, diuresis and emotional reactions during visual sexual stimulation in human females and males. *Psychosomatic Medicine*, **31**, 251–68.

Lev-Ran, A. (1974). Sexuality and educational levels of women with the late-treated adrenogenital syndrome. *Archives of Sexual Behavior*, **3**, 27–32.

Lewis, D. A. & Smith, R. E. (1983). Steroid-induced psychiatric syndromes. A report of 14 cases and a review of the literature. *Journal of Affective Disorders*, **5**, 319–32.

Lewy, A. J. (1984a). Human melatonin secretion (II): a marker for the circadian system and the effects of light. In *Neurobiology of Mood Disorders*, ed. R. M. Post & J. C. Ballenger, pp. 215–26. Baltimore: Williams & Wilkins.

Lewy, A. J. (1984b). Human melatonin secretion (I): a marker for adrenergic function. In *Neurobiology of Mood Disorders*, ed. R. M. Post & J. C. Ballenger, pp. 207–14. Baltimore: Williams & Wilkins.

Leyendecker, G. & Wildt, L. (1983). Induction of ovulation with chronic intermittent (pulsatile) administration of Gn-RH in women with hypothalamic amenorrhoea. *Journal of Reproduction and Fertility*, **69**, 397–409.

Lidz, T. (1949). Emotional factors in the etiology of hyperthyroidism. *Psychosomatic Medicine*, **11**, 2–8.

Lightman, S. L., Jacobs, H. S. & Maguire, A. K. (1982). Down-regulation of gonadotrophin secretion in postmenopausal women by a superactive LHRH analogue: lack of effect on menopausal flushing. *British Journal of Obstetrics and Gynaecology*, **89**, 977–80.

Lindström, L. H., Gunne, L.-M., Öst, L.-G. & Persson, E. (1977). Thyrotropin-releasing hormone (TRH) in chronic schizophrenia: a controlled study. *Acta Psychiatrica Scandinavica*, **55**, 74–80.

Linsell, C. R. & Lightman, S. L. (1983). Postmenopausal flashes: studies of chronological organization. *Psychoneuroendocrinology*, **8**, 435–40.

Loosen, P. T. & Prange, A. J. (1982). Serum thyrotropin response to thyrotropin-releasing hormone in psychiatric patients: a review. *American Journal of Psychiatry*, **139**, 405–16.

Lowy, M. T. & Yim, G. K. W. (1983). Stimulation of food intake following opiate agonists in rats but not hamsters. *Psychopharmacology*, **81**, 28–32.

Luttinger, D., Hernandez, D. E., Nemeroff, C. B. & Prange, A. J. (1984). Peptides and nociception. *International Review of Neurobiology*, **25**, 185–241.

Lynch, A. & Mychalkiw, W. (1978). Prenatal progesterone. II. Its role in the treatment of pre-eclamptic toxaemia and its effect on the offspring's intelligence: a reappraisal. *Early Human Development*, **2**, 323–39.

Lynch, A., Mychalkiw, W. & Hutt, S. J. (1978). Prenatal progesterone. I. Its effect on development and on intellectual and academic achievement. *Early Human Development*, **2**, 305–22.

Lytle, L. D. (1977). Control of eating behavior. In *Nutrition and the Brain*, vol. 2, ed. R. J. Wurtman & J. J. Wurtman, pp. 1–145. New York: Raven Press.

McAdoo, B. C., Doering, C. H., Kraemer, H. C., Dessert, N., Brodie, H. K. H. & Hamburg, D. A. (1978). A study of the effects of gonadotropin-releasing hormone on human mood and behavior. *Psychosomatic Medicine*, **40**, 199–209.

McCance, R. A., Luff, M. C. & Widdowson, E. E. (1937). Physical and emotional periodicity in women. *Journal of Hygiene*, **37**, 571–611.

McCann, S. M. (1982). The role of brain peptides in the control of anterior pituitary hormone secretion. In *Neuroendocrine Perspectives*, vol. 1, ed. E. E. Müller & R. M. MacLeod, pp. 1–22. Amsterdam: Elsevier Biomedical Press.

McCann, S. M., Lumpkin, M. D., Mizunuma, H., Khorram, O., Ottlecz, A. & Samson, W. K. (1984), Peptidergic and dopaminergic control of prolactin release. *Trends in Neurosciences*, **7**, 127–31.

McCann, S. M., Mizunuma, H., Samson, W. K. & Lumpkin, M. D. (1983). Differential hypothalamic control of FSH secretion: a review. *Psychoneuroendocrinology*, **8**, 299–308.

McConnell, R. J., Menendez, C. E., Smith, F. R., Henkin, R. I. & Rivlin, R. S. (1975). Defects of taste and smell in patients with hypothyroidism. *American Journal of Medicine*, **59**, 354–64.

MacCrimmon, D. J., Wallace, J. E., Goldberg, W. M. & Streiner, D. L. (1979). Emotional disturbance and cognitive deficits in hyperthyroidism. *Psychosomatic Medicine*, **41**, 331–40.

McEwen, B. S. (1980). The brain as a target organ of endocrine hormones. In *Neuroendocrinology*, ed. D. T. Krieger & J. C. Hughes, pp. 33–42. Sunderland, Mass.: Sinauer Associates.

McEwen, B. S. (1981). Neural gonadal steroid actions. *Science*, **211**, 1303–11.

McEwen, B. S., Biegon, A., Davis, P. G., Krey, L. C., Luine, V. N., McGinnis, M. Y., Paden, C. M., Parsons, B. & Rainbow, T. C. (1982). Steroid hormones: humoral signals which alter brain cell properties and functions. *Recent Progress in Hormone Research*, **38**, 41–83.

McEwen, B. S. & Parsons, B. (1982). Gonadal steroid action on the brain: neurochemistry and neuropharmacology. *Annual Review of Pharmacology and Toxicology*, **22**, 555–98.

McGaugh, J. L. (1983). Hormonal influences on memory. *Annual Review of Psychology*, **34**, 297–323.

McGeer, P. L. & McGeer, E. G. (1980). Chemistry of mood and emotion. *Annual Review of Psychology*, **31**, 273–307.

MacKinnon, P. C. B. & MacKinnon, I. L. (1956). Hazards of the menstrual cycle. *British Medical Journal*, **i**, 555.

MacLean, P. D. (1976). Sensory and perceptive factors in emotional functions of the triune brain. In *Biological Foundations of Psychiatry*, vol. 1, ed. R. G. Grenell & S. Gabay, pp. 177–98. New York: Raven Press.

McLennan, M. T. & McLennan, C. E. (1971). Estrogenic status of menstruating and menopausal women assessed by cervicovaginal smears. *Obstetrics and Gynecology*, **37**, 325–31.

Major, R. H. (1945). *Classic Descriptions of Disease*, 3rd edn. Springfield, Ill.: Thomas.

Malina, R. M. (1983). Menarche in athletes: a synthesis and hypothesis. *Annals of Human Biology*, **10**, 1–24.

Mancia, G. & Zanchetti, A. (1981). Hypothalamic control of autonomic functions. In *Behavioral Studies of the Hypothalamus*, ed. P. L. Morgane & J. Panksepp, pp. 147–202. New York: Marcel Dekker.

Martin, J. B., Reichlin, S. & Brown, G. M. (1977). *Clinical Neuroendocrinology*. Philadelphia: Davis.

Mashio, Y., Inada, M., Tanaka, K., Ishii, H., Naito, K., Nishikawa, M., Takahashi, K. & Imura, H. (1982). High affinity 3,5,3,'-L-triiodothyronine binding to synaptosomes in rat cerebral cortex. *Endocrinology*, **110**, 1257–1261.

Mason, J. W. (1968a). A review of psychoendocrine research on the pituitary–adrenal cortical system. *Psychosomatic Medicine*, **30**, 576–607.

Mason, J. W. (1968b). A review of psychoendocrine research on the sympathetic–adrenal medullary system. *Psychosomatic Medicine*, **30**, 631–53.

Mason, J. W. (1970). Strategy in psychosomatic research. *Psychosomatic Medicine*, **32**, 427–39.

Mason, S. T. (1983). The neurochemistry and pharmacology of extinction behavior. *Neuroscience and Biobehavioral Reviews*, **7**, 325–47.

Mason, S. T. & Fibiger, H. C. (1979). Current concepts. I. Anxiety: the locus coeruleus disconnection. *Life Sciences*, **25**, 2141–7.

Mathews, A., Whitehead, A. & Kellett, J. (1983). Psychological and hormonal factors in the treatment of female sexual dysfunction. *Psychological Medicine*, **13**, 83–92.

Matthews, R. (1979). Testosterone levels in aggressive offenders. In *Psychopharmacology of Aggression*, ed. M. Sandler, pp. 123–30. New York: Raven Press.

Mazur, A. & Lamb, T. A. (1980). Testosterone, status and mood in human males. *Hormones and Behavior*, **14**, 236–46.

Medvei, V. C. (1982). *A History of Endocrinology*. Lancaster: MTP Press.

Meisenberg, G. & Simmons, W. H. (1983a). Centrally mediated effects of neurohypophyseal hormones. *Neuroscience and Biobehavioral Reviews*, **7**, 263–80.

Meisenberg, G. & Simmons, W. H. (1983b). Peptides and the blood–brain barrier. *Life Sciences*, **32**, 2611–23.

Meites, J., Donovan, B. T. & McCann, S. M. (eds.) (1975). *Pioneers of Neuroendocrinology*. New York: Plenum Press.

Meltzer, H. Y., Sachar, E. J. & Frantz, A. G. (1974). Serum prolactin levels in unmedicated schizophrenic patients. *Archives of General Psychiatry*, **31**, 564–9.

Mendlewicz, J., Van Cauter, E., Linkowski, P., L'Hermite, M. & Robyn, C. (1980). The 24-hour profile of prolactin in depression. *Life Sciences*, **27**, 2015–24.

Metcalf, G. & Dettmar, P. W. (1981). Is thyrotropin releasing hormone an endogenous ergotropic substance in the brain? *Lancet*, **i**, 586–9.

Meyer-Bahlburg, H. F. L. (1978). Behavioral effects of estrogen treatment in human males. *Pediatrics*, **62**, 1171–7.

Meyer-Bahlburg, H. F. L. (1981). Androgens and human aggression. In *The Biology of Aggression*, ed. P. F. Brain & D. Benton, pp. 263–90. Alphen aan den Rijn: Sijthoff & Noordhoff.

Meyer-Bahlburg, H. F. L. (1982). Hormones and psychosexual differentiation: implications for the management of intersexuality, homosexuality and transsexuality. *Clinics in Endocrinology and Metabolism*, **11**, 681–701.

Meyer-Bahlburg, H. F. L. & Ehrhardt, A. A. (1982). Prenatal sex hormones and human aggression: a review, and new data on progestogen effects. *Aggressive Behavior*, **8**, 39–62.

Meyer-Bahlburg, H. F. L., Feinman, J. A., MacGillivray, M. H. & Aceto, T. (1978). Growth hormone deficiency, brain development, and intelligence. *American Journal of Diseases of Children*, **132**, 565–72.

Michael, R. P., Bonsall, R. W. & Zumpe, D. (1976). Evidence for chemical communication in primates. *Vitamins and Hormones*, **34**, 137–86.

Michael, R. P. & Gibbons, J. L. (1963). Interrelationships between the endocrine system and neuropsychiatry. *International Review of Neurobiology*, **5**, 243–302.

Michael, R. P., Zumpe, D., Keverne, E. B. & Bonsall, R. W. (1972). Neuroendocrine factors in the control of primate behavior. *Recent Progress in Hormone Research*, **28**, 665–706.

Mogensen, G. J. (1977). *The neurobiology of behavior: an introduction*. Hillsdale, New Jersey: Lawrence Erlbaum Associates.

Money, J. (1975a). *Ablatio penis:* normal male infant sex-reassigned as a girl. *Archives of Sexual Behavior*, **4**, 65–71.

Money, J. (1975b). Intellectual functioning in childhood endocrinopathies and related cytogenetic disorders. In *Endocrine and Genetic Disorders of Childhood and Adolescence*, 2nd edn, ed. L. I. Gardner, pp. 1207–18. Philadelphia: Saunders.

Money, J. (1983). The genealogical descent of sexual psychoneuroendocrinology from sex and health theory: the eighteenth to the twentieth centuries. *Psychoneuroendocrinology*, **8**, 391–400.

Money, J., Annecillo, C. & Kelley, J. F. (1983). Growth of intelligence: failure and catch-up associated respectively with abuse and rescue in the syndrome of abuse dwarfism. *Psychoneuroendocrinology*, **8**, 309–19.

Money, J. & Ehrhardt, A. A. (1972). *Man and Woman, Boy and Girl*. Baltimore: Johns Hopkins University Press.

Money, J., Hampson, J. G. & Hampson, J. L. (1955). Hermaphroditism: recommendations concerning assignment of sex, change of sex, and psychologic management. *Bulletin of the Johns Hopkins Hospital*, **97**, 284–300.

Money, J. & Lewis, V. (1966). IQ, genetics and accelerated growth: adrenogenital syndrome. *Bulletin of the Johns Hopkins Hospital*, **118**, 365–73.

Money, J. & Mathews, D. (1982). Prenatal exposure to virilizing progestins: an adult follow-up study of twelve women. *Archives of Sexual Behavior*, **11**, 73–83.

Money, J. & Schwartz, M. (1976). Fetal androgens in the early treated adrenogenital syndrome of 46XX hermaphroditism: influence on assertive and aggressive types of behavior. *Aggressive Behavior*, **2**, 19–30.

Money, J., Wiedeking, C., Walker, P. A. & Gain, D. (1976). Combined antiandrogenic and counselling program for treatment of 46,XY and 47,XYY sex offenders. In *Hormones, Behavior and Psychopathology*, ed. E. Sachar, pp. 105–20. New York: Raven Press.

Moore, R. Y. (1982). Catecholamine neuron systems in brain. *Annals of Neurology*, **12**, 321–7.

Moore, R. Y. (1983). Organization and function of a central nervous system circadian oscillator: the suprachiasmatic hypothalamic nucleus. *Federation Proceedings*, **42**, 2783–9.

Moore-Ede, M. C. (1983). The circadian timing system in mammals: two pacemakers preside over many secondary oscillators. *Federation Proceedings*, **42**, 2802–8.

Moore-Ede, M. C., Czeisler, C. A. & Richardson, G. S. (1983). Circadian time-keeping in health and disease. *New England Journal of Medicine*, **309**, 469–76; 530–6.

Moran, T. H. & McHugh, P. R. (1982). Cholecystokinin suppresses food intake by inhibiting gastric emptying. *American Journal of Physiology*, **242**, R491–7.

Morley, J. E. (1980). The neuroendocrine control of appetite: the role of the endogenous opiates, cholecystokinin, TRH, γ-amino-butyric-acid and the diazepam receptor. *Life Sciences*, **27**, 355–68.

Morley, J. E. (1981). Neuroendocrine control of thyrotropin secretion. *Endocrine Reviews*, **2**, 396–436.

Morley, J. E. (1983). Neuroendocrine effects of endogenous opioid peptides in human subjects: a review. *Psychoneuroendocrinology*, **8**, 361–79.

Morley, J. E. & Levine, A. S. (1983). The central control of appetite. *Lancet*, **i**, 398–401.

Morley, J. E., Levine, A. S. & Rowland, N. E. (1983). Stress induced eating. *Life Sciences*, **32**, 2169–82.

Morley, J. E., Levine, A. S., Yim, G. K. & Lowy, M. T. (1983). Opioid modulation of appetite. *Neuroscience and Biobehavioral Reviews*, **7**, 281–305.

Mortimer, C. H., McNeilly, A. S., Fisher, R. A., Murray, M. A. F. & Besser, G. M. (1974). Gonadotrophin-releasing hormone therapy in hypogonadal males with hypothalamic or pituitary dysfunction. *British Medical Journal*, **iv**, 617–21.

Moses, A. M. (1980). Diabetes insipidus and ADH regulation. In *Neuroendocrinology*, ed. D. T. Krieger & J. C. Hughes, pp. 141–8. Sunderland, Mass.: Sinauer Associates.

Moss, R. L. (1979). Actions of the hypothalamic–hypophysiotropic hormones on the brain. *Annual Review of Physiology*, **41**, 617–31.

Moyer, K. E. (1981). Biological substrates of aggression and implications for control. In *The Biology of Aggression*, ed. P. F. Brain & D. Benton, pp. 47–67. Alphen aan den Rijn: Sijthoff and Noordhoff.

Müller, E. E., Camanni, F., Genazzani, A. R., Cocchi, D., Casanueva, F., Massara, F., Locatelli, V., Martinez-Campos, A. & Mantegazza, P. (1981). Dopamine agonist and antagonist drugs and hypothalamic pituitary dysfunction. In *Neuroendocrine Regulation and Altered Behaviour*, ed. P. D. Hrdina & R. L. Singhal, pp. 51–94. London: Croom Helm.

Munck, A., Guyre, P. M. & Holbrook, N. J. (1984). Physiological functions of glucocorticoids in stress and their relation to pharmacological actions. *Endocrine Reviews*, 5, 25–44.

Murray, G. R. (1920). The life-history of the first case of myxoedema treated by thyroid extract. *British Medical Journal*, i, 359–60.

Nadler, R. D. (1973). Further evidence on the intrahypothalamic locus for androgenization of female rats. *Neuroendocrinology*, 12, 110–19.

Naftolin, F., Ryan, K. J., Davies, I. J., Reddy, V. V., Flores, F., Petro, Z. & Kuhn, M. (1975). The formation of estrogens by central neuroendocrine tissues. *Recent Progress in Hormone Research*, 31, 295–315.

Naftolin, F., Ryan, K. J. & Petro, Z. (1971a). Aromatization of androstenedione by limbic system tissue from human foetuses. *Journal of Endocrinology*, 51, 795–6.

Naftolin, F., Ryan, K. J. & Petro, Z. (1971b). Aromatization of androstenedione by the diencephalon. *Journal of Clinical Endocrinology and Metabolism*, 33, 368–70.

Nance, D. M., White, J. P. & Moger, W. H. (1983). Neural regulation of the ovary: evidence for hypothalamic asymmetry in endocrine control. *Brain Research Bulletin*, 10, 353–5.

Nebes, R. D., Reynolds, C. F. & Horn, L. C. (1984). The effect of vasopressin on memory in the healthy elderly. *Psychiatry Research* 11, 49–59.

Nemeroff, C. B., Youngblood, W. W., Manberg, P. J., Prange, A. J. & Kizer, J. S. (1983). Regional brain concentrations of neuropeptides in Huntington's chorea and schizophrenia. *Science*, 221, 972–5.

Nishizuka, M. & Arai, Y. (1982). Synapse formation in response to estrogen in the medial amygdala developing in the eye. *Proceedings of the National Academy of Sciences, USA*, 79, 7024–6.

Nock, B. & Feder, H. H. (1981). Neurotransmitter modulation of steroid action on target cells that mediate reproduction and reproductive behavior. *Neuroscience and Biobehavioral Reviews*, 5, 437–47.

Nordeen, E. J. & Yahr, P. (1982). Hemispheric asymmetries in the behavioral and hormonal effects of sexually differentiating mammalian brain. *Science*, 218, 391–4.

Norgren, R. & Grill, H. (1982). Brain-stem control of ingestive behavior. In *The Physiological Mechanisms of Motivation*, ed. D. W. Pfaff, pp. 99–131. New York: Springer-Verlag.

Oliverio, A., Castellano, C. & Puglisi-Allegra, S. (1984). Psychobiology of opioids. *International Review of Neurobiology*, 25, 277–337.

Olweus, D., Mattsson, A., Schalling, D. & Löw, H. (1980). Testosterone, aggression, physical, and personality dimensions in normal adolescent males. *Psychosomatic Medicine*, 42, 253–69.

van Ophuisen, J. H. W. (1951). A new phase in clinical psychiatry. Part I and Introduction. Endocrinologic orientation to psychiatric disorders. *Journal of Clinical and Experimental Psychopathology*, 12, 1–4.

Page, R. B. (1982). Pituitary blood flow. *American Journal of Physiology*, 243, E427–42.

Panksepp, J., Bishop, P. & Rossi, J. (1979). Neurohumoral and endocrine control of feeding. *Psychoneuroendocrinology*, 4, 89–106.

Pardridge, W. M. (1983). Neuropeptides and the blood–brain barrier. *Annual Review of Physiology*, 45, 73–82.

Parlee, M. B. (1983). Menstrual rhythms in sensory processes: a review of fluctuations in vision, olfaction, audition, taste and touch. *Psychological Bulletin*, 93, 539–48.

Parra-Covarrubias, A., Rivera-Rodriguez, I. & Almarez-Ugalde, A. (1971). Cephalic phase of insulin secretion in obese adolescents. *Diabetes*, 20, 800–2.

Pavasuthipaisit, K., Norman, R. L., Ellinwood, W. E., Oyama, T. T., Baughman, W. L. & Spies, H. G. (1983). Different prolactin, thyrotropin, and thyroxine responses after prolonged intermittent or continuous infusions of thyrotropin-releasing hormone in rhesus monkeys. *Journal of Clinical Endocrinology and Metabolism*, 56, 541–8.

Penfield, W. & Milner, B. (1958). Memory deficit produced by bilateral lesions in the hippocampal zone. *Archives of Neurology and Psychiatry*, 79, 475–97.

Pepper, G. M. & Krieger, D. T. (1984). Hypothalamic–pituitary–adrenal abnormalities in depression: their possible relation to central mechanisms regulating ACTH release. In *Neurobiology of Mood Disorders*, ed. R. M. Post & J. C. Ballenger, pp. 245–70. Baltimore: Williams & Wilkins.

Persky, H. (1974). Reproductive hormones, moods, and the menstrual cycle. In *Sex Differences in Behavior*, ed. R. C. Friedman, R. M. Richart & R. L. Vande Wiele, pp. 455–66. New York: Wiley.

Persky, H., Charney, N., Lief, H. I., O'Brien, C. P., Miller, W. R. & Strauss, D. (1978a). The relationship of plasma estradiol level to sexual behavior in young women. *Psychosomatic Medicine*, 40, 523–35.

Persky, H., Driesbach, L., Miller, W. R., O'Brien, C. P., Khan, M. A., Lief, H. I., Charney, N. & Strauss, D. (1982). The relation of plasma androgen levels to sexual behaviors and attitudes of women. *Psychosomatic Medicine*, 44, 305–19.

Persky, H., Lief, H. I., Strauss, D., Miller, W. R. & O'Brien, C. P. (1978b). Plasma testosterone level and sexual behavior of couples. *Archives of Sexual Behavior*, 7, 157–173.

Petersen, P. (1968). Psychiatric disorders and primary hyperparathyroidism. *Journal of Clinical Endocrinology and Metabolism*, 28, 1491–5.

Petty, F. & Sherman, A. D. (1984). Plasma GABA levels in psychiatric illness. *Journal of Affective Disorders*, 6, 131–8.

Pfaff, D. W. (1982). Motivational concepts: definitions and distinctions. In *The Physiological Mechanisms of Motivation*, ed. D. W. Pfaff, pp. 3–24. New York: Springer-Verlag.

Pfaff, D. W. & McEwen, B. S. (1983). Actions of estrogens and progestins on nerve cells. *Science*, 219, 808–14.

Phoenix, C. H., Goy, R. W., Gerall, A. A. & Young, W. C. (1959). Organizing action of prenatally administered testosterone propionate on the tissues mediating mating behavior in the female guinea pig. *Endocrinology*, 65, 369–82.

Pirke, K. M., Kockott, G. & Dittmar, F. (1974). Psychosexual stimulation and plasma testosterone in man. *Archives of Sexual Behavior*, 3, 577–84.

Plaut, S. M. & Friedman, S. B. (1981). Psychosocial factors in infectious disease. In *Psychoneuroimmunology*, ed. R. Ader, pp. 3–30. New York: Academic Press.

Plum, F. & van Uitert, R. (1978). Nonendocrine diseases and disorders of the hypothalamus. In *The Hypothalamus*, ed. S. Reichlin, R. J. Baldessarini & J. B. Martin, pp. 415–73. New York: Raven Press.

Plutchik, R. (1980). A general psychoevolutionary theory of emotion. In *Emotion. Theory, Research and Experience. 1. Theories of Emotion*, ed. R. Plutchik & H. Kellerman, pp. 3–33. New York: Academic Press.

Plutchik, R. & Kellerman, H. (eds.) (1980). *Emotion. Theory, Research and Experience. 1. Theories of Emotion*. New York: Academic Press.

Poeck, K. & Pilleri, G. (1965). Release of hypersexual behaviour due to lesion in the limbic system. *Acta Neurologica Scandinavica*, 41, 233–44.

Porte, D. & Woods, S. C. (1981). Regulation of food intake and body weight by insulin. *Diabetologia*, 20, 274–80.

Powley, T. L. & Laughton, W. (1981). Neural pathways involved in the hypothalamic integration of autonomic responses. *Diabetologia*, 20, 378–86.

Prange, A. J., Nemeroff, C. B., Loosen, P. T., Bissette, G., Osbahr, A. J., Wilson, I. C. & Lipton, M. A. (1979). Behavioral effects of thyrotropin-releasing hormone in animals and man: a review. In *Central Nervous Effects of Hypothalamic Hormones and Other Peptides*, ed. R. Collu, A. Barbeau, J. R. Ducharme & J.-G. Rochefort, pp. 75–96. New York: Raven Press.

Pratt, J. P., (1939). Sex functions in man. In *Sex and Internal Secretions*, ed. E. Allen, C. H. Danforth & E. A. Doisy, pp. 1263–1334. London: Baillière, Tindall & Cox.

Przewlocki, R., Lasón, W., Konecka, A. M., Gramsch, C., Herz, A. & Reid, L. D. (1983). The opioid peptide dynorphin, circadian rhythms, and starvation. *Science*, 219, 71–3.

Pullan, P. T. (1984). Ectopic hormone production. In *Clinical Endocrinology*, ed.
W. M. Keynes & P. B. S. Fowler, pp. 587–602. London: Heinemann.

Pyle, R. L., Mitchell, J. E. & Eckert, E. D. (1981). Bulimia: a report of 34 cases. *Journal of Clinical Psychiatry*, **42**, 60–4.

Quadagno, D. M., Briscoe, R. & Quadagno, J. S. (1977). Effect of perinatal gonadal hormones on selected nonsexual behavior patterns: a critical assessment of the nonhuman and human literature. *Psychological Bulletin*, **84**, 62–80.

Quadagno, D. M., Shubeita, H. E., Deck, J. & Francoeur, D. (1981). Influence of male social contacts, exercise and all-female living conditions on the menstrual cycle. *Psychoneuroendocrinology*, **6**, 239–44.

Quarton, G. C., Clark, L. D., Cobb, S. & Bauer, W. (1955). Mental disturbances associated with ACTH and cortisone: a review of explanatory hypotheses. *Medicine*, **34**, 13–50.

Querido, A., Bleichrodt, N. & Djokomoeljanto, R. (1978). Thyroid hormones and human mental development. *Progress in Brain Research*, **48**, 337–44.

Raboch, J., Mellan, J. & Starka, L. (1979). Klinefelter's syndrome: sexual development and activity. *Archives of Sexual Behavior*, **8**, 333–9.

Raboch, J. & Stárka, L. (1973). Reported coital activity of men and levels of plasma testosterone. *Archives of Sexual Behavior*, **2**, 309–15.

Raisman, G. & Field, P. M. (1973). Sexual dimorphism in the neuropil of the preoptic area of the rat and its dependence on neonatal androgen. *Brain Research*, **54**, 1–29.

Ramsden, D. B. & Hoffenberg, R. (1983). The actions of thyroid hormones mediated via the cell nucleus and their clinical significance. *Clinics in Endocrinology and Metabolism*, **12**, 101–15.

Rausch, J. L., Janowsky, D. S., Risch, S. C., Judd, L. L. & Huey, L. Y. (1982). Hormonal and neurotransmitter hypotheses of premenstrual tension. *Psychopharmacological Bulletin*, **18**, No. 4, 26–34.

Rebar, R. W. & Cumming, D. C. (1981). Reproductive function in women athletes. *Journal of the American Medical Association*, **246**, 1590.

Redmond, D. E. & Huang, Y. H. (1979). Current concepts II. New evidence for a locus coeruleus–norepinephrine connection with anxiety. *Life Sciences*, **25**, 2149–62.

van Ree, J. M. & De Wied, D. (1981). Endorphins in schizophrenia. *Neuropharmacology*, **20**, 1271–7.

Rees, L. H. & Smith, R. (1982). Endogenous opiates: β-endorphin and methionine enkephalin. In *Recent Advances in Endocrinology and Metabolism*, vol. 2, ed.
J. L. H. O'Riordan, 1–15. Edinburgh: Churchill Livingstone.

Reichlin, S. (1983). Somatostatin. *New England Journal of Medicine*, **309**, 1495–1501; 1556–63.

Reid, I. A. & Schwartz, J. (1984). Role of vasopressin in the control of blood pressure. In *Frontiers in Neuroendocrinology*, ed. L. Martini & W. F. Ganong, pp. 177–97. New York: Raven Press.

Reinisch, J. M. (1974). Fetal hormones, the brain, and human sex differences; a heuristic, integrative review of recent literature. *Archives of Sexual Behavior*, **3**, 51–90.

Reinisch, J. M. (1976). Effects of prenatal hormone exposure on physical and psychological development in humans and animals: with a note on the state of the field. In *Hormones, Behavior, and Psychopathology*, ed. E. J. Sachar, pp. 69–94. New York: Raven Press.

Reinisch, J. M. & Karow, W. G. (1977). Prenatal exposure to synthetic progestins and estrogens: effects on human development. *Archives of Sexual Behavior*, **6**, 257–88.

Reiss, M. (1958). Psychoendocrinology. In *Psychoendocrinology*, ed. M. Reiss, pp. 1–40. New York: Grune & Stratton.

Reiter, R. J. (1983). The pineal gland: an intermediary between the environment and the endocrine system. *Psychoneuroendocrinology*, **8**, 31–40.

Resko, J. A. (1975). Fetal hormones and their effect on the differentiation of the central nervous system in primates. *Federation Proceedings*, **34**, 1650–5.

Richter, C. P. (1943). Total self-regulatory functions in animals and human beings. *Harvey Lectures*, **38**, 63–103.

Risch, S. C. (1982). β-Endorphin hypersecretion in depression: possible cholinergic mechanisms. *Biological Psychiatry*, **17**, 1071–9.

Rivier, J., Spiess, J., Thorner, M. & Vale, W. (1982). Characterization of a growth hormone-releasing factor from a human pancreatic islet cell tumour. *Nature*, **300**, 276–8.

Roberts, F. & Calcutt, C. R. (1983). Histamine and the hypothalamus. *Neuroscience*, **9**, 721–39.

Roberts, G. W., Ferrier, I. N., Lee, Y., Crow, T. J., Johnstone, E. C., Owens, D. G. C., Bacarese-Hamilton, A. J., McGregor, G., O'Shaughnessey, D., Polak, J. M. & Bloom, S. R. (1983). Peptides, the limbic lobe and schizophrenia. *Brain Research*, **288**, 199–211.

Robertson, G. L., Shelton, R. L. & Athar, S. (1976). The osmoregulation of vasopressin. *Kidney International*, **10**, 25–37.

Rogel, M. J. (1978). A critical evaluation of the possibility of higher primate reproductive and sexual pheromones. *Psychological Bulletin*, **85**, 810–30.

Rogers, P. W. & Kurtzman, N. A. (1973). Renal failure, uncontrollable thirst and hyperreninemia. *Journal of the American Medical Association*, **225**, 1236–8.

Rolls, B. J. & Rolls, E. T. (1982). *Thirst*. Cambridge University Press.

Rose, R. M. (1980). Endocrine responses to stressful psychological events. *Psychiatric Clinics of North America*, **3**, 251–76.

Rose, R. M., Jenkins, C. D., Hurst, M., Herd, J. A. & Hall, R. P. (1982a). Endocrine activity in air traffic controllers at work. II. Biological, psychological and work correlates. *Psychoneuroendocrinology*, **7**, 113–23.

Rose, R. M., Jenkins, C. D., Hurst, M., Livingston, L. & Hall, R. P. (1982b). Endocrine activity in air traffic controllers at work. I. Characterization of cortisol and growth hormone levels during the day. *Psychoneuroendocrinology*, **7**, 101–11.

Rosenthal, N. E., Sack, D. A., Gillin, J. C., Lewy, A. J., Goodwin, F. K., Davenport, Y., Mueller, P. S., Newsome, D. A. & Wehr, T. A. (1984). Seasonal affective disorder. *Archives of General Psychiatry*, **41**, 72–80.

Ross, D. A., Glick, S. D. & Meibach, R. C. (1981). Sexually dimorphic brain and behavioral asymmetries in the neonatal rat. *Proceedings of the National Academy of Sciences, USA*, **78**, 1958–61.

Roth, J., Le Roith, D., Shiloach, J., Rosenzweig, J. L., Lesniak, M. A. & Havrankova, J. (1982). The evolutionary origins of hormones, neurotransmitters, and other extracellular chemical messengers. Implications for mammalian biology. *New England Journal of Medicine*, **306**, 523–7.

Roth, J., Le Roith, D., Shiloach, J. & Rubinovitz, C. (1983). Intercellular communication: an attempt at a unifying hypothesis. *Clinical Research*, **31**, 354–63.

Roth, J. & Taylor, S. I. (1982). Receptors for peptide hormones: alterations in diseases of humans. *Annual Review of Physiology*, **44**, 639–51.

Rubin, R. T. & Poland, R. E. (1982). The chronoendocrinology of endogenous depression. In *Neuroendocrine Perspectives*, vol. 1, ed. E. E. Müller & R. M. MacLeod, pp. 305–37. Amsterdam: Elsevier Biomedical Press.

Rubin, R. T., Reinisch, J. M. & Haskett, R. F. (1981). Postnatal gonadal steroid effects on human behavior. *Science*, **211**, 1318–24.

Rubinow, D. R., Gold, P. W., Post, R. M., Ballenger, J. C. & Cowdry, R. W. (1984). Somatostatin in patients with affective illness and in normal volunteers. In *Neurobiology of Mood Disorders*, ed. R. M. Post & J. C. Ballenger, pp. 369–87. Baltimore: Williams & Wilkins.

Rubinow, D. R., Gold, P. W., Post, R. M., Ballenger, J. C., Cowdry, R., Bollinger, J. & Reichlin, S. (1983). CSF somatostatin in affective illness. *Archives of General Psychiatry*, **40**, 409–12.

Rubinow, D. R. & Roy-Byrne, P. (1984). Premenstrual syndromes: overview from a methodologic perspective. *American Journal of Psychiatry*, **141**, 163–72.

Ruble, D. N. (1977). Premenstrual symptoms: a reinterpretation. *Science*, **197**, 291–2.

Russell, M. J., Switz, G. M. & Thompson, K. (1980). Olfactory influences on the human menstrual cycle. *Pharmacology Biochemistry & Behaviour*, **13**, 737–8.

Sachar, E. J. (1980). Hormonal changes in stress and mental illness. In *Neuroendocrinology*, ed. D. T. Krieger & J. C. Hughes, pp. 177–83. Sunderland, Mass.: Sinauer Associates.

Salmimies, P., Kockott, G., Pirke, K. M., Vogt, H. J. & Schill, W. B. (1982). Effects of testosterone replacement on sexual behavior in hypogonadal men. *Archives of Sexual Behavior*, **11**, 345–53.

Sanders, D. & Bancroft, J. (1982). Hormones and the sexuality of women – the menstrual cycle. *Clinics in Endocrinology and Metabolism*, **11**, 639–59.

Sanders, D., Warner, P., Backström, T. & Bancroft, J. (1983). Mood, sexuality, hormones, and the menstrual cycle. 1. Changes in mood and physical state: description of subjects and method. *Psychosomatic Medicine*, **45**, 487–501.

Sandman, C. A., Kastin, A. J. & Schally, A. V. (1981). Neuropeptide influences on the central nervous system: a psychobiological perspective. In *Neuroendocrine Regulation and Altered Behaviour*, ed. P. V. Hrdina & R. L. Singhal, pp. 3–27. London: Croom Helm.

Sano, K., Mayanagi, Y., Sekino, H., Ogashiwa, M. & Ishijima, B. (1970). Results of stimulation and destruction of the posterior hypothalamus in man. *Journal of Neurosurgery*, **33**, 689–707.

Santen, R. J. & Bardin, C. W. (1973). Episodic luteinizing hormone secretion in man. Pulse analysis, clinical interpretation, physiologic mechanisms. *Journal of Clinical Investigation*, **52**, 2617–28.

Schachter, S. (1967). Cognitive effects on bodily functioning: studies of obesity and eating. In *Neurophysiology and Emotion*, ed. D. C. Glass, pp. 117–44. New York: Rockefeller University Press.

Schachter, S. (1975). Cognition and peripheralist–centralist controversies in motivation and emotion. In *Handbook of Psychobiology*, ed. M. S. Gazzaniga & C. Blakemore, pp. 529–64. New York: Academic Press.

Schachter, S. & Singer, J. E. (1962). Cognitive, social, and physiological determinants of emotional state. *Psychological Review*, **69**, 379–99.

Scharrer, B. (1974). The concept of neurosecretion past and present. In *Recent Studies of Hypothalamic Function*. International Symposium, Calgary, 1973, pp. 1–7. Basel: Karger.

Scharrer, E. & Scharrer, B. (1963). *Neuroendocrinology*. New York: Columbia University Press.

Schiavi, R. C., Theilgaard, A., Owen, D. R. & White, D. (1984). Sex chromosome anomalies, hormones, and aggressivity. *Archives of General Psychiatry*, **41**, 93–9.

Schreiner, L. & Kling, A. (1956). Rhinencephalon and behavior. *American Journal of Physiology*, **184**, 486–90.

Schreiner-Engel, P. (1980). Female sexual arousability: its relation to gonadal hormones and the menstrual cycle. Unpublished Ph.D. thesis, New York University, quoted by Sanders & Bancroft, 1982.

Schreiner-Engel, P., Schiavi, R. C., Smith, H. & White, D. (1981). Sexual arousability and the menstrual cycle. *Psychosomatic Medicine*, **43**, 199–214.

Schwartz, M. F., Bauman, J. E. & Masters, W. H. (1982). Hyperprolactinemia and sexual disorders in men. *Biological Psychiatry*, **17**, 861–76.

Scott, J. P. (1980). The function of emotions in behavioral systems: a systems theory analysis. In *Emotion. Theory, Research and Experience. 1. Theories of Emotion*, ed. R. Plutchik & H. Kellerman, pp. 35–56. New York: Academic Press.

Scott, J. P., Stewart, J. M. & de Ghett, V. J. (1974). Critical periods in the organization of systems. *Developmental Psychobiology*, **7**, 489–513.

Selye, H. (1957). *The Stress of Life*. London: Longmans, Green.

Serra, G. & Gessa, G. L. (1983). Role of brain monoamines and peptides in the regulation of male sexual behavior. In *Psychoneuroendocrine Dysfunction*, ed. N. S. Shah & A. G. Donald, pp. 141–55. New York: Plenum Medical Book Company.

Shaffer, D., Meyer-Bahlburg, H. F. L. & Stokman, C. L. J. (1980). The development of aggression. In *Scientific Foundations of Developmental Psychiatry*, ed. M. Rutter, pp. 353–68. London: Heinemann.

Shepherd, G. M. (1983). *Neurobiology*. New York: Oxford University Press.

Sheridan, P. J. (1983). Androgen receptors in the brain: what are we measuring? *Endocrine Reviews*, **4**, 171–8.

Shillabeer, G. & Davison, J. S. (1984). The cholecystokinin antagonist, proglumide, increases food intake in the rat. *Regulatory Peptides*, **8**, 171–6.

Sigusch, V., Schorsch, E., Dannecker, M. & Schmidt, G. (1982). Official statement by the German Society for Sex Research (*Deutsche Gesellschaft für Sexualforschung, e.V.*) on the research of Prof. Dr Gunter Dörner on the subject of homosexuality. *Archives of Sexual Behavior*, **11**, 445–9.

Sirinathsinghji, D. J. S., Rees, L. H., Rivier, J. & Vale, W. (1983). Corticotropin-releasing factor is a potent inhibitor of sexual receptivity in the female rat. *Nature*, **305**, 232–5.

Sirinathsinghji, D. J., Whittington, P. E., Audsley, A. & Fraser, H. M. (1983). β-Endorphin regulates lordosis in female rats by modulating LH-RH release. *Nature*, **301**, 62–4.

Skakkebaek, N. E., Bancroft, J., Davidson, D. W. & Warner, P. (1981). Androgen replacement with oral testosterone undecanoate in hypogonadal men: a double blind controlled study. *Clinical Endocrinology*, **14**, 49–61.

Smith, C. K., Barish, J., Correa, J. & Williams, R. H. (1972). Psychiatric disturbance in endocrinologic disease. *Psychosomatic Medicine*, **34**, 69–86.

Smith, G. P. (1983). The peripheral control of appetite. *Lancet*, **ii**, 88–90.

Smith, I. (1983). Indoles of pineal origin: biochemical and physiological status. *Psychoneuroendocrinology*, **8**, 41–60.

Smith, K. & Sines, J. O. (1960). Demonstration of a peculiar odor in the sweat of schizophrenic patients. *Archives of General Psychiatry*, **2**, 184–8.

Smith, O. A. & DeVito, J. L. (1984). Central neural integration for the control of autonomic responses associated with emotion. *Annual Review of Neuroscience*, **7**, 43–65.

Snyder, S. H. (1982). Schizophrenia. *Lancet*, **ii**, 970–3.

Sokoloff, L. & Kennedy, C. (1973). The action of thyroid hormones and their influence on brain development and function. In *Biology of Brain Dysfunction*, vol. 2, ed. G. E. Gaull, pp. 295–332. New York: Plenum Press.

Sørensen, P. S., Hammer, M. & Bolwig, T. G. (1982). Vasopressin release during electroconvulsive therapy. *Psychoneuroendocrinology*, **7**, 303–8.

Soules, M. R., Steiner, R. A., Clifton, D. K., Cohen, N. L., Aksel, S. & Bremner, W. J. (1984). Progesterone modulation of pulsatile luteinizing hormone secretion in normal women. *Journal of Clinical Endocrinology and Metabolism*, **58**, 378–83.

Spark, R. F., Wills, C. A. & Royal, H. (1984). Hypogonadism, hyperprolactinaemia and temporal lobe epilepsy in hyposexual men. *Lancet*, **i**, 413–18.

Spies, H. G., Norman, R. L., Clifton, D. K., Ochsner, A. J., Jensen, J. N. & Phoenix, C. H. (1976). Effects of bilateral amygdaloid lesions on gonadal and pituitary hormones in serum and on sexual behavior in female rhesus monkeys. *Physiology and Behavior*, **17**, 985–92.

Stein, M., Keller, S. & Schleifer, S. (1981). The hypothalamus and the immune response. In *Brain, Behavior, and Bodily Disease*, ed. H. Weiner, M. A. Hofer & A. J. Stunkard, pp. 45–63. New York: Raven Press.

Steiner, M., Haskett, R. F., Carroll, B. J., Hays, S. E. & Rubin, R. T. (1984). Plasma prolactin and severe premenstrual tension. *Psychoneuroendocrinology*, **9**, 29–35.

Stephan, H. (1983). Evolutionary trends in limbic structures. *Neuroscience and Biobehavioral Reviews*, **7**, 367–74.

Sterling, K. (1979). Thyroid hormone action at the cell level. *New England Journal of Medicine*, **300**, 173–7.

Stevens, J. R., Mark, V. H., Erwin, F., Pacheco, P. & Suematsu, K. (1969). Deep temporal stimulation in man. *Archives of Neurology*, **21**, 157–69.

Studd, J., Chakravarti, S. & Oram, D. (1977). The climacteric. *Clinics in Obstetrics and Gynaecology*, **4**, 3–29.

Stumpf, W. E. (1980). Anatomical distribution of steroid hormone target neurons and circuitry in the brain. In *The Endocrine Functions of the Brain*, ed. M. Motta, pp. 43–9. New York: Raven Press.

Stunkard, A. J. & Stellar, E. (eds.) (1984). *Eating and its Disorders*. New York: Raven Press.

Swanson, L. W. & Mogensen, G. J. (1981). Neural mechanisms for the functional coupling of autonomic, endocrine and somatomotor responses in adaptive behavior. *Brain Research Reviews*, **3**, 1–34.

Swanson, L. W. & Sawchenko, P. E. (1983). Hypothalamic integration. *Annual Review of Neuroscience*, **6**, 269–324.

Symonds, E. M. (1981). Pre-menstrual tension. *Oxford Reviews of Reproductive Biology*, **3**, 156–81.

Taché, Y. & Brown, M. (1982). On the role of bombesin in homeostasis. *Trends in Neurological Sciences*, **5**, 431–3.

Tattersall, R. B. (1981). Psychiatric aspects of diabetes – a physician's view. *British Journal of Psychiatry*, **139**, 485–93.

Terzian, H. & Ore, G. D. (1955). Syndrome of Klüver and Bucy. Reproduced in man by bilateral removal of the temporal lobes. *Neurology*, **5**, 373–80.

Timiras, P. S. & Cons, J. M. (1982). Hormones during prenatal and neonatal development. In *Hormones in Development and Aging*, ed. A. Vernadakis & P. S. Timiras, pp. 25–79. Lancaster: MTP Press.

Toran-Allerand, C. D. (1978). Gonadal hormones and brain development: cellular aspects of sexual differentiation. *American Zoologist*, **18**, 553–65.

Tromp, S. W. (1975). Possible extra-terrestrial triggers of interdisciplinary cycles on earth. A review. *Journal of Interdisciplinary Cycle Research*, **6**, 303–15.

Tsitouras, P. D., Martin, C. E. & Harman, S. M. (1982). Relationship of serum testosterone to sexual activity in healthy elderly men. *Journal of Gerontology*, **37**, 288–93.

Turner, C. D. & Bagnara, J. T. (1976). *General Endocrinology*, 6th edn. Philadelphia: Saunders.

Udry, J. R., Morris, N. M. & Waller, L. (1973). Effect of contraceptive pills on sexual activity in the luteal phase of the human menstrual cycle. *Archives of Sexual Behavior*, **2**, 205–14.

Ungar, A. & Phillips, J. H. (1983). Regulation of the adrenal medulla. *Physiological Reviews*, **63**, 787–843.

Vague, J. (1983). Testicular feminization syndrome. *Hormone Research*, **18**, 62–8.

Vale, W., Rivier, C., Brown, M. R., Spiess, J., Koob, G., Swanson, L., Bilezikjian, L., Bloom, F. & Rivier, J. (1983). Chemical and biological characterization of corticotropin releasing factor. *Recent Progress in Hormone Research*, **39**, 245–70.

Vale, W., Spiess, J., Rivier, C. & Rivier, J. (1981). Characterization of a 41-residue ovine hypothalamic peptide that stimulates secretion of corticotropin and β-endorphin. *Science*, **213**, 1394–7.

Veith, J. L., Buck, M., Getzlaf, S., van Dalfsen, P. & Slade, S. (1983). Exposure to men influences the occurrence of ovulation in women. *Physiology and Behavior*, **31**, 313–15.

Verbanck, P. M. P., Lotstra, F., Gilles, C., Linkowski, P., Mendlewicz, J. & Vanderhaeghen, J. J. (1984). Reduced cholecystokinin immunoreactivity in the cerebrospinal fluid of patients with psychiatric disorders. *Life Sciences*, **34**, 67–72.

Verebey, K., Volavka, J. & Clouet, D. (1978). Endorphins in psychiatry. An overview and hypothesis. *Archives of General Psychiatry*, **35**, 877–88.

Vermeulen, A. (1983). Androgen secretion after age 50 in both sexes. *Hormone Research*, 18, 37–42.

Vernadakis, A. & Culver, B. (1982). Neuroendocrine control systems in the adult. In *Hormones in Development and Aging*, ed. A. Vernadakis & P. S. Timiras, pp. 371–449. Lancaster: MTP Press.

Vernadakis, A. & Timiras, P. S. (1967). Effects of estradiol and cortisol on neural tissue in culture. *Experientia*, 23, 467–8.

Vogel, G. W., Thurmond, A., Gibbons, P., Sloan, K., Boyd, M. & Walker, M. (1975). REM sleep reduction effects on depression syndromes. *Archives of General Psychiatry*, 32, 765–77.

Wade, N. (1981). *The Nobel Duel*. New York: Anchor Press.

Walker, J. M., Moises, H. C., Coy, D. H., Baldrighi, G. & Akil, H. (1982). Non-opiate effects of dynorphin and des-tyr-dynorphin. *Science*, 218, 1136–8.

Walsh, B. T. (1982). Endocrine disturbances in anorexia nervosa and depression. *Psychosomatic Medicine*, 44, 85–91.

Ward, M. M., Mefford, I. N., Parker, S. D., Chesney, M. A., Taylor, C. B., Keegan, D. L. & Barchas, J. D. (1983). Epinephrine and norepinephrine responses in continuously collected human plasma to a series of stressors. *Psychosomatic Medicine*, 45, 471–86.

Wardlaw, S. L., Thoron, L. & Frantz, A. G. (1982). Effects of sex steroids on brain β-endorphin. *Brain Research*, 245, 327–31.

Warren, M. P. (1980). The effects of exercise on pubertal progression and reproductive function in girls. *Journal of Clinical Endocrinology and Metabolism*, 51, 1150–7.

Wathes, D. C., Swann, R. W., Pickering, B. T., Porter, D. G., Hull, M. G. R. & Drife, J. O. (1982). Neurohypophysial hormones in the human ovary. *Lancet*, ii, 410–12.

Watson, S. J., Khachaturian, H., Akil, H., Coy, D. H. & Goldstein, A. (1982). Comparison of the distribution of dynorphin systems and enkephalin systems in brain. *Science*, 218, 1134–6.

Wehr, T. A., Lewy, A. J., Wirz-Justice, A., Craig, C. & Tamarkin, L. (1982). Antidepressants and a circadian rhythm phase-advance hypothesis of depression. In *Brain Neurotransmitters and Hormones*, ed. R. Collu, J. R. Ducharme, A. Barbeau & G. Tolis, pp. 263–76. New York: Raven Press.

Wehr, T. A., Sack, D., Rosenthal, N., Duncan, W. & Gillin, J. C. (1983). Circadian rhythm disturbances in manic–depressive illness. *Federation Proceedings*, 42, 2809–14.

Wehr, T. A., Wirz-Justice, A., Goodwin, F. K., Duncan, W. & Gillin, J. C. (1979). Phase advance of the circadian sleep–wake cycle as an antidepressant. *Science*, 206, 710–13.

Wehrenberg, W. B., Wardlaw, S. L., Frantz, A. G. & Ferin, M. (1982). β-Endorphin in hypophyseal portal blood: variations throughout the menstrual cycle. *Endocrinology*, 111, 879–81.

Weichsel, M. E. (1977). The therapeutic use of glucocorticoid hormones in the perinatal period: potential neurological hazards. *Annals of Neurology*, 2, 364–6.

Wetzel, R. D. & McClure, J. N. (1972). Suicide and the menstrual cycle: a review. *Comprehensive Psychiatry*, 13, 369–74.

Whalley, L. J., Rosie, R., Dick, H., Levy, G., Watts, A. G., Sheward, W. J., Christie, J. E. & Fink, G. (1982). Immediate increases in plasma prolactin and neurophysin but not other hormones after electroconvulsive therapy. *Lancet*, ii, 1065–8.

White, F. J. & Wang, R. Y. (1983). Differential effects of classical and atypical antipsychotic drugs on A9 and A10 dopamine neurons. *Science*, 221, 1054–7.

Whybrow, P. C. & Prange, A. J. (1981). A hypothesis of thyroid–catecholamine–receptor interaction. *Archives of General Psychiatry*, 38, 106–13.

Whybrow, P. C., Prange, A. J. & Treadway, C. R. (1969). Mental changes accompanying thyroid gland dysfunction. *Archives of General Psychiatry*, 20, 48–63.

Wiegant, V. M. & De Wied, D. (1981). Behavioural effects of pituitary hormones. In *Neuroendocrine Regulation and Altered Behaviour*, ed. P. D. Hrdina & R. L. Singhal, pp. 29–49. London: Croom Helm.

Wiesenfeld-Hallin, Z. & Södersten, P. (1984). Spinal opiates affect sexual behaviour in rats. *Nature*, **309**, 257–8.

Wilkins, L. & Richter, C. P. (1940). A great craving for salt by a child with corticoadrenal insufficiency. *Journal of the American Medical Association*, **114**, 866–8.

Wilkinson, D. G. (1981). Psychiatric aspects of diabetes mellitus. *British Journal of Psychiatry*, **138**, 1–9.

Williams, R. H. (1970). Metabolism and mentation. *Journal of Clinical Endocrinology and Metabolism*, **31**, 461–79.

Wilson, J. D. (1982). Gonadal hormones and sexual behavior. In *Clinical Neuroendocrinology*, vol. 2, ed. G. M. Besser & L. Martini, pp. 1–29. New York: Academic Press.

van Wimersma-Griedanus, Tj. B., Bohus, B., Kovács, G. L., Versteeg, D. H. G., Burbach, J. P. H. & De Wied, D. (1983). Sites of behavioral and neurochemical action of ACTH-like peptides and neurohypophyseal hormones. *Neuroscience and Biobehavioral Reviews*, **7**, 453–63.

Winokur, A., Amsterdam, J. D., Mihailović, V. & Caroff, S. N. (1982). Improvement in ratings of tension after TRH administration in healthy women. *Psychoneuroendocrinology*, **7**, 239–44.

Wirz-Justice, A. & Campbell, I. C. (1982). Antidepressant drugs can slow or dissociate circadian rhythms. *Experientia*, **38**, 1301–9.

Wirz-Justice, A. & Richter, R. (1979). Seasonality in biochemical determinations: a source of variance and a clue to the temporal incidence of affective illness. *Psychiatry Research*, **1**, 53–60.

Wolff, C. T., Friedman, S. B., Hofer, M. A. & Mason, J. W. (1964). Relationship between psychological defenses and mean urinary 17-hydroxycorticosteroid excretion rates. I. A predictive study of parents of fatally ill children. *Psychosomatic Medicine*, **26**, 576–91.

Wolff, C. T., Hofer, M. A. & Mason, J. W. (1964). Relationship between psychological defenses and mean urinary 17-hydroxycorticosteroid excretion rates. II. Methodological and theoretical considerations. *Psychosomatic Medicine*, **26**, 592–609.

Wolkin, A., Peselow, E. D., Smith, M., Lautin, A., Kahn, I. & Rotrosen, J. (1984). TRH test abnormalities in psychiatric disorders. *Journal of Affective Disorders*, **6**, 273–81.

Woods, S. C., West, D. B., Stein, L. J., McKay, L. D., Lotter, E. C., Porte, S. G., Kenney, N. J. & Porte, D. (1981). Peptides and the control of meal size. *Diabetologia*, **20**, 305–13.

Yalom, I. D., Green, R. & Fisk, N. (1973). Prenatal exposure to female hormones: effect on psychosexual development in boys. *Archives of General Psychiatry*, **28**, 554–61.

Yarbrough, G. G. (1983). Thyrotropin releasing hormone and CNS cholinergic neurons. *Life Sciences*, **33**, 111–18.

Yates, A., Leehey, K. & Shisslak, C. M. (1983). Running–an analogue of anorexia? *New England Journal of Medicine*, **308**, 251–5.

Yates, F. E. (1981). Analysis of endocrine signals: the engineering and physics of biochemical communication systems. *Biology of Reproduction*, **24**, 73–94.

Yen, S. S. C. (1980). Neuroendocrine regulation of the menstrual cycle. In *Neuroendocrinology*, ed. D. T. Krieger & J. C. Hughes, pp. 259–72. Sunderland, Mass.: Sinauer Associates.

Young, J. K. (1982). A comparison of hypothalami of rats and mice: lack of gross sexual dimorphism in the mouse. *Brain Research*, **239**, 233–9.

Zeman, W. & King, F. A. (1958). Tumors of the septum pellucidum and adjacent structures with abnormal affective behavior: an anterior midline structure syndrome. *Journal of Nervous and Mental Disease*, **127**, 490–502.

Zuger, B. (1970). Gender role determination: a critical review of the evidence from hermaphroditism. *Psychosomatic Medicine*, **32**, 449–67.

Zussman, L., Zussman, S., Sunley, R. & Bjornson, E. (1981). Sexual response after hysterectomy–oophorectomy: recent studies and reconsideration of psychogenesis. *American Journal of Obstetrics and Gynecology*, **140**, 725–9.

INDEX